HEALING
for the
HEART

Crossway books by Cheryl V. Ford

The Pilgrim's Progress Devotional
Treasures from the Heart
Healing for the Heart

WOMEN OF THE WORD

HEALING

for the

HEART

The Hope of
Full Surrender

CHERYL V. FORD

CROSSWAY BOOKS • WHEATON, ILLINOIS
A DIVISION OF GOOD NEWS PUBLISHERS

Cover design: Liita Forsyth

Cover photo: Gary Irving

First printing 2001

Printed in the United States of America

Library of Congress Cataloging-in-Publication Data
Ford, Cheryl V.
    Healing for the heart : the hope of full surrender / Cheryl V. Ford.
      p.   cm.— (Women of the Word)
    ISBN 1-58134-260-8 (pbk. : alk. paper)
    1. Women in the Bible—Biography. 2. Christian women—Religious life.
I. Title.
BS575.F665   2001
248.8'43—dc21   2001001182
                                       CIP

15	14	13	12	11	10	09	08	07	06	05	04	03	02	01
15	14	13	12	11	10	9	8	7	6	5	4	3	2	1

In memory of my mother,
Dorothy Verkler,

a struggling lamb in God's flock.
Her troubles are now behind her,
and her heart is fully healed.
How I look forward to seeing her again in heaven.

Thank You, Jesus.

Contents

ACKNOWLEDGMENTS

Thanks to my husband, Clay, the wisest man I know. Your guidance and editing expertise provided invaluable contributions. Your perspective of God's grace and your gentle and generous heart toward women provided abundant inspiration.

Again I would be lost without those who prayed for me. Thank you to my E-mail buddies—Pat Schmitz, Janine Kramer, Jean Bailes, Terry Temple, Sharon Schlotzhauer, Jean Wilson, Kathleen DeVita, Lory Chaves, Helen Mooradkanian, Kersti Stoen, Linda Storm, Cheri Cole, Marie Dainow, my wonderful mother-in-law Virginia Ford, and my daughter Hannah. Also, thanks so much to Jean Abercrombie and the rest of my incredible AFBC church family. Many of you prayed for me faithfully, and I didn't even know it. Because of your prayers, I trust the Lord to bless many hurting women through these pages.

Also, thanks to my son and daughter-in-law, Billy and Denise, for their love and support.

I am so grateful for Crossway Books. I still can scarcely believe they trusted me with this message. I praise the Lord for Marvin Padgett, Jill Carter, and other Crossway staff who serve the Lord diligently in their calling to produce quality books for God's glory. I really appreciate your patience and gentleness with me. I am especially thankful to my editor and friend, Lila Bishop. I really appreciate your wisdom and expertise. It's a joy and comfort to entrust a manuscript to your able hands.

Most of all, I thank You, Jesus. How can words describe how wonderful You are? Without You, this book and my life would be blank. How You have touched and healed my heart.

INTRODUCTION

Living near a secular university campus, I sometimes hear hostile students voice their opinion that Christians are ignorant and intolerant. Female students especially like to declare that the Christian faith oppresses women. While I believe they are mistaken, I do not think they are the only ones confused about the issue. Often, either directly or indirectly, Christian women are made to feel like second-class citizens in God's kingdom.

If you have bought into this view, I believe this book will surprise you. Through these pages I hope your heart will hear God's shout: "I LOVE YOU! I WILL NEVER FORSAKE YOU! HAVE I GOT A PLAN FOR YOUR LIFE!" I hope that hearts of women everywhere, especially those who are hurting, will become convinced that God is *for* them, not against them. I hope they will see that He *loves* His daughters, that they are *eternally significant* to Him, that He *never* abandons them, and that He even goes to *great lengths* to care for them.

The biblical record abounds with illustrations of God's intervention in the lives of women. Included are numerous incidents of those whose aching hearts He touched and healed. In these pages you will meet some of these women. You will feel their pain but will also witness and experience their ultimate victory and restoration as you see God graciously extend His love and compassion to them.

When our picture of life shatters, it's easy to think that God has changed toward us, that He has somehow turned against us. But God has another picture. His is much larger, and He wants to reveal it to us. Seeing the big picture, seeing our lives from His perspective, will encourage us and give us hope. Paul's prayer for the Ephesian Christians (and for *us*, too) was: "I pray also that the eyes of your heart may be enlightened in order that you may know the hope to which he has called you" (Ephesians 1:18). Yes, Lord. In the midst of our pain, please open the eyes of our hearts to see this larger picture, this broader perspective.

There are some who teach that God wants us to live pain-free lives. "Pain, after all, is part of the Fall, and—praise God!—we have been redeemed from the Fall." We may not consciously subscribe to that teaching, but in our love for comfort and security, we may be more affected by it than we realize. Idealizing the lives of other Christians who appear to live on some blissful plane above human difficulty, we conclude that they are the ones whom God has truly blessed and that something must be terribly amiss with our own walk with God.

In reality *no one* is immune from life's tragedies and pain. Jesus said, "In this world you will have trouble" (John 16:33). We might put on a happy face, but we all must live in this world with its universal troubles. This book does not presume to have all the answers to our suffering and does not seek to offer answers and insights that are glib, easy, and short-sighted.

But this book does offer *hope*. In the midst of our disappointments, unfulfilled dreams, shattered ideals, and broken hearts, we can take comfort and find encouragement. There is a sovereign and loving God who knows and loves us, who feels our pain, and who does not ignore, slight, or neglect His children. Come what may, He still reigns—not only over the universe but over our own lives as well. Whatever our trial, no matter how faltering our faith, His love holds firm. His power is infinite, and the hope He offers is a candle of light that can never be extinguished.

As we surrender our hearts to the Lord, we will come to see that He is able to turn all our painful circumstances and trials into ultimate blessings. We may not understand all that He is doing in and through us, but we will come to trust His wise and loving sovereignty over our lives. We will even learn to glorify Him in the midst of our difficulties. Let me encourage you to open your heart now as we begin to interact with various biblical women. You will be able to relate to them because they were ordinary women like you and me.

They were real women; they felt real pain; they cried real tears. But their tears of sorrow turned to tears of joy!

Journey with these dear sisters of faith, and see how they came to experience God's miraculous intervention in their lives. Their stories will inspire you with hope and encouragement. Your faith will grow as you reach out to experience new depths of healing for your own heart and life.

Before reading this book, if you are uncertain as to your relationship with Christ, let me encourage you to start this journey by surrendering your heart to Him. You can turn to Appendix A at the end of this book, where you will find a suggested prayer to help you do this. Our healing begins and ends with open hearts to Jesus Christ.

1

Hannah

THE HARASSED HEART

1 SAMUEL 1—2:10, 19-21

HANNAH SAT IN THE corner quietly weeping, praying, and wiping her tears. *I can't take any more. Lord, what have I done to deserve this?* She looked up as another woman entered the room.

"Oh, there you are pitying yourself again!" Peninnah said in her blustery, taunting way. Squealing children skipped and danced through the room on their way outside. They didn't notice the sad woman; they never did. Smiling after them, Peninnah shook her finger at Hannah and started in again: "If you had children of your own, you'd learn to carry your weight. But God knew—didn't He?—who would make a better mother to Elkanah's children. It's good he took *me* for a wife—with *you* he'd have nothing!" Every day it was the same. Peninnah assailed Hannah mercilessly.

"How long will you torment me and crush me with words?"

JOB 19:2

It was a dark period in Israel's history. The nation had fallen largely into idolatry, moral collapse, and infighting. For its sin God let Israel's neighbors oppress them. It was hardly a time that inspired faith and commitment to God: "In those days the word of the LORD was rare" (1 Samuel 3:1). Yet during this period of the Judges, pockets of those who loved and honored God could still be found. Hannah was such a one.

Following God does not always mean that life is easy, and life was certainly not easy for Hannah. Although her husband, Elkanah, loved her dearly, Hannah carried deep pain in her heart—and for good reason. First, she was childless: "The LORD had closed her womb" (1 Samuel 1:5). Second, she shared Elkanah with Peninnah, his second wife. Third, while she was infertile, Peninnah had borne Elkanah many children. Fourth, Peninnah saw Hannah as a rival, constantly belittling her as a failure and a lesser woman. Hannah's failure daily stared her in the face as she lived with Peninnah's clamoring offspring.

So unrelenting was Peninnah's persecution that Hannah's life became intolerable. She could never make her house a home; it was an endless torture chamber. Thus, we call Hannah's heart The Harassed Heart.

The law of Moses tolerated polygamy (Deuteronomy 21:15-17), and it had become a fact of life in ancient Israel, especially in this time when "all the people did what was right in their own eyes" (Judges 21:25 NRSV). Family lines were extremely important. Where one wife might fail to produce a son for a man, or his sons might die in battle, an additional wife provided extra insurance that someone would carry the family name to another generation. But polygamy was never God's intent for marriage—and for good reason! When a man married more than one wife, he could expect much unhappiness. Usually at odds with each other, his wives jealously vied for his affections. The rivalry under Elkanah's roof portrays this dark side of polygamy.

While Hannah longed for a child of her own to cherish, with each passing year it seemed more out of reach. As her hope disintegrated, her agony intensified—for "hope deferred makes the heart sick" (Proverbs 13:12). She was heartsick, all right. She not only bore the inward sense of failure, but her husband's marriage to Peninnah landed a devastating blow to her already bruised ego. As the Bible lists Hannah's name first, she was likely Elkanah's first wife, but due to her infertility, he married Peninnah. Sharing her home with this harassing nemesis was no easy task; thinking of her in Elkanah's arms must have been unbearable.

Israel's various tribes at this time formed a loose confederacy with the center of their worship located in Shiloh. Elkanah was a God-fearing man who annually took his family on a ten-mile pilgrimage to worship God and offer Him sacrifices in Shiloh. Under normal circumstances, this would be a much anticipated trip for Hannah. Yet the high point in the family's year was her low point. Year by year her woes compounded as it marked yet another anniversary of her barrenness. Flourishing Peninnah went to Shiloh, often thanking God for another child. Traveling with this mean-spirited woman and her children proved increasingly torturous for lonely Hannah. The trip was all the more painful because it brought her face to face with God—and her wounded heart toward Him.

After offering their sacrifice at the Shiloh tabernacle, the family culminated their pilgrimage with a feast. Receiving back a part of their fellowship (or peace) offering (Leviticus 7:11-18), they ate the meat in celebration of their restored fellowship with God. Elkanah always gave portions to Peninnah and her children, but he reserved the best portion for Hannah. He loved her, and this was his way of trying to comfort and affirm her.

Of course, this special treatment offended Peninnah. Jealously stepping up her persecution, she made Hannah feel worthless. Jabbing at Hannah's heart with acid words, she drove her to despair. God's Word says, "And because the LORD had closed her womb, her rival kept provoking her in order to irritate her. This went on year after year. Whenever Hannah went up to the house of the LORD, her rival provoked her till she wept and would not eat" (1 Samuel 1:6-7). So it went, year after miserable year of Hannah's existence.

Where was God in Hannah's life? Had He abandoned her, saying, "Peninnah's right; you're a loser"? Was He preoccupied with other interests? Had He judged her by "closing her womb"? No, never! God was there all along, intensely concerned for her. *Some comfort!* you might think. But while it seemed to Hannah that her life was over, God had an immense plan for her life. Hannah's name means "grace" and "favor," but before she could be a testimony of grace and favor, she had to be prepared. Her character had to be refined, her will broken, her devotion tested to the roots of her being. She had to come to the place of surrendering her all to the Lord.

In Old Testament times, people considered women like Hannah as failures. Crucial to the society's economic and social structure, children provided labor for families and cared for parents in old age. A social embarrassment, Elkanah could have legally divorced Hannah for disgracing him in this way. Instead, he stayed lovingly supportive of her. Hearing her sobs, he would implore, "Hannah, why are you weeping? Why don't you eat? Why are you downhearted? Don't I mean more to you than ten sons?" (1 Samuel 1:8).

Nice try, Elkanah. But how could he understand? After all, he was satisfied; he had children. She, on the other hand, had to bear watching him bounce "their" children on his knee. So his reassuring words fell flat; the years of abuse took their toll. Nothing he tried lifted the blanket of oppression from Hannah's seriously depressed soul.

It was that time again—time for the family's annual trek to Shiloh. Hannah could have whined to Elkanah, "You go this year. God never answers my prayers, so just go without me." Yet despite her escalating sorrow, she faithfully presented herself in Shiloh because the Lord was still worthy of her worship. He had shut her womb, but her heart stayed open to Him.

One day in Shiloh, as the family dined, Hannah had a breakthrough moment. Peninnah and Elkanah were discussing the day's events. Their happy children giggled and chattered, ever ignoring Hannah, likely treating her with the polite tolerance Elkanah demanded. Unable to eat and feeling lonely and isolated, she came to a decision.

After the meal "Hannah stood up" (1 Samuel 1:9). No one else understood her action, but God did. This stand was a moment of resolve. She had finally had enough—enough of feeling like an unnecessary appendage to the family, enough of pining away, enough of feeling forsaken by God, enough of Elkanah's pity, enough of

Peninnah's contempt, enough of leaving Shiloh with a broken heart. ENOUGH!

Casting off her sense of victimhood, Hannah became a woman of mission. She would go to the tabernacle with a special plea. Bypassing her husband and even the high priest, she would wrestle with God until He answered. After all, the patriarchs' wives Sarah and Rachel had been long barren, but God remembered them. Surely God understood her pain, too. She must find Him; only He could help her. The Creator of children was the only one who made barren women mothers. Going out the door, she literally fled to God, thinking, *I will get in touch with the Lord or die!*

Eli, the high priest and judge, sat at the tabernacle door, ready to judge any cases brought to him. Hannah arrived and stood some distance from him. As she stood before the Lord, she was overcome with emotion. "In bitterness of soul Hannah wept much and prayed to the LORD" (1 Samuel 1:10). She vehemently cried to Him, believing He knew her situation and had the power to give her a son. Never had she so agonized in prayer, crying for Him to look on her misery and remember her. She made a desperate promise: "O LORD Almighty, if you will only look upon your servant's misery and remember me, and not forget your servant but give her a son, then I will give him to the LORD for all the days of his life, and no razor will ever be used on his head" (1 Samuel 1:11).

This was a Nazirite vow. Like Samson, also a Nazirite, Hannah's son would be "set apart to God from birth" (Judges 13:5). She would consecrate him to God's service, for His exclusive use, from early childhood. Unlike a Levite whose service spanned from about age twenty-five to fifty, Samuel would serve the Lord "all the days of his life" (1 Samuel 1:11).

Eli was not used to seeing deeply distressed people pray like this. With much of the nation in a backslidden state, few prayed fervently at all. Observing Hannah's behavior, he thought it strange that her lips moved rapidly without speaking aloud. He was used to hearing audible prayers, pretentiously offered perhaps. She was "praying in her heart" (1 Samuel 1:13), but he thought this swaying, tormented figure must be drunk. So adding to Hannah's woes, he said, "How long will you keep on getting drunk? Get rid of your wine" (1 Samuel 1:14).

Eli didn't know it, but Hannah was offering the Lord utmost respect. This is the first time in Scripture that someone directly addresses God as the Lord Almighty or Lord of Hosts (Yahweh *tsaba'*). Using this name, Hannah expressed faith in His infinite resources and power to work on her behalf. The Jewish Talmud says that from the day God created the world, no one had called Him this until Hannah (Talmud: Berachot 31b).

Hannah's prayer is noteworthy for another reason. She had yearned for a child for so long, and yet her yearning reached beyond her own distress to the needs of her nation. Righteous people like Hannah wondered whether hope remained for the nation. Israel's religion had become corrupt. The priesthood had lost its meaning. Eli's sons who would succeed him were perverse. For its sin, God let Israel's neighbors oppress them. Israel desperately needed a godly, consecrated man to mediate between the Lord and His people, to serve as His representative and mouthpiece, and to point the nation back to Him.

Offering God a cosmic covenant, Hannah was saying, "Give me a son, and I will exchange him for the greater glory of Israel. As a gift not only to me but to all Israel, You can take and use him to lead your people back to You." In seeking not just a son for herself but a man for God, Hannah lined up perfectly with the divine intent to raise up just such a one.

For Eli's part, he showed his own sunken state by correcting a poor distraught woman while failing to correct his own degenerate sons who flagrantly disgraced the priesthood on a continual basis. Much to his surprise, Hannah looked up with clear eyes and soberly and rationally defended herself against his accusation. "Not so, my lord," she asserted. "I am a woman who is deeply troubled. I have not been drinking wine or beer; I was pouring out my soul to the LORD. Do not take your servant for a wicked woman; I have been praying here out of my great anguish and grief" (1 Samuel 1:15-16).

Eli saw his mistake at once. When he recognized her deep devotion, a light went on in him, and he acted as the priest God had called him to be. As the Lord's representative, he sensed that God was there for her. "Go in peace," he told her. Then, wanting her to go home expecting God to answer her prayer, he agreed with her petition, saying, "And may the God of Israel grant you what you have asked of him" (1 Samuel 1:17).

Hearing Eli's blessing, Hannah had a revelation of God's character. She saw that He is faithful, that He listened to her prayers, that He was engaged behind the scenes in her life's circumstances, and that He was committed to her well-being. She had known the right doctrines, but now the missing pieces came together in her heart; a healing took place. It was not Eli but the Lord giving her His blessing! With rising faith, she gratefully replied to Eli, "May your servant find favor in your eyes" (1 Samuel 1:18).

Leaving her place of prayer, Hannah went back to rejoin her family with a whole new attitude. She believed the Lord had heard her request and would answer it. While nothing had changed externally, her heart assured her that *everything* had changed.

What a sight the family saw when Hannah came back through the door! How could they not notice the difference? The sorrowful countenance, the sad lines, had been erased. She looked like a new woman; her face glowed, and her eyes sparkled. Happy and buoyant, she finally felt like eating. As she devoured her meal, even Peninnah must have been struck speechless.

The next morning the family worshiped at the tabernacle before returning home to Ramah. Elkanah was, no doubt, thrilled at Hannah's new hope-filled outlook. Once home he slept with her, "and the LORD remembered her" (1 Samuel 1:19) by giving her the power to conceive. She gave birth to a son whom she named Samuel, perhaps meaning "heard of God" and "asked of God," because she said, "I asked the LORD for him" (1 Samuel 1:20). At last her ordeal was over.

As Hannah nursed her little one, she gave him all the affection a mother would give her firstborn. Enjoying a delightful time with him, she did all she could to prepare him for a lifetime of service to God. When it was again time for the annual trip to Shiloh, she wanted to stay home with young Samuel. Ever mindful that he had come from God and belonged to God, she told Elkanah, "After the boy is weaned, I will take him and present him before the LORD, and he will live there always"(1 Samuel 1:22).

The period of weaning usually lasted two to three years. When the time was up, Hannah made good on her commitment. Remarkably, she not only gave God her word, but she kept it. Wouldn't it be easy to have second thoughts when it came time to turn little Samuel over to the Shiloh tabernacle? She could find many plausible excuses to renege. High Priest Eli was a sorry father and protector of his people. Surely, God wouldn't want young Samuel left in the care of this pitiful role model. Worse, his sons had made the tabernacle the religious equivalent of a brothel. If they had not kept their commitment to God, why should she? How could God want her precious son raised in that environment? Bargaining with God had worked once. Why not again? "I promise to do a much better job of raising little Sammy for you, Lord, than they would," she might have prayed.

Yet Hannah was a woman of her word who had come to trust God's sovereignty. She would entrust Samuel into God's hands. Bravely she took her child up to Shiloh for the yearly festival just as she said she would. Hannah and Elkanah offered their sacrifice at the tabernacle and then approached Eli with Samuel. It had been several years since she had seen Eli, and she explained, "As surely as you live, my lord, I am the woman who stood here beside you praying to the LORD. I prayed for this child, and the LORD has granted me what I asked of him. So now I give him to the LORD. For his whole life he will be given over to the LORD" (1 Samuel 1:26-28).

Hannah gave up what she had most wanted in life—her son. Leaving him behind with Eli must have been trying for her, adding to her list of painful experiences. In dedicating her only child to God, she surrendered her entire life and hope for the future to Him, giving up her right to have a son to care for her if Elkanah should die.

Would this be enough to sink her back into depression? No. We do not see her dwell on her loss or her sacrifice for a moment. The Lord had fulfilled her longing for a son; she had proved by experience that He had not abandoned her but regarded her cry. Believing she was not really giving Samuel *up* to God but giving him *back* to God, she gratefully released her best and most costly gift to Him without fear or regret. She had the peace that comes to those who surrender their all to the Blessed Controller. Knowing God in a new way, she realized that He really did order her life. With unshakable faith, she knew that God would take care of Samuel and even sensed that he had an important destiny in Israel.

With her heart freed of harassment, Hannah rejoiced over the Lord's goodness toward her. Overflowing with grateful praise, she composed a song that described how He took her on a painful journey from disgrace to honor. Extolling His majesty, power, omniscience, grace, and faithfulness, she sang:

> My heart rejoices in the Lord; in the Lord my horn is lifted high. My mouth boasts over my enemies, for I delight in your deliverance. There is no one holy like the Lord; there is no one besides you; there is no Rock like our God. Do not keep talking so proudly or let your mouth speak such arrogance, for the Lord is a God who knows, and by him deeds are weighed. The bows of the warriors are broken, but those who stumbled are armed with strength. Those who were full hire themselves out for food, but those who were hungry hunger no more. She who was barren has borne seven children, but she who has had many sons pines away. The Lord brings death and makes alive; he brings down to the grave and raises up. The Lord sends poverty and wealth; he humbles and he exalts. He raises the poor from the dust and lifts the needy from the ash heap; he seats them with princes and has them inherit a throne of honor. For the foundations of the earth are the Lord's; upon them he has set the world. He will guard the feet of his saints, but the wicked will be silenced in darkness. It is not by strength that one prevails; those who oppose the Lord will be shattered. He will thunder against them from heaven; the Lord will judge the ends of the earth. He will give strength to his king and exalt the horn of his anointed. (1 Samuel 2:1-10)

What a magnificent expression of praise to God! How marvelous that Hannah chose to worship, not at Samuel's birth when she was happiest, but upon fulfilling her vow when she walked away from Samuel. Now that is a healed heart! A thousand years later we detect the Virgin Mary's familiarity with Hannah's song as we find echoes of it in her Magnificat (Luke 1:46-55).

We can see God's overarching plan in what God's Word describes next: "Then Elkanah went home to Ramah, but the boy ministered before the LORD under Eli the priest. Eli's sons were wicked men; they had no regard for the LORD" (1 Samuel 2:11-12). With no godly successor for the office of high priest, God was moving ahead with His plan to groom Samuel for that role.

At home in Ramah, Hannah surely yearned for young Samuel in her heart. But the pain she felt came not from a broken heart but from a mended heart, one satisfied and fulfilled in God's purpose. Knowing the corruption around her beloved son, she no doubt prayed for his protection and spiritual nurture. Visiting him each year during her annual pilgrimage, she would present him, not a toy, but a priestly robe she had made for him. These visits meant a lot not only to her but to Samuel, too. His mother's godly influence helped to hold him steady throughout the years.

Each year Eli praised Elkanah and Hannah's unselfish sacrifice by blessing them and saying, "May the LORD give you children by this woman to take the place of the one she prayed for and gave to the LORD" (1 Samuel 2:20). Subsequently, the Lord graciously gave Hannah three more sons and two daughters. Meanwhile Samuel, unsullied by the influence of Eli's wicked sons, grew up to share his mother's faith.

Little did Hannah know that her desperate cry for a son not only marked a turning point in her life but in her nation's. Samuel became a powerful representative for God. The record attests to this fact: "The LORD was with Samuel as he grew up, and he let none of his words fall to the ground. And all Israel from Dan to Beersheba recognized that Samuel was attested as a prophet of the LORD. The LORD continued to appear at Shiloh, and there he revealed himself to Samuel through his word. And Samuel's word came to all Israel" (1 Samuel 3:19—4:1).

Like his mother who prevailed in prayer, Samuel became a dedicated man of prayer and intercession. He told the people of Israel, "As for me, far be it from me that I should sin against the LORD by failing to pray for you" (1 Samuel 12:23). As one of the greatest men in Israel's history, Samuel was its faithful prophet, priest, and judge. Later he was the counselor and adviser who led the nation back to God. He was the last and most effective of its judges and the anointer of its first two kings, Saul and David. The New Testament book of Hebrews includes him in its "Hall of Faith" (Hebrews 11:32).

The Lord gave Hannah an extra blessing to enjoy. Samuel faithfully continued to serve the nation all the days of his life and traveled a circuit to various places throughout Israel. Yet he moved his headquarters from Shiloh to Ramah, her hometown: "But he always went back to Ramah, where his home was, and there he also judged Israel" (1 Samuel 7:17).

The harassed and brokenhearted woman who thought God had forgotten her received blessing and wholeness beyond measure. She left a mark of eternal significance through her prayer and sacrifice. While we never hear of Peninnah again, multiplied millions have found hope through Hannah's endearing example of one with a broken heart healed by God. I for one, inspired by her life, named my own daughter after her.

LESSONS FOR OUR OWN HEARTS

For Hannah there was no escape. Her life was hopelessly bound to Peninnah. It's bad enough to have someone you must associate with continually jabbing at you for your failures, but how much worse to have this person under your roof. The harassment Hannah endured so distressed her that she became physically ill and could not eat. But though Peninnah clearly hankered for a cat fight, we see none here. Wisely refraining from growing mean-spirited and lashing back, Hannah took her problem to God.

Do you suffer from a "Peninnah pain"—those who drive you to grief with relentless criticism? They keep unloading their shotgun of one-upmanship at you, and you don't know what to do. Maybe you suffer a "barrenness" unrelated to the issue of children. You lack something significant to you, and your hard effort never seems to bear the fruit you so earnestly long to see. Perhaps you even live or work with one who abuses you with cruel words and deeds.

I think we all endure these trying people at times. My first full-time job was in downtown Los Angeles. A cute young co-worker with an outgoing personality was the "teacher's pet." She somehow saw my "barrenness" of inner confidence and chose to exploit it. Thinking to make herself look better by making me look worse, my rival did everything she could to ruin my reputation as a good worker. She maligned me to the boss and sabotaged my work. Her strategy worked. I was so crushed that rather than defending myself against the little opportunist, I quit.

Much later at another company, a co-worker nitpicked about everything I did. I tried hard to keep a godly witness by working hard and receiving my blows with grace. But I became the "whipping boy" for every problem. My boss began to harass me mercilessly until I dreaded going to work. Finally I felt the Lord release me to give notice.

On my last day of work, I wondered all day if my persecutors would give me any kind of a sendoff. Quitting time came and went with not so much as a good-bye. I sadly went to my boss's office to say farewell. She looked up, shocked, and said, "Cheryl, you weren't serious, were you? We need you too badly. I never bothered sending your resignation to the personnel office, and we have no one to replace you." Well, it was a struggle to extricate myself, but I finally did.

I can think of other stories in my life, too, but none compare with the harassment that some of you must bear. Perhaps you live in a family where no one loves or accepts you; so-called friends might contemptuously needle you for your commitment to a Christian lifestyle; you might suffer ridicule for your faith from co-workers; perhaps you are passed over for promotions, demoted, or receive threats for honoring Christ. Maybe you have chosen Christian service for your vocation or decided to give generously to God's interests, but rather than experiencing peace and joy, insults are burying you alive.

There is an even more devastating harassment that sometimes comes from spiritual foes. All persecution is at root spiritually motivated. Yet while the enemy of our souls can use human emissaries to defeat us, he often bypasses them altogether and comes at us directly. Here we can be our own worst enemy. Evil spirits cruelly harass us with inner accusations, and we not only listen, but we even side with their judgments!

A particular area of vulnerability for me is perfectionism. Judging life by God's perfect standards often puts me right in Satan's line of fire. Failing to meet those standards, I readily accepted demonic accusations: "You're a poor excuse for a Christian; you're a failure; you're no good; God is fed up with you, etc." Guilt and condemnation buffeted me. Thinking I was getting my just deserts, I had no shield of faith protecting me from the cruel darts. From personal experience, I know how this can drive a Christian to complete despair.

We probably cannot keep others from unjustly ridiculing us for whatever reasons; nor can we keep evil spirits from hurling their fiery darts at our hearts. But we can learn to respond wisely. Let's look to Hannah's story for some keys to victory over the harassing voices that try to drive us to despair.

Recognize God

Let's remember that Hannah's story is not so much about what she did to remedy her situation, but about God's sovereignty, grace, and faithfulness. Hannah sat under heaping abuse for years before the light turned on in her soul. God was the one who flicked the switch to "on" and gave her a revelation. She suddenly realized that there was a solution for her, and it rested in God. Without His intervention, Hannah would never have enjoyed victory.

Like Hannah, we cannot find our way past our afflictions without a move of God upon our hearts. When does God so move? I believe it begins when we come to the end of ourselves. Recognizing our complete helplessness, we depend on Him as our loving provider. When we rest our faith in His ability and His willingness, we begin to see breakthroughs in our lives. God gave Hannah whatever victory she experienced, and she knew it. He prepared her for her day of triumph, and she gave Him the glory.

The prophet Isaiah explains to God's people, "You were sold for nothing, and without money you will be redeemed" (Isaiah 52:3). Our hopes for victory rest completely on our redemption. We were spiritually sold into bondage, but through the precious blood of Christ, without any payment on our part, He has secured eternal redemption for us. We are free not only from eternal death and hell but from defeated lives of captivity to sin and the powers of darkness.

Come to the end of your effort to solve your problem; look to Christ. Think great thoughts of Him; think noble thoughts of Him. Believe He loves you and has not abandoned you, that He has some overriding purpose in allowing your trials, that He will make them work for your ultimate good.

Rise up

Predicated upon the foundational truth of God's redemption, the people of Israel had certain rights. As New Testament believers, we take these rights as our own. "Awake, awake, O Zion," Isaiah exhorts, "clothe yourself with strength. Put on your garments of splendor. . . . Shake off your dust; *rise up*, sit enthroned, O Jerusalem. Free yourself from the chains on your neck, O captive Daughter of Zion" (Isaiah 52:1-2, emphasis added). After God redeems, He esteems. His people become His prized possession, and He wants them to regard themselves as such.

Hannah "rose up" (1 Samuel 1:9). This "captive daughter of Zion" could not address God with her problem of barrenness until she finally had enough of the ridicule, browbeating, and provocation that bound her heart to defeat. She had to stop her pining, whining, and resigning. Once she flung her "chains" of oppression aside, turned her ear from Peninnah's voice, and went out the door to do business with God, things changed quickly for Hannah.

The devil, taunting and accusing me, used to make me feel so bad about myself that I could barely lift my eyes to heaven. I could not bear to face God, so I sat in a pool of self-pity and just kept receiving Satan's blows. Completely overwhelmed with feelings of failure and despondency, God had let me reach the end of my hopes for personal achievement.

But one day light dawned as the Holy Spirit fought through the dark plague in my heart, crying, "Enough is enough!" I rose up in faith and walked out of my accuser's presence. Standing to my feet, I ordered, "Satan, be gone! True, in myself I *am* unworthy, but I stand under the blood of Christ as a redeemed child of God. I refuse to take your harassment any longer and cast off your oppression. God loves me and His grace is sufficient for me! Go, go, go, in Jesus' name!"

Yes, I had to be forceful; I had to believe; I had to mean it. Unwilling to agree any longer with the devil's assessment of my relationship with God, I turned the eyes of my heart toward God and His promises. As I proceeded from Satan's cruel arena into the arena of God's truth, guess what I discovered? The black cloud had gone! Does this mean I never fought this battle again? No. But I had found an important key to my personal victory.

Press In to God

To recognize God as our answer, to rise up from our bed of affliction, and to actually receive God's gracious provision are separate things. Hannah could not receive her provision until she slipped off the manacles of accusation and went out to meet God at the tabernacle. Still in our distress, praying in faith is hard to do. But God understands. That is why He helps us: "In the same way, the Spirit helps us in our weakness. We do not know what we ought to pray for, but the Spirit himself intercedes for us with groans that words cannot express" (Romans 8:26). God's Spirit responds best to our wholehearted, if not ineloquent, cries when we rely on Him as our resource.

The prophet Hosea urged Israel to seek God with these words:

"Let us know, let us press on to know the Lord." The Hebrew word *radaph*, translated here as "press on," means to pursue ardently, to aim eagerly to secure, and to chase after. So strong is it that it can even mean "to persecute." Hosea closes out this verse, prophesying God's response to such earnestness: "His appearing is as sure as the dawn; he will come to us like the showers, like the spring rains that water the earth" (Hosea 6:3 NRSV).

Even when nothing outwardly seems to change, keep pressing in to "know" God—to love Him, trust Him, see His purpose, and believe His promise. Remember, "faith is being sure of what we hope for and certain of what we do not see" (Hebrews 11:1). As Hannah wrestled in prayer for her miracle, she found that perseverance, spiritual strength, and faith began to percolate in her spirit.

Fully Surrender

Who can understand God's purposes? His ways are so much higher than ours. Sometimes we hit a wall and feel stuck there. Beset by feelings of pain and rejection, we can think ourselves cursed, unloved, and guilty. We introspect, trying to dig up what we did wrong, but we just feel more lost. Our problem, however, might not be any sin at all. It might be that God is drawing us to a deeper spiritual level so He can better use us to impact our world.

What no one in our story could see was that God had a plan for Hannah all along. It wasn't just any old plan; it was a fabulous plan. But it involved postponing her years of childbearing. Samuel was conceived in God's heart long before he was conceived in Hannah's womb. But He waited. Why? For one thing: He waited for her to become willing to give her son to His service. A devout woman, she likely had her own good ideas, even wonderful ideas. But God had a better idea. Jesus said, "I tell you the truth, unless a kernel of wheat falls to the ground and dies, it remains only a single seed. But if it dies, it produces many seeds" (John 12:24). Hannah died to her plans and got hooked into God's plan. Moving beyond her own interests, she offered her child completely for the sake of His kingdom. "The child's yours, Lord!" she cried.

Isn't it amazing? God used even Peninnah's hammering for His purpose. Her sinful harassment drove Hannah to the place of full surrender. Hannah's travailing prayer became prevailing prayer when she offered God her best. By then it was no sacrifice at all; He had literally prepared her heart to make her astonishing vow. After she gave her only child to God with a psalm of praise, He gave her five more children to cherish. Truly, one who surrenders everything to the Lord receives much more in return!

What do you give to God—tokens, or your best? If you have children, have you truly "dedicated" them to Him, giving Him authority over their lives to shape them and send them on His chosen course? What about your own life? Does the Lord have your whole life—all you are, all you have, all you hope for? Until He does, you will suffer a spiritual "barrenness." Don't accept it! You will be ready for miracles when your heart truly cries, "I surrender all."

The Lord tested me years ago related to my son Billy. During a very lonely and difficult period of my life, I had to let him go to college. "Cutting the apron strings" seemed to happen at the worst possible time for me. I was extremely sad. Billy served as a part-time youth pastor, and the Bethel Christian Fellowship youth group was in revival mode.

One night I watched an animated cartoon version of the life of Samuel, and I felt Hannah's pain as Samuel, now a young man, came for a visit. She said to him, "Oh, Samuel, I miss you so much." Thinking of my own son, I tried to hold back my tears.

I was shocked to hear Samuel reply, "Oh, but, Mom, God is doing such great things at Bethel." It was just too much to be coincidence. Recalling how I had offered my son to God as an infant but was trying to take him back, I surrendered him afresh to God and to his Bethel.

Believe for God's Blessing

Eli's blessing greatly encouraged Hannah's faith for the Lord's blessing. A loving Father, God delights to give us signposts of His grace and favor as we await His plan's fulfillment. In transforming faith, Hannah believed that God had heard her prayer; she believed Him for her miracle. She went back to her family with a light heart and faced Peninnah with unruffled confidence. In faith she conceived and received her miracle.

God has miracles for you, too. Stop heeding the devil's lies: You're unworthy; you're not right; something's wrong with you. Believe the truth: God loves you; His ear is open to you; He will respond to your heart's cry. While Hannah feared that God had completely forgotten her, He accomplished everything she wanted and so much more. His plan was perfect, His timing perfect for her to bless the entire nation.

Will you recognize God in your situation, rise up against your harassment, press in to God, fully surrender to Him, and believe for His blessing? He delights to do good things for you: "If you, then, though you are evil, know how to give good gifts to your children, how much more will your Father in heaven give good gifts to those who ask him!" (Matthew 7:11).

As Samuel later moved back to his hometown, much to his mother's delight, I had a similar joy. Billy graduated from college and seminary. Beyond my wildest dreams, he moved his family to our town and is doing a great work for the Lord as he serves on our church's staff. What more could I ask for?

Heart Check

1. Do you suffer from some sort of debilitating harassment?

2. How does Hannah's story encourage you?

3. What steps might you take to overcome your affliction?

4. How can God use this trial for ultimate good?

5. Compose a prayer to God in response to this chapter's lessons.

2

Naomi

THE DEVASTATED HEART

BOOK OF RUTH

"IT'S OVER. What more could go wrong? I've lost everything . . . everything!" Of late Naomi could have filled bottles with her tears. Each night she cried herself to sleep, only to awaken again to unrelenting heartache. For ten years calamities had dogged her footsteps, and she had bravely forced herself to go on. But blow after disastrous blow had hit, until she was old and helpless—too old, she felt, to take any more. Something had to change, or she would die of a broken heart. Oh, but what could she do? What hope was there? Bitter thoughts chased through her mind: *I'd better just accept it. The Lord's hand is against me. He has consigned me to a life of misery. I'm under His curse.*

Naomi could not help thinking her life was over. She and her family had moved from her own country to a foreign land with hopes for a brighter future. But now her husband and two dear sons had died, leaving her alone with her sons' two idol-worshiping Moabite widows. Desperately clinging together, they felt lost, abandoned, and confused. They had no means of support—no jobs, no death benefits, no welfare system to bail them out.

Widowhood in the ancient world was a fate almost worse than death. Widows were often exploited and nearly always poverty-stricken. But worse than this, with her sons gone, Naomi had no one left to pass on her husband's name. To Israelites, having the family line cut off was nearly tantamount to extinction. It meant Naomi's family was lost from history, almost as if they had never existed.

To Naomi it seemed that God had turned His back on her, too. She had every reason to feel devastated. Thus, we call her aching heart The Devastated Heart. She was so deeply distraught by her extremely painful experiences and circumstances that she wanted to change her name, a charming name meaning "My delight," to Mara, meaning "bitterness."

This period of Israel's history was "when the judges ruled" (Ruth 1:1). When a ruinous famine swallowed Judah, even in Bethlehem (Hebrew for "House of Bread") little food could be found. Elimelech, Naomi's husband, felt responsible for his family, including his two sons, Kilion and Mahlon, who likely were sickly from birth (their names possibly mean "weak" and "pining"). Looking to the horizon from his home, he could see the fertile plateau of Moab about fifty miles away. The drought had not reached those parts, and it looked inviting. A time when "people did what was right in their own eyes" (Judges 17:6 NRSV), Elimelech did what seemed right for his family by deciding to emigrate to Moab for a while.

Naomi could remember vividly the day they bade their neighbors farewell. Elimelech had seemed so sure of himself. "You're sure you won't join us?" he had asked them confidently. "The Lord will provide for us well in Moab, and we'll return as soon as He restores His blessing to Judah." No one joined their little party though. As they pulled out, Naomi felt afraid. *Should we really venture into a pagan land for refuge? How can this be the Lord's will?* she wondered. But she kept her peace and quietly prayed for the famine to end quickly so they could come home soon and resume their lives.

Leaving Bethlehem, they crossed the Jordan River into the country of Moab and kept going until they were out of the famine zone. Naomi loved the Lord and had a strong attachment to the traditions of her people, so leaving her homeland to live among foreigners must have been difficult for her. She particularly did not want her beloved sons getting involved with Moabite women and their heathen gods.

After the initial difficulties of settling among strangers in a foreign land, we can almost hear Elimelech and Naomi in conversation:

"See, Naomi, it was a good decision; while our countrymen suffer from famine, we have plenty."

"Yes, Eli, but could not the Almighty have provided for us back home?"

"Oh, Naomi, have faith; we will return home soon, and everyone will wish they had been so wise."

Humph! How differently things turned out. How the Lord proved her husband wrong. If only she could turn back the clock! She would insist that they not step one foot beyond Israel's border. In those days famines were interpreted as a punishment visited on God's people for their sin, and this was a sinful period. Some say Elimelech should have stayed put instead of dragging his family off to Moab. Yet Scripture lays no blame on him. Whether or not he made the wisest choice, he did what seemed best for his family and surely did not think he was in any way forsaking the Lord.

Things, nonetheless, went disastrously for them in Moab. Elimelech had not foreseen that he might die and leave his family stranded there. But die he did, leaving a grieving widow with two sons in a foreign land without the support of friends and relatives who believed in the Lord. Naomi surely relied on her sons more than ever before for support.

Rather than struggling to return to Israel in a time of famine and personal distress, they stayed put in Moab. Perhaps the two young men had prevailed on Naomi to stay because they had fallen for local women. Their subsequent marriages to Moabites, Orpah and Ruth, must have further distressed Naomi, bringing her worst fears to pass. How she wished they had waited to marry God-fearing Hebrew girls, not idolatrous Moabites!

Despite her pain at the young women's different faith and culture, Naomi proved a godly example and a loving mother to all four young people. Pulling together as a family, they lived in mutual love and respect. But their short stay in Moab dragged into ten long years. Then tragedy struck again. This time Kilion and Mahlon died, leaving all three women childless widows. Oh, what grief filled Naomi's heart!

While God's law provided for a widow by compelling the nearest relative of the deceased husband to care for her, no such law existed in Moab. Suffering the desolation of widowhood with Ruth and Orpah in Moab, Naomi felt hopeless. She had no hope for grandchildren, no hope for anyone to carry on the family line, no hope of rising above the poverty level. She didn't even know if relatives in Bethlehem who might be charitably disposed toward her were still alive.

Naomi had often inquired about conditions in Israel, only to hear dismal news. One day, however, she heard a good report from the land of Judah. The Lord had visited His people, and the famine had ended. Food was once again in abundant supply. Reminded of the Lord's goodness, she longed to go home and share in His blessing. For ten years she had been away from God's people, God's land, and God's blessing. How her stricken heart yearned to retrieve the past when God had smiled on her. While she had little hope of finding help in Israel, she viewed this as her only hope. "Enough!" she decided. "This heathen land has brought my family to the grave, and if I stay here, I will soon join them. I'm going home. Perhaps the Lord will still have mercy on me. If not, I'd still rather die there than here."

Despite the tensions that can exist in mother/daughter-in-law relationships, we see only tenderness and love between the three women. They had been through so much together—working, weeping, enduring together—that their hearts were closely knit to each other. Still when Naomi approached her daughters-in-law with her decision, she thought they would want to stay in Moab. But they surprised her. They loved her so dearly that they both wanted to go with her. What a tribute to Naomi!

So the three packed up and left with what little they could carry. But barely making it to the road that would take them to Israel, Naomi came to a standstill. She had come to a realization that caused her fresh grief. Her daughters-in-law were all she had left, but they must stay in Moab. Loving them like her own daughters, she wished she could somehow provide for them. But she had nothing to offer. Foreseeing little hope for her own future in Bethlehem, she saw less

for them. Not only were they poor widows, but they would be foreigners, likely suffering prejudice, rejection, and poverty. What God-
honoring Israelite would marry an unbelieving pagan? No, from the
outset their future would be doomed. Thinking it selfish to take them
with her, she thought, *I can't do that to them; I must spare them this miserable fate.*

The two were still young; they could still find a life in Moab. If
their parents were still living, they had homes to go to where they
could be cared for. There they would also have a good prospect for a
second marriage. She, after all, was only a mother-in-law, and an old
homeless one at that. Besides, in her present state, she was miserable
company. Why should they walk this trail of tears with her?

"Go back, each of you, to your mother's home," she implored.
Commending them for being good wives to her sons and wonderful
daughters-in-law, she went on to bless them affectionately. "May the
LORD show kindness to you, as you have shown to your dead and to
me," she said. "May the LORD grant that each of you will find rest in
the home of another husband" (Ruth 1:8-9). She kissed them both,
assuming they would bow at once to her advice and start their lives
over among their own people and gods.

Instead, Orpah and Ruth both wept aloud, unable to bear the
thought of parting with their dear mother-in-law. They loved her
deeply, not for her happy spirit or wealth, but for her selfless character and love. "We will go back with you to your people," they cried
(Ruth 1:10).

Naomi would not hear of it. Even though she was old and
needed their support, and losing them meant more misery to her, she
wanted what was best for them. Concerned for their future, she persisted: "Return home, my daughters. Why would you come with me?
Am I going to have any more sons, who could become your husbands?" (Ruth 1:11).

To her way of thinking, it might have been worth a try for them
to go with her if she had other sons or even near kinsmen who might
marry them. Then they could take advantage of the levirate marriage
provision where a brother (or nearest relative) of a man who died

childless might marry the widow. The *go'el*, as he was called, would redeem the family's estate and raise up an heir for the dead husband (the first male child of this union). This law provided a way for the deceased man's name to continue and to keep his widow from poverty. But how could this apply to Orpah and Ruth? Naomi had no more sons and could think of no other kinsmen-redeemers. And further, she was too old to marry and produce offspring for them to marry later.

Naomi shook her head. No, she could do nothing at all for her beloved daughters-in-law, especially since, as she believed, the Lord was against her. Thinking that she had caused their grief by coming to Moab in the first place only compounded her sorrow. Therefore, she would much rather see herself left destitute and alone than to drag these whom she loved any further into her hopeless situation. Again, she urged, "Return home, my daughters. . . . It is more bitter for me than for you, because the LORD's hand has gone out against me!" (Ruth 1:12-13).

Even through the tragedies, Naomi's life and witness had impressed Orpah and Ruth. She had remained loyal to her God and had faithfully shared her faith with them. They appreciated her convictions and had even considered her claims, but they had never made a break with their own gods. While their differences had never become significant enough to divide them, Naomi probably doubted that the two had ever received her witness.

Now the women stood at their last crossroads together. This was the moment of truth for them all. Naomi was going home to her people and her God, and the two younger women had to make a choice. As Joshua had challenged Israel, "Choose this day whom you will serve," they must choose. Orpah and Ruth finally realized the gravity of the moment, that they must dig deeper than their surface emotions, that this decision involved their destinies. As Orpah assessed the cost, her resolve collapsed. Naomi's argument persuaded her. After weeping and kissing Naomi good-bye, Orpah left.

Yet Ruth would not so easily be shaken. Seeing how Naomi had put their interests first, Ruth loved her all the more. Naomi's efforts on her behalf only strengthened her resolve. She had never admired Naomi more than at this moment. In no way would she let Naomi dissuade her from going with her. Watching Orpah leave, she clung more tightly to her. As Naomi had forgotten her own interests for her sake, Ruth forgot hers for Naomi's sake. She wanted only one thing in life—to go with Naomi.

"Look," Naomi told her, "your sister-in-law is going back to her people and her gods. Go back with her" (Ruth 1:15). What Naomi did not yet realize was that as Ruth clung to Naomi, Ruth was expressing her deep desire to cling to Naomi's God as well.

She pleaded with Naomi, "Don't urge me to leave you or to turn back from you. Where you go I will go, and where you stay I will stay. Your people will be my people and your God my God. Where you die I will die, and there I will be buried." Then binding herself by an oath to stand by Naomi till death, she testified, "May the LORD deal with me, be it ever so severely, if anything but death separates you and me" (Ruth 1:16-17).

What a powerful witness Naomi had provided Ruth. The young Moabite was so taken with her that she would risk and perhaps forfeit any future opportunity to find security and have children. She would, under strictest oath, go wherever Naomi went; sleep wherever she slept; join herself to Naomi's people, land, and God; and even die and be buried in the same grave with her. Truly, this was the moment of Ruth's conversion. Dumbstruck, Naomi said no more.

The two widows, with hearts bound to one another and to the Lord, made their journey together. Their arrival in Bethlehem caused a stir, especially among the women of the community. News traveled quickly that Naomi had returned. "Have you heard the news?" they asked each other. The whole town turned out to meet her.

How dark and depressing for Naomi! As her old friends and acquaintances gathered to welcome her, they could scarcely believe their eyes. Before them stood a broken and destitute old woman, a sad shell of the one they remembered. "Can this be Naomi?" (Ruth 1:19) they asked in shocked disbelief. How different she was from the dignified woman who had left them ten years earlier. Then she had dreamed of being the matriarch of a happy and prosperous clan, with plenty of grandchildren running around her spacious home. Instead, her pride, her possessions, and her family had perished. All she had left was one equally destitute Moabite daughter-in-law.

As Naomi stood pathetically before the gawking crowd, the discrepancy between her name—meaning "my delight"—and the reality of her devastating experience weighed heavily on her heart. Wanting her former friends to know that she was not the person she used to be, she lamented, "Don't call me Naomi. . . . Call me Mara, because the Almighty has made my life very bitter. I went away full, but the LORD has brought me back empty. Why call me Naomi? The LORD has afflicted me; the Almighty has brought misfortune upon me" (Ruth 1:20-21).

Was she bitter against God? Maybe a little. But despite her severe depression, it is hard to believe that her heart ever became seriously embittered against Him. She complained of her bitter trials, that the Lord had dealt bitterly with her, and that bitterness best described her experience—but not her heart. To her, the Lord was the source of her affliction, and rather than fighting Him, she submitted to Him, even thinking to change her name to fit His will for her life.

Still as with any devastated heart, Naomi's perception had become distorted. She had lost faith in God's love for her and saw her suffering as a sure sign of His disapproval. Wanting to change her name showed she had lost hope for a better future. With little more than the clothes on her back, she foresaw nothing but grinding poverty and despair. Saying she "went away full," she idealized the past and forgot that she had left her country in a time of famine, not fullness. Also, she failed to realize what she *did* have left. She was not as empty as she thought. She had precious Ruth who would do anything for her, and she had God who put love for her in Ruth's heart. He had not forgotten her.

God had led Naomi and Ruth back to Bethlehem as the spring barley harvest began. Bethlehem, a farming community about five miles southwest of Jerusalem, was surrounded by lush fields that provided abundant harvests. There were two major harvests each year, spring and fall. The law designated that the poor could glean grain left by reapers (Leviticus 23:22). Since the fields had plenty of leftover grain at this time, Ruth saw an opportunity to eke out an existence by gleaning them.

Wanting to spare Naomi the hard work and humiliation of gleaning, Ruth gladly went out to the fields herself. She labored cheerfully and tirelessly at this menial task, counting it a privilege. Why? Because she loved Naomi. She would never be tempted to abandon her mother-in-law; she would never complain that she had given up her country, her people, her way of life in Moab; she would never look back. Naomi would soon realize the wondrous gift the Lord had given her in this amazing daughter-in-law.

Fortunately, the field God had led Ruth to glean belonged to a rich landowner who just "happened" to be related to Naomi's late husband, Elimelech. Having heard of Ruth's love for Naomi and her conversion to Israel's God, this man, Boaz, wanted to encourage her. He provided for the two women, first by letting Ruth glean and then by giving her extra privileges, including food and protection. He even invoked a blessing on Ruth, saying, "May the LORD repay you for what you have done. May you be richly rewarded by the LORD, the God of Israel, under whose wings you have come to take refuge" (Ruth 2:12).

Naomi would soon learn that she, too, was still under the Lord's wings. Ruth came home the first night loaded with more grain than a gleaner could normally collect. When Ruth told of Boaz's kindness, the despair in Naomi's heart cracked. For the first time in months, she saw a ray of sunshine, a flicker of hope. Astonished, she wondered what the Lord might be doing. "The LORD bless him!" she cried. She then praised the Lord for Boaz's kindness and remembered that he was a close relative, a kinsman-redeemer.

After this, Ruth kept working in Boaz's field. Like a shriveled plant needing but a little water to revive, Naomi's devastated heart began to heal. Her hope in God and for her future was reborn as her daughter-in-law lovingly cared for her and won the respect of the community. Townsfolk would ask her, "Naomi, do you realize how the Lord has blessed you with Ruth?" God's favor had been restored.

But the harvest season would soon end, and Naomi knew that gleaning fields was but a temporary remedy for her and Ruth. With renewed confidence in the Lord, she began to think and pray about a more permanent provision. She could not stop thinking about Boaz. As far as she knew, he was next of kin to her deceased husband and sons; he could serve as their *go'el*. He was an older man who might not have minded taking her for a wife. But again putting Ruth's interests first, she entrusted her own needs to God and eagerly embarked on a mission to get Boaz and Ruth together.

Fond of Ruth, Boaz had been treating her with special kindness. And this was the time for winnowing the harvested grain, a joyful time of plenty when he would feel especially magnanimous. The timing seemed perfect to remind him of his duty to either marry Ruth or find someone to marry her. Approaching Ruth one day, Naomi asked, "My daughter, should I not try to find a home for you, where you will be well provided for?" (Ruth 3:1). She had planned carefully and was sure Boaz would be working that night. Preparing Ruth to make a bold move to win him for her husband, she continued, "Is not Boaz . . . a kinsman of ours? Tonight he will be winnowing barley on the threshing floor. Wash and perfume yourself, and put on your best clothes. Then go down to the threshing floor, but don't let him know you are there until he has finished eating and drinking. When he lies down, note the place where he is lying. Then go and uncover his feet and lie down. He will tell you what to do" (Ruth 3:2-4).

Though Naomi's advice sounded strange to Ruth, she was telling her to act in conformity to Israel's custom and law. Still it was a risky move with opportunity for moral compromise and even scandal. Naomi knew both participants in the drama she was staging, however. She knew Boaz to be a God-fearing man, honorable and generous, and Ruth to be a wise and virtuous woman.

Ruth trusted Naomi's wisdom and integrity. "I will do whatever you say," she told Naomi (Ruth 3:5). When she got to the threshing floor, things went just as Naomi had predicted. Boaz, protecting his grain, stayed the night. When he awakened in the night to find Ruth at his feet, he asked, "Who are you?" (Ruth 3:9).

"I am your servant Ruth," she replied. Then she requested, "Spread the corner of your garment over me, since you are a kinsman-redeemer" (Ruth 3:9). Surely, this request for a pledge of marriage came as a shock to a man awaking from a sound sleep. How would he respond?

Ruth could not have hoped for a better response. Feeling honored, he gladly accepted her bold yet humble advance, promising, "I will do for you all you ask" (Ruth 3:11). But there was one possible wrinkle. A closer kinsman-redeemer existed. He reassured her that he would try to resolve the problem in the morning. Meanwhile for her safety, he advised her to stay there until daybreak.

When Ruth got home, Naomi asked, "How did it go, my daughter?" (Ruth 3:16). Their future seemed to hinge on the answer, but this was no anxious, fretful question. A healing had taken place in her heart, and she felt renewed trust in God's providential care. When Ruth explained the evening's events and showed her a gift of barley from Boaz, Naomi reassured her that the matter would be settled quickly.

True to his word, Boaz went straight to the city gate and found the other kinsman-redeemer. Presenting his case to him before the city elders, he explained that Elimelech still had property that Naomi now wanted to sell. Selling the field to a *go'el* would assure that the land would stay in the family name. As the nearest kin, he could serve as the *go'el* and redeem it.

The man agreed to the transaction until Boaz added that Ruth came with the property. Fearing this might jeopardize his own estate, he told Boaz, "You redeem it yourself. I cannot do it" (Ruth 4:6). He then removed his sandal and gave it to Boaz, signifying that he transferred all rights to Boaz.

Boaz at once made a public declaration: "Today you are witnesses that I have bought from Naomi all the property of Elimelech, Kilion and Mahlon. I have also acquired Ruth the Moabitess, Mahlon's widow, as my wife, in order to maintain the name of the dead with his property, so that his name will not disappear from among his family or from the town records. Today you are witnesses" (Ruth 4:9-10). The elders and everyone present replied, "We are witnesses." Then they gave Boaz their blessing.

Ruth and Boaz then married. Far from being abandoned, Naomi kept her mother-in-law status and continued as a principal participant in the joys that followed. When Ruth bore a son, Obed, it was Naomi whom the women congratulated. She now had a "son" and a whole new lease on life. Crediting the birth specifically to God's blessing to her, the women told her, "Praise be to the LORD, who this day has not left you without a kinsman-redeemer. May he become famous throughout Israel! He will renew your life and sustain you in your old age. For your daughter-in-law, who loves you and who is better to you than seven sons, has given him birth" (Ruth 4:14-15). Comforted from her sorrows, Naomi took baby Obed on her knee, symbolizing that she had adopted him.

She had been stripped of life's every blessing, but God did not leave Naomi devastated. He restored her life in every way. Enjoying His manifold blessing, she was now a woman of joy and plenty. Ruth and Boaz would always love and provide for her. She even got to hold a grandson after all. Through little Obed, her husband's line would continue to be passed on in Israel's genealogies. Little did Naomi know that the precious, tiny babe she held in her lap would later become the grandfather of Israel's great King David and that from David would come Jesus Christ, Israel's Messiah, the Savior of the world. This is how God honored and restored Naomi.

LESSONS FOR OUR OWN HEARTS

Have you ever thought that you made a wise decision, only to see it end in disaster? Casting blame at people like Elimelech and Naomi, who risk and fail, is so easy. "They went out of God's will for their lives," we self-righteously assert. We are certain that if they had listened to the Lord and obeyed Him, their lives never would have taken such a terrible turn. Yet Job's life experience proves that terrible things often happen to very godly people.

The primary lesson of the book of Ruth, therefore, is not correction to the self-willed, but rather reassurance of God's love and care for those who suffer. Most of us can probably feel compassion toward the characters in this story because we, too, at one time or another have suffered devastation for what some might call a poor decision. Clay and I surely have!

Fortunately, no one died in our case. We just died what seemed like a thousand deaths—and that was bad enough! Like Elimelech and Naomi, we once did what seemed best to us. Young and enthusiastic Christians, we had prayed and sought God with all of our hearts for direction. We would not have knowingly stepped out of His perfect will for anything, and we were sure that we were making the right decision.

Clay had been a street missionary in Berkeley one summer and had just published a book about his ministry experience. Subsequently, seminary and denominational officials alike saw him as a rising star to brag about. Many churches showed interest in hiring Clay following his seminary graduation.

As exciting as the future looked, however, we had a growing dissatisfaction with traditional church life. Like Elimelech, we tired of the struggle of living in a spiritual "famine zone." Searching for greener pastures, we looked longingly at the early church. Then we came in contact with what appeared to be a truly New Testament church. It was a church "on fire" for the Lord, where a mighty revival was taking place, souls were being saved, and abundant ministries flourished. Since the church happened to be in our denomination, we decided it must be right. We were ready to pay any price to join. We sought His will, and it seemed, despite the persecution we received, that He was leading us to make this radical decision. We confidently and expectantly left for our "Moab."

As it turned out, there was, indeed, a price to pay. For the privilege of joining this church where God was restoring New Testament Christianity, we confused our relatives and friends and tarnished our reputations by moving into a Christian "community household" associated with the church. Submerged in this life, we forfeited worldly resources, died to self, and became part of the revival. We were, so we thought, on the "cutting edge" of what God was doing.

Moving into one of the church's dozen households with some thirty other Christians, we knew we had lots to learn. Teachings seemed strange and radical, but as young Christians amid vastly more mature ones, we struggled but finally accepted teachings that said to submit to your earthly authority as you would to the Lord. Our egos suffered many blows, but in time we adjusted, and they sent us to head up our own household.

We saw God work in the structured environment to do miraculous healing in broken lives. God honored our efforts, setting captives free from drugs, alcohol, eating disorders, and demonic afflictions. Riding the vibrant wave of revival, the church experienced an exceedingly fruitful time.

Yet we had bought into a theology with seeds of error. Having given our spiritual superiors ultimate authority to hear God for us, our task was to submit and trust God. We managed to live this way until, increasingly, our consciences clashed with the church direction. Having surrendered our right to disagree, however, our Moab became an unfriendly and oppressive environment in which to live. We could not just leave because our pastor and elders, God's delegated authorities, would not release us. We feared being declared "in rebellion."

The church was suffering. What had begun in the Spirit was ending in the flesh; the crushing letter of the law bore down and squeezed the life from us. Ministries dried up; the Holy Spirit seemed to depart; the unity of the households, including ours, crumbled. All we had was an enslaving legalism whipping and driving us to press on.

I hoped I could find a solution by trying harder, digging deeper, pulling out a greater commitment. Continually striving, I did all the "right stuff": I prayed, fasted, worshiped, read through the entire Bible, memorized promises, repented of sins that I had and had not committed. I cried out to God with my whole heart. Like a pilgrim walking a journey of a thousand miles on her knees for God, I was certain that with a little more effort God would finally notice our plight and turn things around. After all, God was faithful . . . wasn't He?

Conditions only turned more brutal. After four years of living this way, Clay and I were in desperate emotional and spiritual distress. I also suffered physically, having developed severe chronic head and neck aches requiring me to down ten aspirins a day. For over a year, I woke up in pain and went to bed in pain. Finally thinking I was dying of a brain tumor, I went to a specialist who concluded that I must change my lifestyle. But I *couldn't* change my lifestyle. God had called us, after all, to a lifetime commitment to this church and way of living.

In the deepening crisis, I cried bitterly to God—yes, I would have changed my name to Mara, too! When I was not whining and lamenting, I was rebelliously shaking my fist at God. Optimism surrendered to doom, hope to gloom. One day I asked Clay, "What would God do if we just walked away? Do you think we would go to hell?" Showing the extent of our deception, Clay replied, "I don't know."

Finally, the lid blew off our church, revealing just how deeply cultlike tendencies had taken control of us. Confused, disillusioned, and broken, we were at the end of ourselves, the end of our resources, the end of our legalistic striving. Our devastation was complete. That is when, after five long years, the Lord graciously let us see the light. Although we had to leave our hellhole "in rebellion," we made our break.

Like Naomi, we shamefacedly limped out of Moab back to our gawking friends and family, forced to declare that we "went out full," only to return "empty." While our peers had bought homes and prospered, we had given up everything. Now, fractured and humiliated, we wondered why God had laid us waste. Like caged bees clamoring to get out, unanswered questions furiously banged around in our confused hearts. "Why, Lord, did You let us go there?" "Why did You disgrace us?" "Why did You let us get deceived?" "Why did we suffer such hellish bondage?" Clay's frustration and anger had been repressed so long, he sometimes screamed into his pillow for relief.

Naomi needed to go back to where she could find hope in God. For her, it meant getting out of Moab and going home to Bethlehem. Likewise, we needed to reclaim our heritage. Clay wanted to return to his roots, and he applied for the doctoral program at Eastern Baptist Seminary in Philadelphia where we knew several professors. But that meant I had to give up *my* roots in Southern California. Struggles over this decision alone almost doomed our fragile marriage.

Like broken refugees with little more than our two young children and an old blue van, we made our way east. That frigid February I felt small hope for a better future. Since our old clunker didn't even have a heater, we kept ourselves bundled with coats, caps, gloves, and blankets. Trying hard to keep my children warm, I cried at their rosy cheeks. How we had provided for our dear children! We couldn't even keep them warm! They were so sweet, so trusting, such gifts from God. How would it all end for them? I kept crying out to the Lord to spare them from the foolishness of our disastrous mistakes.

Was I bitter? Yes. In fact, the aching coldness in my heart posed a far greater hazard to us than the snowy outdoors. I just knew that this was not the way our lives were supposed to unfold, and I was angry about it. I had thrown away five of the best years of my life, and now I was headed across the country to who knew where. In my mind, God had required too much of me. All of my grandiose dreams and ideals lay shattered; in fact, my whole life lay shattered. "Why, God?"

Clay enrolled in seminary to work on his doctorate, and he became the pastor of a very small struggling church. As he preached to the little congregation, saying, "We can be fruitful again; we can live," he was preaching to himself and to me. Over the months and years, our healing came, not in turning inward or cursing our mistakes, but in loving and serving the Lord and others in our little church and community.

Eventually we returned to California where the Lord repaid us "for the years the locusts have eaten" (Joel 2:25). Today Clay serves as the senior pastor of a vibrant church of over five hundred where

God has often led hurting, dispossessed spiritual refugees to find restoration. Our church is a safe haven, a place of grace, of truth, and of God's restoring power. Why? A big part of it is that a young family who many years ago suffered devastation also by God's grace lived to recover.

We have escaped like a bird out of the fowler's snare; the snare has been broken, and we have escaped.

PSALM 124:7

Like us, many of you have stories of devastation. Some have come through to the other side testifying to God's faithfulness. You can join the apostle Paul in declaring, "And we know that in all things God works for the good of those who love him" (Romans 8:28). Others, however, in the throes of devastation feel that you are losing the battle, holding on only by the skin of your teeth. Naomi's story offers you, dear friend, hope for restoration.

It does not matter whether Naomi was perfect or imperfect, whether she should or should not have moved to Moab, or whether she did or did not do the right things to recover. What matters is that this is not a story about Naomi's goodness, her decision-making savvy, or her masterful self-effort to gain recovery. This is a story about the faithful God who led her back home, healed her broken heart, and restored her life.

What are some lessons devastated hearts can learn from Naomi?

We Can Keep Hoping in God

Naomi might have thought her life was over, her witness ruined. Yet all was not lost, and even in the ugly clouds of her devastating circumstances, silver linings can be seen. Isn't it interesting that right when she felt most miserable, when she thought that all was lost, when she could see nothing left in her of a worthy witness to her daughters-in-law, that both Orpah and Ruth clung to her?

Through all her trials, Naomi's life still provided a powerful witness to the reality of God. She had steadfastly loved and cared for her daughters-in-law, and, despite her faltering faith in His love for her, she had never turned away from her Lord. Obviously the two younger women retained great respect for both her and her faith. Ruth's steadfast refusal to heed Naomi's advice to return to her people and gods proved that, despite all the heartache, she chose to embrace Naomi's faith.

Just think: If Ruth had not grown to so love and respect Naomi, she would have stayed in Moab, an eternally lost pagan. She would not have come to faith in the true God. She would not have married Boaz. David, Israel's beloved psalmist and king, would never have been born! What a profound impact Naomi's life made!

How often do we think our life and witness are completely botched, that whatever light we might have had has been snuffed out forever. Yet God's Word promises, "A bruised reed he will not break, and a smoldering wick he will not snuff out" (Isaiah 42:3; also see Matthew 12:20). Even at our wit's end, God is making a testimony in us for His glory.

In hope Naomi turned her heart toward God's country, putting one foot in front of the other until she reached it. Though she could not perceive it then, God walked her back to her homeland. He still had a plan for her life. It was a painful time for her, but look at her ultimate blessing! Did she just happen to decide to come home at harvest time? Did she just happen to have an industrious daughter-in-law who loved and supported her? Did she just happen to have a kinsman-redeemer willing to make the right choice? These things were not luck or coincidence but God's sovereign and loving intervention.

In bitter times try to catch sight of God's provision for you. Don't let your devastating circumstances or sorrows and tragedies blind you to His love or His ability to restore and bless you. When severe trials hit, be like Naomi who resisted turning her back on God. Let your roots grow deep in the knowledge that He still loves you and is with you. In the darkness He will still bring light; among your woes He will still give you blessings to count. Hope in Him.

Surrender Brings Recovery

Surrendering to God in the happy seasons when life is going our way is pretty easy. Doing it in times of distress, however, when life spins out of control, when God no longer seems on the throne—well, that is another story! Perhaps you tried to do everything right. You served God, you prayed, you tithed, you obeyed, you turned the other cheek. You tried everything you could think of to pull out of your nosedive. Still you crashed and burned. Not only do you feel devastated, but you feel disappointed and disillusioned with God. You can't understand how or why He let this happen to you. Your heart feels cold and indifferent to Him.

When her loved ones died, Naomi learned to surrender to God. Although she tried to make a go of it in Moab, it just didn't work. When all was lost, she finally gave up trying to do it her way and set her heart toward home. God's Word tells us, "Listen to me, you who pursue righteousness and who seek the LORD: Look to the rock from which you were cut and to the quarry from which you were hewn; look to Abraham, your father, and to Sarah, who gave you birth" (Isaiah 51:1-2). When Naomi set her heart toward returning to Israel, this was her point of full surrender. This was the route that would lead to her restoration. In your time of distress, turn your heart toward home; bend toward God, not away from Him.

Despite Naomi's devastation, she never shook her fist and walked away from God, but she accepted her afflictions as His sovereign will. As it was in her best interest, it is in ours to bow our heads and our hearts to the Almighty. If we can somehow accept our crises as from God, we can find hope to believe He will also bring us through them as He did Naomi and a host of other biblical figures. Devastated, Job cried, "Surely, O God, you have worn me out; you have devastated my entire household. . . ." Later, however, a restored Job confessed, "My ears had heard of you but now my eyes have seen you" (Job 16:7; 42:5).

Today is a new opportunity for you to surrender your life, your questions, your pain and burdens to God and to trust Him to care for you. Believe He is at work in your life. Have faith. Your time of distress is no time to give up. It is a time to trust the Lord and to surrender anew to Him. Why not give Him a "sacrifice" of praise: "Through Jesus, therefore, let us continually offer to God a sacrifice of praise—the fruit of lips that confess his name" (Hebrews 13:15). "Give thanks in all circumstances, for this is God's will for you in Christ Jesus" (1 Thessalonians 5:18). When you begin to thank and praise the Lord again, even though it is a sacrifice to do so, you will have surrendered your heart to Him. You will have begun to trust Him again. You will be on the road to a recovery where you will know Him in a whole new way.

You will forget the shame of your youth and remember no more the reproach of your widowhood. For your Maker is your husband—the LORD Almighty is his name—the Holy One of Israel is your Redeemer; he is called the God of all the earth.

ISAIAH 54:4-5

We Have a Kinsman-Redeemer

When Naomi thought about Boaz, she must have asked herself numerous times, "Will he or will he not be my *go'el*?" When Ruth proceeded to the threshing floor to make her proposition, she, too, wondered how he might respond. The *go'el* of this story had the right to redeem but not the obligation. In that Boaz responded generously, he in some way foreshadows Jesus Christ, the great *Go'el*, who would one day descend from Boaz.

Unlike Naomi and Ruth, we do not have to wonder about our Kinsman-Redeemer. In faith we can go to His threshing floor, lay at His feet, and know for a certainty His response. Jesus Christ, our eternal Redeemer, looked upon our wretched condition with compassion. At great expense to Himself he redeemed us. Remember this: "For you know the grace of our Lord Jesus Christ, that though he was rich, yet for your sakes he became poor, so that you through his poverty might become rich" (2 Corinthians 8:9).

What amazing love! Rather than being ashamed of us in our hopeless and helpless state, our divine *Go'el* purchased us for His possession, thereby raising us to a place of honor and restoring to us our lost inheritance. As Naomi perceived that Ruth had won Boaz's heart, how much more you should know that even amid devastating circumstances, God's heart is directed toward you. Yes, He has heard your cries, and He understands your pain; He wants to comfort you and longs to embrace you in His arms of love; He wants to touch your heart, dry your tears, and draw you into His rest. Whatever sacrifices you have made for Him He appreciates and will not forget. He loves you beyond words. You are precious to Him. Run to your divine *Go'el*. Let Him love and restore you.

First Corinthians 13:8 promises that "love never fails." How Naomi discovered this truth! Much is made—and rightly so—of Ruth's incredible love for Naomi. But Naomi reaped what she had sown. Through all her pain, Naomi kept loving her daughters-in-law. Even while still grieving, she tried her best to comfort them and to put their interests before her own.

Are you heartbroken, crying your heart out? Try following Naomi's example, and invest yourself in showing God's love to others. You will be surprised by the love, joy, healing, and deliverance that come back to you. God promises, "Cast your bread upon the waters, for after many days you will find it again" (Ecclesiastes 11:1). Go ahead—you have an opportunity to give love away and discover how this one resource just keeps growing the more you give it away.

After Clay and I escaped the church that nearly claimed our lives, I studied everything I could about deception. I wanted to sound the alarm far and wide; I wanted to shatter the darkness; I wanted to launch a crusade and destroy the movement I saw decimating God's people. But Clay said, "Cheri, God has a *positive* call on our lives. This is what we need to focus on." Later I thanked God for Clay's wisdom. I still needed healing, something I never would have found by cursing the darkness.

Love is what I needed more than anything, and love restored me. Clay and I gave what we had—and it wasn't a lot—to our little church and community. He preached. I taught Sunday school. We knocked on doors, shared the love of Jesus, and sponsored outreach events. Instead of constantly licking my own wounds, I began to feel compassion again for the wounds of others. The little church grew. We saw the fruit of God's transforming grace—yes, in our own lives and in the lives of those being saved.

Incredibly, love has as much healing power for the one who gives it away as for the one who receives it. Did not our Lord Jesus say, "It is more blessed to give than to receive" (Acts 20:35)? Paul called love "the most excellent way" (1 Corinthians 12:31).

Naomi would never fully understand why she went through her devastating trials. You may never understand why you have gone through yours. Clay and I certainly never came to fully understand why we went through ours. Still God is faithful. An old hymn that we leaned heavily on after our devastating experience, "How Firm a Foundation," has a lot to offer us:

> *How firm a foundation, ye saints of the Lord,*
> *Is laid for your faith in His excellent Word!*
> *What more can He say than to you He hath said—*
> *To you, who for refuge to Jesus have fled?*
>
> *"Fear not, I am with thee—O be not dismayed,*
> *For I am thy God, I will still give thee aid;*
> *I'll strengthen thee, help thee, and cause thee to stand,*
> *Upheld by My gracious, omnipotent hand.*
>
> *"When through the deep waters I call thee to go,*
> *The rivers of sorrow shall not overflow,*
> *For I will be with thee thy trials to bless,*
> *And sanctify to thee thy deepest distress.*
>
> *"When through fiery trials thy pathway shall lie,*
> *My grace all sufficient shall be thy supply;*
> *The flame shall not hurt thee—I only design*
> *Thy dross to consume and thy gold to refine.*

"The soul that on Jesus hath leaned for repose,
I will not, I will not desert to his foes;
That soul, though all hell should endeavor to shake,
I'll never, no never, no never forsake!"

For we do not want you to be ignorant, brethren, of the affliction we
experienced in Asia; for we were so utterly, unbearably crushed that we
despaired of life itself. Why, we felt that we had received the sentence of
death; but that was to make us rely not on ourselves but on God who
raises the dead; he delivered us from so deadly a peril, and he will deliver
us; on him we have set our hope that he will deliver us again.

2 CORINTHIANS 1:8-10 RSV

Heart Check

1. Do you need healing from a devastated heart?

2. Have you in any way pulled away from the Lord in your heart?

3. How does Naomi's story encourage you?

4. What steps might God be leading you to take in your journey to restoration?

5. Compose a prayer to God in response to this chapter's lessons.

3

The Woman with the Issue of Blood

THE LANGUISHING HEART

MATTHEW 9:20-22; MARK 5:25-34; LUKE 8:43-48

IT IS A UNIVERSALLY disconcerting female affliction. That "time of the month" sometimes means relief, sometimes distress, throwing us into a constant love-hate relationship with our own bodies. Each month it can mean cramps, PMS, extra expense. It restricts our freedom, curtails our activity, and sometimes embarrasses us. Later in life, when we finally live to see our day of liberation, we find a mixed blessing where we are forced to decide between hormones and hot flashes!

The once-a-month ordeal is enough for most women to endure, but what if it never ended? Here is a pitiable woman, nameless to us, whose natural cycle was all out of kilter. It wasn't just a hormonal imbalance. Some uterine malady made her female plumbing go totally haywire. It was as if she had a nonstop menstrual period day in and day out for weeks, months, and years—twelve to be exact. Can you imagine twelve years of chronic physical torment like this?

Such a predicament required a great deal of discretion and personal care on her part. She was exhausted, wasting away under the burden of her constant affliction. She was debilitated, pale, and sickly. With sad eyes cast downward, she had the look of one completely beaten by her life experiences.

From a Jewish point of view, aside from leprosy she could not have had a more horribly humiliating and debasing condition. Since many viewed such maladies as a stigma, a punishment by God for some sin, she paid an immense emotional toll. Largely living in isolation, her life had become a social disaster. She was barred from fellowship, deprived in marriage, shunned by the community—all for this one medical condition. As a social and religious outcast, one of society's "untouchables," she would pay any price to get rid of her ailment. She had tried every treatment and regimen the world had to offer, and it had all come to nothing. Perhaps wealthy once, she had spent it all, only to be left impoverished and uncured.

The apostle Mark says of her, "She had suffered a great deal under the care of many doctors and had spent all she had, yet instead of getting better she grew worse" (Mark 5:26). Imagine how she felt: She had "suffered a *great* deal," "under the care of *many* doctors," "spent *all* she had," "yet instead of getting better she *grew worse*." The apostle Luke, a physician himself, said, "No one could heal her" (Luke 8:43). Because she continued so long in this miserable and disheartening condition, we call her heart The Languishing Heart.

To grasp the depth of her distress, we must know the cultural context. Jewish law regulated what menstruating women could and could not do in public or even in private (Leviticus 12; 15:19-27). A woman was considered ritually unclean during her period. While this did not imply sinfulness on her part, it still impressed her psyche with feelings of dirtiness. For seven days she was "unclean." Others could not touch her, sit in the same chair she had occupied, or even touch what she had touched. Her bed was unclean, anything she sat on was unclean, and anyone touching her was unclean. If someone even brushed against her, they had to wash their clothes, bathe, and be considered unclean until evening. For this reason many Jewish teachers avoided touching women altogether, lest they become unwittingly contaminated.

If a woman had a discharge that went beyond the days of her monthly cycle, she would be considered unclean for as long as she kept bleeding. On the eighth day after her discharge had stopped, she would have to go through a ritual cleansing, with a priest making a sacrifice for her. Only then could she be "clean" and return to normal community life. The Law concluded: "Thus you shall keep the people of Israel separate from their uncleanness, so that they do not die in their uncleanness" (Leviticus 15:31 NRSV).

Such an affliction would be depressing enough today, though most of us could still live somewhat normally. But think what it meant to one living in a culture that counted her an object of uncleanness for twelve years! Denied access to God in His temple or synagogue and kept from fellowship and worship with His people, she felt completely ostracized. Even her close friends and family, tired of cleansing themselves after contact with her, would avoid her. Any marital relationship had surely ended in divorce. She couldn't even go to market but needed someone to shop for her and leave the supplies on her doorstep.

She had never been one to simply sit back and accept her sickness. Somewhere in her languishing heart, she had persisted in her hope that God might provide her a solution, that as a daughter of Abraham she could be healthy. Refusing to leave one stone unturned, she had fought her affliction with every ounce of her strength. Physician after physician had treated her, but since many treatments by Jewish and Gentile physicians alike were no more than superstitious remedies, they had not worked.

In the Jewish Talmud (the collection of ancient rabbinic teachings), no less than eleven different treatments were given for this malady. Some were tonics that may have shown some effectiveness, and others were merely based on superstition. One was to carry the ashes of an ostrich egg in a bag; another was to carry a barleycorn that had been found in the dung of a white female ass (according to William Barkley's *The Gospel of Matthew*, Vol. 1, p. 346, and Alice Mathews's *A Woman God Can Lead*, p. 271). How far had this woman traveled to find an ostrich egg? How much donkey doo-doo had she waded through to find her barleycorn?

"I should give up," she may have told herself. But she began to hear stories, awesome stories of miracles. People everywhere were beginning to sing the praises of a young rabbi, Jesus of Nazareth, who was said to have an amazing healing ministry. Skeptical at first, she kept listening. The more she heard, the more she believed in Him.

One story in particular would have interested her a great deal—the story of a leper. He, too, had been "unclean." This leper had asked Jesus, "If you are willing, you can make me clean." How did Jesus respond? He reached out His hand and *touched* the man—a leper! "I am willing," Jesus had replied. He healed the man with a mere touch (Mark 1:40-42).

If Jesus had healed the leper, just maybe this compassionate Healer would have mercy on her, too. Faith built in her heart as she thought to herself, *The next time Jesus comes this way, I will get to Him, cast myself at His feet, and plead for mercy. If He is all that people say He is, He will help me.*

One day she heard shouting outside in the street: "The miracle-worker is coming! Jesus of Nazareth is here!" People tore from their homes and from the marketplace, racing from every direction toward the Sea of Galilee where He was arriving. An excited crowd gathered around the shore even before Christ and His disciples had disembarked.

Now was this woman's best and perhaps last opportunity for healing. We do not know any details of her approach to Christ, but it may have happened like this:

Her heart racing in adrenaline-induced anticipation, she threw her cloak over her and went out the door. Trying her best to avoid contact with others, she made her way toward the shore as quickly as she could move in her weakened state. As she went, she could remember back before her illness had struck. Young and vibrant then, she now dragged along like a ninety-year-old. *Oh, to be free!*

When she got to the shore, she found a huge crowd. Standing away from the horde, she wondered if Jesus of Nazareth might help her. As she sized up the situation, however, she became very sad, for the crowd was so great that she could not even see Him. Serious questions flooded her mind: *How can I get to Him? What should I do? What if I touch somebody?*

Having learned to distance herself from humiliation and pain, she found doubts assailing her mind: *This is a loathsome disease; what if He won't want to heal me? Why would He care about a poor hemorrhaging woman? What if He rebukes me in front of everyone? He'll probably prove to be one more letdown, and so why dare to hope? Wouldn't it be better to give up now than to have my hopes dashed again—before the whole town?* Then she remembered the lepers whom Christ had graciously restored, and hope recaptured her heart. Casting her doubts aside, her heart cried, *Enough! If I can just get to Him, I know He won't reject me. He will heal me—yes, even me! I WILL get to Him!*

But there was only one way to get to Jesus, and it meant breaking the law to do it. This would take faith—bold faith. For not only was she considered unfit to be in the presence of others, but she was especially unfit to approach a teacher or any person of rank or title. But she would do it! With pulse-pounding determination she stepped forward. No one noticed as she crept cautiously to the edge of the crowd. *What can they do to me that I have not already suffered—stone me? It's worth the risk!* In a recklessly daring move that revealed her desperation, she entered the crowd—something she had not done in twelve long years—and in a moment was swallowed up in it.

If anyone had noticed her, they would have known something was amiss. But they were too occupied with Jesus and with pushing and shoving each other. With her head completely covered to avoid detection, she began to weave her way toward Jesus. An unseen hand seemed to guide her forward, opening the way to her, and she made great progress, getting past even the disciples, who were doing their best at crowd control.

But then she came to a stop. Weak and exhausted, she had no strength to fight her way any further. The crowd was simply too tightly packed. *How can I get to Him? And once I do get to Him, what will I do?* Unlike others who could openly appeal to Jesus for healing, her condition was of an embarrassing and shameful nature. To publicly state her need was something she could not bring herself to do. If she attracted attention, the crowd might angrily thrust her away.

Suddenly a commotion interrupted her thoughts. A voice rose

above the cacophony, a desperate voice, a sobbing voice: "Let me through! Let me through! Please, please, let me through!" a man pleaded.

Then she heard other voices commanding, "Make way; make way for him." She could not see what was taking place, but she heard someone gasp, "It's Jairus, the ruler of the synagogue!" The crowd grew silent.

People around her seemed to crush in all the more to hear Jairus plead with Jesus: "My daughter has just died. But come and put your hand on her, and she will live" (Matthew 9:18).

Everyone, including the woman, stood amazed at Jairus's faith in Jesus, but when Jesus agreed to go with him, she could not help protesting in her heart: *Wait! What about me, Lord! I need You, too!"* But Jairus was important. She was nobody—no, she was less than nobody. Dismayed and fearful of her opportunity slipping away, she wanted to scream, "JESUS!"

Just then, to her astonishment, the crowd parted before her, and she could see Him! He and Jairus were coming *her* way! As they approached, she studied their faces. Jairus had hope in his eyes, and Jesus had certainty. Just seeing Christ, her own heart surged with dynamic faith. She believed He could do anything. *Jesus of Nazareth has the power to heal that dead girl, and His power will heal me, too!*

She knew what to do. It would not interrupt Him or create a scene. She would simply sneak up unnoticed, reach out her hand, and touch Him. That would do it! He had so much healing power that it would just spill over onto her if she reached for it. Why, she did not even have to touch His body. *If I only touch his cloak, I will be healed* (Matthew 9:20-21).

What gave her such faith? We know that "faith comes from hearing the message" (Romans 10:17). The message of Christ's ministry was everywhere; testimonies of His miracles abounded. There were even reports of others being healed by simply touching Him (see Mark 6:56; Luke 6:19). For whatever reason, her faith was greatly encouraged, and the Holy Spirit moved powerfully on her.

Along with everyone else, she stepped aside to let Jesus and Jairus pass. As she watched the Great Physician go by, she felt His power-ful presence that further convinced her. Touching Jesus, or anyone else for that matter, was unlawful for her, but now she no longer cared. Casting aside all fears, doubts, and inhibitions, she quickly positioned herself behind Jesus as the crowd again closed ranks to fol-low Him.

Looking down, she eyed the hem of His garment. In obedience to the Law, every good Jewish male's outer garment was fringed on its corners with four tassels along the bottom edge as a reminder that he belonged to God (Numbers 15:37-41; Deuteronomy 22:12). In a startling impulse of faith and courage, she bent down, reached out her frail hand, and not only touched but grasped the fringing. The Greek word used here, *haptomai*, means to fasten one's self, adhere or cling to something. Clutching His holy garment, she called forth her miracle.

Instantly, in a breathless moment of release, she felt a jolt—not a destructive jolt but a healing jolt. Healing energy gushed into her, coursing through her body, and she knew instinctively that she was free. Her longstanding disease was gone! Her incurable flow had stopped! But she had no time to enjoy her miracle. Jesus came to an abrupt halt. Wheeling around, He asked, "Who touched me?" (Luke 8:45).

Oh no, He noticed! Terrified, she wanted to run. The healing sen-sation had been so powerful that she thought she must have taken what was not hers. Perhaps she had even drained Jesus dry. He looked shocked, determined, demanding. Everyone nervously denied His charge, and she dared not admit it either.

That day the disciples acted as bodyguards, and it was all they could do to protect their Master from being crushed by the crowd. They looked at Him, perplexed, wondering how He could ask such a crazy question. *Lots* of people were touching Him! They protested, "You see the crowd pressing in on you; how can you say, 'Who touched me?'" (Mark 5:31 NRSV).

But Jesus Christ knew the difference between the touch of the crowd and the touch of faith. He knew there was one person there who knew *exactly* what He meant. Refusing to take another step, He replied, "Someone touched me; I know that power has gone out from me" (Luke 8:46).

We should not think that Christ was less than fully in charge of this situation. He did not need the woman to identify herself. Nothing really could escape the Son of God's detection. As the Great Physician, He knew His patient. He simply wanted the one in the crowd who had faith enough to claim His divine power to admit it. Her confession of healing would not only bring glory to God, but it would provide an opportunity to commend great faith.

The dear woman would have been more than happy to go away unnoticed, having received what she came for. But Jesus wanted more for her. With years of rejection still locked up in her heart, she needed more than physical health. She needed her wounded heart healed. This could not come by an impersonal touch of His garment but only through a personal relationship with Him. True, an unclean woman had violated the Law by touching Him. But He was not angry with her, as the heart of the Law is love. "For the law was given through Moses; grace and truth came through Jesus Christ" (John 1:17).

But the woman knew none of this. She thought, *Oh, what a mistake I've made! I just broke all the rules! How could I, an unclean woman, have presumed to think I could get away with defiling a holy man of God?*

Jesus stood waiting. She tried hard to be inconspicuous and avoided looking at Him. But feeling His scrutinizing gaze, she guiltily stepped forward and fell at His feet in trepidation. A very private matter turned embarrassingly public as right before everyone she confessed how and why she had touched Him and that she had been healed instantaneously. She told "the whole truth" (Mark 5:33). Wondering what He might do to her, she looked into His eyes and saw something startling, something that melted her fear. He exhibited not even a hint of anger. Instead, His countenance showed compassion and acceptance.

Jesus did not want His shy patient groveling on the ground before Him. Far from denouncing her scandalous act, He tenderly addressed her before the crowd, calling her "daughter." What a lovely salutation to one who for twelve long years may have heard no sweet words of endearment. That one word told her that He invited her into relationship with Him, that He claimed her as His own. He had the affection of a father toward her; she was, indeed, a daughter of God—worthwhile, included, affirmed, cherished. In that moment her restoration went beyond her body to include her soul and spirit. She found mercy, acceptance, approval, a new identity—and her languishing heart was cured. This is the only place in Scripture where Jesus ever addressed a woman as "daughter."

I will be a Father to you, and you will be my sons and daughters, says the Lord Almighty.

2 CORINTHIANS 6:18

Jesus publicly commended her faith: "Your faith has healed you" (Luke 8:48). How often did He lament those, even among His disciples, who were of little faith. Given the recurrent failures of their faith, this woman's faith all the more impressed Him. He honored it; He cherished it deeply. "Go in peace," He told her warmly before going on with Jairus.

Oh, the grace of our Lord Jesus! This woman had been cut off from the courts of God's house but not from Him. If He had allowed her to leave without confronting her, not only would her witness have been lost, but she might have suffered guilt and shame over her action despite her physical healing. It was a humiliating confession that Christ forced her to make, but, oh, the freedom she enjoyed in her full surrender. The truth had set her free; what she had done need not remain hidden but could now be freely proclaimed.

Her fear was gone, and a wave of relief must have flooded her soul. With her heart suffused with gratitude, her life infused with vitality, and her world transfused with sunshine, she ran home rejoicing. She was a new woman, a true believer, a complete daughter of Abraham.

Come, ye disconsolate, where'er ye languish—
Come to the mercy seat, fervently kneel;
Here bring your wounded hearts, here tell your anguish:
Earth has no sorrow that heav'n cannot heal.

THOMAS MOORE

LESSONS FOR OUR OWN HEARTS

Have you ever been in a discussion about which gifts of the Holy Spirit are the most important and which are the least? One thing is certain: For those who desperately need healing, this gift quickly leaps to the top of the list. No matter what the cost, people will spend their livelihoods, even traveling the world over, looking for a cure to their diseases. And when every human recourse fails, their appetite for God and His healing power becomes ferocious.

So it was with the woman in our story. Every other option had dried up. Jesus was "it." We can imagine that once she caught on to the fact that Jesus offered her hope, she lived and breathed Jesus. And God saw it. She may have been a nameless face in the crowd to others that day, but she was not to Him. Aware of her languishing heart, He heard her prayers, let her faith develop, and got her to the right place at the right time. Sufficiently prepared, she did not hesitate at her opportunity.

I can only imagine the torment this poor woman had gone through for twelve years. I suppose the closest I have come to languishing under a longstanding physical affliction is with my chronic back problems for over twenty-five years. Even then, however, I only languish sometimes. If things get too bad, I can always stay in bed for a few days to get my body back to a tolerable state.

Still there have been times when it has become a depressing health issue for me. I know what it is like to be prayed for, to have hands laid on me, to be anointed with oil on a hundred different occasions in a hundred different places and still come up empty. I know what it is like to have those praying for me ask, "Are you better? Do you feel anything?" I feel the responsibility to somehow encourage *their* faith. I know what it is like to feel the guilt, the failure, and the shame of letting *them* down, of not having enough faith, of not being quite perfect enough to "receive my healing." I know what it is like to have Satan whisper in my ear that I did not repent deeply enough, did not pray sincerely enough, and that surely I had committed some terrible sin that had grieved God's Spirit.

I know what it is like to claim my healing, to praise the Lord for it, to assert that as God's child, who stands under the atoning blood of Jesus Christ, I deserve healing because it is my birthright. I know what it is like to admit I deserve nothing, to humbly plead for healing, to say, "Thy will be done." I know what it is like just to grin and bear it. I even know what it is like to avoid opportunities for prayer in order to escape another disappointment. Yes, to some degree I know what it is like!

I also know what it is like to try various treatments and remedies. I will never forget languishing in physical pain, finally going to one doctor who made me keep a journal of my emotions. Week after week he psychoanalyzed me, only to ultimately tell me I had "chronic pain syndrome" and to take antidepressants.

I thought, *Well, if I were not depressed before seeing this man, I certainly am now!* How *happy* I was when an MRI ordered by another doctor showed a disk problem, when a neurological test showed a pinched nerve affecting my legs, when a blood test showed arthritis. I wasn't crazy after all! Yes, to some degree I know what it is like.

At the same time, however, I have *no* idea what it is like. My problems quickly pale when compared to the throbbing pain and distress that some of you must bear. You languish under a seemingly endless sentence of torment that makes me unqualified to offer a word on the subject of misery. Perhaps you desperately need God to come through for you. Perhaps you are so weak and diseased that you can barely sit up in bed. This is not just a matter of inconvenience to you—it is a matter of life and death.

I wish I could come up with the right key, some pat answer, a certain guarantee for you. I want to tell you what you want to hear; I want to assure you that Christ will heal your condition here and now.

The only thing I can say, however, is that though He has never completely healed me, I am encouraged. Why do I feel encouraged?
Because I can say that He has proven His grace to be sufficient, that
He remains my dearest and best Friend, and that I look forward with
full assurance of hope to the day when I am completely whole, either
in this life or in the next.

While I say that God has never *completely* healed me physically,
that is not to say that I don't believe in healing or that I have never
experienced it. Recently my foot kept cramping up. I massaged it,
wore the best shoes, soaked it, took calcium, etc.—all to no avail. It
seemed yet another sign that my body was going to pieces, and I was
unhappy about it. One night at a worship service, however, I forgot
my problems and began to stomp my foot joyfully to the music.
Suddenly my foot screamed to stop. I removed my shoe, rubbed my
contorted foot feverishly, and prayed, "Well, Lord, I'm not going to
let this rob me; I'm praising You anyway." To my amazement my foot
stopped hurting instantly.

Does this experience answer any of my questions about healing?
No, it only raises more! *Why, Lord, did You choose to touch my foot and
not my other longstanding afflictions? Why did You touch me at all? Why don't
You touch other friends who need healing? Why don't You get this world's attention by dramatically emptying hospitals all over the world? Well, why not,
Lord? It sounds like a good plan to me. It would really show Your love and
power.*

This is not yet reality though. In fact, when we take a hard look
at the suffering of this war-ravaged, disaster-torn, disease-ridden
mass of humanity, we might be tempted, along with the rest of the
unbelieving world, to think that believing in a God of love is
Pollyannaish. Don't we wonder how a loving God fails to put an end
to the constant afflictions of His bleeding world? And when the suffering hits us personally, don't we feel intensifying inner conflicts?

By and large, we have embraced a theology today that only adds
to our conflict. The doctrine, uniquely ours in history, tells us that
life—especially the Christian life—should be easy and painless. God
is here, we think, to make sure it works just that way—to His glory,

of course. In the face of suffering, we even feel some moral outrage toward Him. Demanding an accounting, we cry, "Why, God?" Yet this was not the theology of the saints of yesteryear. The early church fathers, a host of missionaries, martyrs, and believers throughout the ages accepted suffering as a normal part of life.

When it comes down to it, suffering is a mystery that defies human reason. Veteran sufferers have learned two things: Striving to understand the "why" is a frustrating and futile effort, and learning to trust the "Who" is a becalming and blessed comfort. In fact, the more we strive to make sense of our suffering, the more likely it is that we become embittered by it. If we focus our efforts more on our response and less on the reason, we will find more peace in our hearts and a growing richness and depth in our lives. "I am suffering; how will I respond?" should be the great question we seek to answer.

Some of the godliest people with long lists of people praying for them continue to suffer intensely. Some never do find the healing they so desperately seek. And God refuses to answer why. Job never found out the why of his loathsome, painful, hideous afflictions. He never found out why he lost his ten children in a single day! Friends thought they knew the reason—obviously he had sin in his life. But they were wrong! When Job finally did get a conference with God, he surely thought God would explain Himself. Yet despite one of God's longest dialogues in Scripture—four long chapters—He never offered Job a reason for his suffering. His answer was simply, "Acknowledge and trust Me."

In a general way God has revealed what He will about our suffering. Right off, the book of Genesis explains where human suffering started. Way back in the Garden God gave our first parents freedom to choose to love and obey Him. But they—and now we—made the wrong choice by defying God and His loving intent for humanity. This sin doomed us and spoiled a perfect planet.

While we can see much beauty in God's creation, that beauty is but a hint of what it once was. Due to our abused freedom, pain and suffering entered the world that was never part of God's original design, and with it came death. In time even bodies that He heals wear out and die. We cannot fault God in this; we are the guilty race. That the world still exists at all testifies to His great mercy, not to injustice. Rather than meting out the justice we deserve, He effected a rescue mission. In sending His Son to die in our place, He proves both His intense hatred for sin and His intense love for sinners. Wanting "everyone to be saved and to come to the knowledge of the truth" (1 Timothy 2:4 NRSV), He offers us eternal life in Christ.

Still this suffering, ruined planet will one day be destroyed and replaced with new heavens and a new earth. But in the meantime its inhabitants groan under its pangs. As my sister Gayle, a volunteer hospital chaplain, tells questioning patients: "We live in a fallen world and in fallen bodies. We're all marching toward final decay in these human tents, and some are running faster than others in that direction—until we all stand before the Lord."

The earth dries up and withers, the world languishes and withers. . . .
ISAIAH 24:4

Although God is sovereign and permits suffering, He does not cause it and even grieves over it. In His great love, He takes the pain we endure in this fallen world and uses it for our good—yes, our good! While none of us enjoys suffering, there are useful purposes in it. Bent on independence from God, our suffering constantly reminds us of our condition. It shouts to us that all is not right on this planet—that we are wrong; we are sinful; we are fallen; we are helpless; we need mercy. We need God!

We may struggle hard to retain our self-sufficiency, but suffering makes us come to terms with our frail and temporary existence here. It compels us to grapple with ultimate issues, transcendent realities . . . God. We are given grace to recognize our desperate need for Him; to respond to His call; to trust Him; to believe that He hears our cries, feels our pain, and really does care about it; to believe that He has some overriding purpose in allowing our suffering. It makes us declare with hope and gratitude that "our citizenship is in heaven. And we *eagerly* await a Savior from there" (Philippians 3:20 italics added).

As I walked along the lovely little country lane where I once lived, I would notice vines growing up the sides of the trees. In fierce storms power lines came down and electricity went out, but those vines were never worse for the wear. Thrashing winds could beat at them, but their tendrils would cling tightly to tree bark. It didn't seem to matter on which side of a tree the vines grew. If they were on the side away from the wind, the tree protected it. If they were on the exposed side, the wind just pressed the vine closer into the tree. Likewise, whether God shelters us from difficulty or allows us to suffer exposure to life's harsh realities, one thing is sure: Being close to Him is our victory.

We may never know the "why" of our personal suffering. But Christ's own passion—His anguish in Gethsemane and agony on the cross—is our eternal assurance that it is not for lack of love that God permits us to suffer.

The Bible offers awesome hope and clear directives concerning our tribulations: "Dear friends, do not be surprised at the painful trial you are suffering, as though something strange were happening to you. But rejoice that you participate in the sufferings of Christ, so that you may be overjoyed when his glory is revealed" (1 Peter 4:12-13). Ultimately all of our pain and affliction will end in glorious triumph. We will go to a much better place where suffering is unheard of. What an awesome hope is ours!

Pain is short, and joy is eternal.
JOHANN CHRISTOPH FRIEDRICH VON SCHILLER

God can use our afflictions for great good, but that doesn't mean that we shouldn't seek Him for healing. The story of the woman with the issue of blood speaks to the fact that God cares about our bodily ailments. Jesus healed her infirmity, and He cares no less about ours. This compassionate Christ, who is "the same yesterday

and today and forever" (Hebrews 13:8), still has power that goes out
from Him to heal.

While this story is simply the testimony of one woman's experience, not a pattern for healing, there are still things we can learn from
her. What did it take for her to receive her healing?

It Took Suffering

If she had not suffered as she did, we never would have heard of her
great faith. In fact, she never would have had great faith at all. How
often we try everything else first, and then the Lord. This woman's
affliction drove her to try everything she could think of to reclaim her
health. But after twelve years of untold misery, after spending her
entire livelihood and ending up impoverished, after having her self-
sufficiency shattered, after losing her entire support network—family, friends, church, community—she was at the end of herself and
her resources. But isn't it amazing that all this did not destroy her?
On the contrary, her poverty of spirit prepared her to see Jesus as her
only hope. Made rich in faith and ready for a miracle, she reached out
and touched the divine Son of God.

God's Word has promises for those with languishing hearts:
"The LORD is close to the brokenhearted and saves those who are
crushed in spirit" (Psalm 34:18) and "The sacrifices of God are a broken spirit; a broken and *contrite* heart, O God, you will not despise"
(Psalm 51:17). "For this is what the high and lofty One says—he who
lives forever, whose name is holy: 'I live in a high and holy place, but
also with him who is *contrite* and lowly in spirit, to revive the spirit of
the lowly and to revive the heart of the *contrite*'" (Isaiah 57:15). In all
these instances, the same Hebrew word is used—*dakah*, meaning to
be broken or crushed, even crushed to pieces. Do you feel as if you
have been ground into powder? Have hope! God is near you.

If the languishing woman had not known suffering, it is likely
she never would have grown strong in faith. Could it be that this hostile planet with so much misery is a suitable place for God to build
people of strong character to rule and reign with Him one day in
heaven? It seems that the School of the Spirit in which we are

enrolled must include suffering, for look what it produces: "Not only so, but we also rejoice in our sufferings, because we know that suffering produces perseverance; perseverance, character; and character, hope" (Romans 5:3-4).

It Took Perseverance

It is good that suffering produces perseverance, because the woman needed perseverance to finally seize her prize. She may have died a thousand deaths, but she did not give up her fight. She was like a welterweight boxer in the ring with a heavyweight champion. The devil kept pummeling her and sending her down for the count, but every time the match seemed over, she got back up. Down but never completely out, she always had enough hope left to try one more thing. Had she given in to thoughts of death and suicide, she would not have been ready for her miracle. No, despite it all, she persevered in the hope that God had a solution for her.

We, too, must never give up in despair. The blessing might seem long in coming, and you may be continually disappointed, but trust Him and His timing. Be a prisoner of hope, not of despair. Even if you have tried all that the world can offer and have already learned to look to Christ, but nothing is happening, don't give up! Your life is not over. God loves you, and He will never send you away empty. He can change your unchangeable situation. The woman's malady was longstanding, but her healing was instantaneous.

The book of James urges us: "Consider it pure joy, my brothers, whenever you face trials of many kinds, because you know that the testing of your faith develops perseverance. Perseverance must finish its work so that you may be mature and complete, not lacking anything" (James 1:2-4).

It Took Overcoming Negativity

The woman had serious wounds in her soul. How could she not? The whole community saw her as a poor, sick nobody who would be better off dead. Yet while they had given up on her, viewing her as a drain on them, she had not given up on herself or on God. She rose above all the negatives and went out to meet the Great Physician. Because she did, she not only found her body healed, but in meeting Christ, she found her heart healed as well. In that encounter she learned that she was known, loved, and valued by Him. He took pleasure in publicly calling her "daughter." Surely, the healing of her broken heart was a far greater miracle than the healing of her broken body.

One of the great tribulations of those who live with afflictions, whether physical or otherwise, is isolation. They think that no one understands, that they have been abandoned. Many withdraw in defeat. Perhaps you can relate well. Do you fight feelings of being forgotten or overlooked? Do your prayers seem to shatter on the ceiling to rain back on your head in broken pieces—or worse, never even make it to the ceiling? Perhaps you feel rejected, worthless, deprived, insignificant, or even condemned and punished by God. These feelings can be so demoralizing!

You need to know: God has *not* forgotten you! That your prayers are not answered in the way you prefer does not reflect on what He thinks of you. True, He sometimes chastens us for sin, but if we have repented, there is no need for languishing under a burden of self-defeating guilt. More than likely, God has you in the crucible to refine you simply because you are so significant and special to Him.

You are dear to God; you are always in His sight. Never withdrawing His love, He cries to *you*, "Can a mother forget the baby at her breast and have no compassion on the child she has borne? Though she may forget, I will not forget you!" Then stretching out His hands to prove the depth of His love, He shows you their marks, saying, "See, I have engraved you on the palms of my hands" (Isaiah 49:15-16). Each of us—no matter how twisted and broken our bodies or souls—is eternally significant to God. No one is a nameless face in the crowd, and that includes you. Whether He chooses to heal you physically or not, He does have healing of some kind for you. It is not fitting for you to shrink back in shame and defeat when you know that Christ loves and accepts you. And He does. Reach out and touch

Him. He cherishes you and calls you "daughter," and there is hope and healing in that alone.

It Took Faith

God rewards faith. Sometimes the faith is ours, sometimes the faith is that of friends and family on our behalf, and sometimes it seems He works unrelated to anyone's faith. He is sovereign and cannot be pinned down to one specific formula.

The woman in our story herself had great faith. We might wonder how she who had suffered so much disappointment in life found such faith. As already expressed, faith often comes alive when we are at the end of our rope, when every other resource has been tried and failed, and we are on the ragged edge of life, stripped of self-sufficiency. Also the woman did not leave herself time for counting her losses, licking her wounds, being a martyr, indulging in self-pity, shrinking back in shame or defeat, or waiting for death to overtake her. She was too busy keeping hope alive in her heart.

The Bible tells us to think on "whatever is true, whatever is noble, whatever is right, whatever is pure, whatever is lovely, whatever is admirable" (Philippians 4:8). She didn't just "think positively"; she thought positively about Jesus Christ. She no doubt listened to faith-building stories about Him, His teachings, and the miracles He performed until she not only believed in His power, but she believed that His power was for *her!*

The woman gave no place to complacency, that generator of spiritual stagnation and exterminator of faith. Some of us might think, *Well, God knows my address; if He wants to touch me, He knows where to find me.* But genuine faith requires positive action. Faith without such action is not faith. The woman went to Christ. Not only that, but she fought her way through a crowd to get to Him, and that took faith on her part; it took determination. Faith is not a matter of strength but of belief. Though she was physically weak, probably dying, she still had strength to catch hold of Jesus.

You, too, can reach out to Christ by faith. Believe in His love for you; set your heart on His promises; reach out in faith, knowing that

His power is sufficient to meet your need. "In this you greatly rejoice, though now for a little while you may have had to suffer grief in all kinds of trials. These have come so that your faith—of greater worth than gold, which perishes even though refined by fire—may be proved genuine and may result in praise, glory and honor when Jesus Christ is revealed" (1 Peter 1:6-7).

It Took Surrender

I believe the woman in our story had a heart surrendered to God. We see no indication, despite her life of torment, that she got angry and blamed God for her woes. She was unhealthy and ostracized, but we do not see her questioning His fairness. In fact, she kept her hope in Him alive, something she could not have done if she had angrily hardened her heart against Him.

Surrendering to God does not mean we passively sit back and succumb to our affliction; it does not mean we raise a white flag and give up on life. We do not see passivity in the woman for an instant. She knew when to storm heaven's gates. We need discernment to know when to let go and when to fight our way through a situation. We will never know exactly what to do unless our heart is kept surrendered.

An elderly woman I once knew got terminal cancer. Her friends were like Job's friends, telling her that if she had enough faith, she would be healed and that she must have some sin in her life that blocked her healing. She took it to the Lord and prayed, "Lord, I don't believe this is true, but if there is sin in my life, I repent. I want to be healed, and I ask to be healed, but it is up to You. If You want to take me home to be with You, then so be it. I surrender my life to You." She rose with peace in her heart, and guess what? God healed her, and she went on to live another fruitful ten years of service for Christ.

On the other hand, the Lord denied the apostle Paul's request for healing of his physical infirmity. Here was the great apostle, faithfully traveling everywhere to spread the Gospel, yet having some limiting ailment. If I were God, I certainly would have healed Paul. In my mind, this would have enabled him to be even more fruitful in his ministry. But God is God, and His ways are not mine. He replied to Paul, "My grace is sufficient for you, for my power is made perfect in weakness" (2 Corinthians 12:9). How did Paul respond to God's denial? He testified, "Therefore I will boast all the more gladly about my weaknesses, so that Christ's power may rest on me" (2 Corinthians 12:9). Now that's a surrendered heart! And look what God did through Paul's life!

Dear one with a languishing heart, have you come to the end of yourself, the end of your effort, the end of your solutions? Do you see Jesus? He is here for you today just as much as He was there for the nameless little woman in the crowd. You do not need to perform some humongous feat to convince Him of your worthiness or to prove your loyalty or your need. You do not need some special formula; you do not need to sneak up behind Jesus and grab the hem of His garment. The Lord simply wants you to surrender your will; He wants you to surrender your burden.

> *You have longed for sweet peace,*
> *and for faith to increase,*
> *And have earnestly, fervently prayed;*
> *But you cannot have rest;*
> *or be perfectly blest,*
> *Until all on the altar is laid.*
>
> *Is your all on the altar of sacrifice laid?*
> *Your heart, does the Spirit control?*
> *You can only be blest*
> *And have peace and sweet rest,*
> *As you yield Him your body and soul.*
>
> ELISHA A. HOFFMAN

This is the story of a woman whose childlike and uncomplicated faith brought her through to wholeness. When she had come to the end of her efforts, there stood Jesus Christ. She did not need to beg or cajole; she did not try to manipulate; she did not ask for a sign or perform a ritual. She simply believed and reached out to Him. She believed she was helpless without Him, and she believed He had the power to do what every other physician, every other earthly resource, had failed to do. And she went home healed in every way after her encounter with Him. Let this inspire your own faith.

Christ intends to bring something beautiful from your unhappiness, distress, and grief. Won't you let Him have your anger, your frustration, your fear and unbelief, your languishing heart? Reach out and let Him heal you, restore you, set you free. Believe that He is there for you. You, too, will hear Him say, "Go in peace."

They shall come and sing aloud on the height of Zion, and they shall be radiant over the goodness of the LORD . . . their life shall become like a watered garden, and they shall never languish again.

JEREMIAH 31:12 NRSV

Heart Check

1. How can you relate to the woman in this story?

2. How does suffering influence your perspective on life, and how does surrendering influence your perspective on suffering?

3. Can you see ways God has used suffering for good in your life?

4. What steps might God lead you to take in your search for wholeness? How can you strengthen your faith in God?

5. Compose a prayer to God in response to this chapter's truths.

4

The Widow of Zarephath

THE CRISIS-STRICKEN HEART

1 KINGS 17:8-24; LUKE 4:25-26

DISTRESS, DREAD, DESPAIR, DOOM, DEATH—these words describe the state of the feeble woman picking up sticks outside her city gate. She had once lived a full, contented life, but that was then and this was now. The land was in a deep crisis, and so was she. In fact, she had never known such agony. Every crop and tree had died, animals had died, and now people were dying.

Staring hopelessly from the parched ground to the cloudless heavens, her heart pleaded for a little rain. She had cried to her gods repeatedly, but they apparently had died, too. Her husband was already dead, and it seemed inevitable that the severe drought would claim her and her beloved son shortly.

Every day nightmarish fear gripped her heart as she tried to cope with their crisis. She rationed every bit of food and prized each crumb. Yet her supplies got lower and lower, and their rations smaller and smaller, until . . . well, all you had to do was look at her to see it had been for nothing. She had wasted away. Rain never came, conditions remained intolerable, and the angel of death was closing in for the kill.

Now the most dreadful day of all had come, the day she had so desperately tried to stave off. Her young son cried for food, and she could deny him no longer. She had to feed him. But the one meager bread-cake she made for the two of them would completely use up their remaining food supply. This would be their last meal.

Filled with despair, the woman hobbled weakly out of the house and made her way down to the city gate to gather sticks for fuel one last time. Then for the last time she would light her oven; for the last time she would reach for her flour and oil; for the last time she would knead her dough into a cake and bake it, and for the last time she would eat with her son at the table. After that they would simply throw themselves on the bed and wait for starvation to finally end their misery.

The Widow of Zarephath, as she was known, had a Crisis-stricken Heart. Yet, as we shall see, even though she was in a deep personal crisis, God had a plan for this traumatized woman and her son. He was about to change their destiny, and He would use His servant Elijah to call it forth.

Elijah the Tishbite, God's great prophet, had just entered the national arena. In his first recorded act, he boldly approached Israel's King Ahab and upbraided him for turning from the Lord to embrace Baal worship with his wicked wife, Jezebel. Under this couple's corrupting influence, most of the nation had sold out to Baal. How tragic for God's people that they so quickly forgot God's strict admonition: "So if you faithfully obey the commands I am giving you today—to love the LORD your God and to serve him with all your heart and with all your soul—then I will send rain on your land in its season. . . . Be careful, or you will be enticed to turn away and worship other gods and bow down to them. Then the LORD's anger will burn against you, and he will shut the heavens so that it will not rain and the ground will yield no produce, and you will soon perish from the good land the LORD is giving you" (Deuteronomy 11:13-17).

So Elijah came on the scene with a divine wake-up call to remind the apostate Israelites of the cost of breaking covenant with the Lord. He declared to Ahab, "As the LORD, the God of Israel, lives, whom I serve, there will be neither dew nor rain in the next few years except at my word" (1 Kings 17:1). This judgment also directly challenged Baal, who supposedly was a god of rain and harvest. The Lord had sent Elijah, and He would do exactly as Elijah had predicted.

Once the drought began, the Lord knew Ahab and Jezebel would hotly pursue Elijah. To protect him from both their anger and from the ravaging drought, He sent him away from Samaria where Ahab ruled to a safe hiding place east of the Jordan River called Kerith Ravine (Cherith in KJV). There God assigned ravens to feed him, and he drank water from a brook. Meanwhile God confirmed Elijah's prediction; the heavens refused to relinquish a drop of water. After a time Israel began to suffer, and even the brook that sustained Elijah dried up. He was wondering what to do next when the Lord spoke to him: "Go at once to Zarephath of Sidon and stay there," He said. "I have commanded a widow in that place to supply you with food" (Zidon in KJV, 1 Kings 17:9).

This command to Elijah is intriguing for several reasons. God may have been testing Elijah's faith in sending him to Zarephath for safe haven. It was a one-hundred-mile trek, a long way to travel on foot to find safety. More surprising than the distance, however, was the direction. This destination was not out of the drought zone. The same drought plaguing Israel had worked its way up the Mediterranean Coast (then called the Great Sea) so that coastal Sidon was in deep distress, too.

Not only that, but Sidon was the most prominent city-state in the Baal-worshiping land of Phoenicia (Lebanon today). Zarephath was a town under Sidonian rule, about eight miles south of the city. Jezebel, Israel's queen by her marriage to Ahab, was the daughter of the Sidonian king and a fanatical worshiper of Baal. The most corrupting influence in Israel, she brazenly led Israel away from God into her pagan religion and waged a bloody campaign to annihilate every prophet of the Lord in the land. How strange that God's prophet should escape to his mortal enemy's own homeland where her ruthless father ruled.

Stranger still, the woman commissioned by God to supply Elijah's need was none other than the poor starving widow of Zarephath! While Jezebel was a powerful and cruel tyrant, this woman was completely powerless and so obscure that we do not even know her name. Nevertheless, she was a good woman, and God's eye was on her. While Jezebel turned Israel from worshiping the Lord to Baal worship, this woman would turn from Baal to worship the Lord. Therefore, God destined Jezebel for destruction and this dear woman for life.

It might have seemed strange to Elijah that God would send him to a widow for support, and a Gentile at that. Widows were nearly always impoverished, and in this time of desolation, one could expect them to be among the first to die of starvation. What could such a one possibly do for him in these hard times? Couldn't God find some rich man in Israel to provide for His prophet? What about Obadiah, a high official in Ahab's palace, who was secretly feeding other prophets (1 Kings 18:3-4)? After being fed by ravens, however, nothing could surprise Elijah. He had plenty of faith to believe that somehow God would supply his need through a poor Sidonian widow.

God's command to Elijah was clear. Thus he began his journey in unquestioning obedience. However, the widow heard no orders from God to provide for Elijah. Such an order would have stupefied her. Yet the Lord said, "I have *commanded* a widow . . ." The Hebrew word used here, *tsavah,* also can be translated "commissioned, ordained, or appointed." God had appointed her, as she would soon learn.

But God's choice of this widow was not just for Elijah's sake; God had heard her heart's cry and would provide for her, too. The Lord has always had a special concern in His heart for widows (see Exodus 22:22-24; Deuteronomy 10:18; Psalm 68:5, 146:9; Malachi 3:5). But she did not know this. She did not know that her deliverance was on its way.

So Elijah obediently traveled to Zarephath. If the brook in Kerith Ravine had dried up, then surely other water sources along the way were dry, too. Such a long, dusty journey would leave Elijah weak, dehydrated, and desperate to find his promised supplier. Surely, he would still prefer the home of some wealthy person where he could ease up awhile from the rigors of living by faith. But God would not let Elijah grow spiritually soft. When he got to the town gate, he immediately saw the poor widow hunting for just enough sticks to cook her last meal. God had let their paths cross at the ordained moment. Looking for assistance but also testing her to see if she were the right woman, he called to her, "Would you bring me a little water in a jar so I may have a drink?" (1 Kings 17:10).

Elijah had lived a long time in the wilds and had just made a very long and arduous trip. When she looked up, she probably saw a weary, weather-beaten, wheezing stranger. His attire, a garment of haircloth cinched about his waist by a leather girdle, made him appear even more unusual. No one she knew dressed this way. In fact, Elijah's apparel was so distinctive that it identified him (see 2 Kings 1:7-8). The woman probably knew at once that he was no ordinary beggar, that instead he must be some type of Israeli holy man.

Israel's God was not her God, but she had heard enough to respect Him. And since her own religion had failed her, she felt an openness toward Elijah and His God. While she was more in a condition to receive charity than to offer it, God had prepared her heart to show generosity. Even in her deepest crisis, she did not complain to Elijah about the scarcity of water, her weak condition, the urgency of her own task, or his being a stranger. She did not just point him in the right direction or ask what he would do in return. Amazingly, at his first request she left to take care of his need.

But then her real test came. As she was going, Elijah called, "And bring me, please, a piece of bread" (1 Kings 17:11). Now he had hit a tender spot. Another might have angrily snapped, "Surely you jest, you heartless beggar! Look at me! Do I look like I have food to spare? Charity begins at home, and my son is dying. You want me to share my last morsels with you? Why, if you believe in your God, let *Him* provide for you!"

Yet this woman was innately hospitable. It must have distressed her to decline his request. "As surely as the LORD your God lives," she replied, "I don't have any bread—only a handful of flour in a jar and a little oil in a jug. I am gathering a few sticks to take home and make a meal for myself and my son, that we may eat it—and die" (1 Kings 17:12).

Clearly, from her oath she believed that the God of Israel was a living God. Unlike proud and stubborn Jezebel who would go to her death vehemently opposing Him, this woman of the same heritage humbly acknowledged Him. Her words *"your* God," however, show that she had no personal hope in Him, thinking His mercy inaccessible to Gentiles like her. She was sure Elijah would understand her hopeless predicament and refrain from pressing her further. Instead he replied, "Don't be afraid. Go home and do as you have said. But first make a small cake of bread for me from what you have and bring it to me, and then make something for yourself and your son" (1 Kings 17:13).

What? Elijah, weren't you listening to this poor woman? Didn't you hear what she said? She has only a handful of flour, enough to make a last morsel of bread for them before they die. How could you expect her to share her last meal with a stranger of another race and religion? You had better go look for another widow because surely you've found the wrong one!

Elijah, however, knew exactly what he was doing. It was not from selfishness on his part that he made his request, but he was testing her faith and obedience. If she cooperated with the Lord's purpose, he had full confidence that the Lord would provide not only for him but for her and her son as well.

With a word from the Lord for the flabbergasted woman, he explained, "For this is what the LORD, the God of Israel, says: 'The jar of flour will not be used up and the jug of oil will not run dry until the day the LORD gives rain on the land'" (1 Kings 17:14).

Wasn't this too much for this pagan woman to believe? After all, Elijah offered her no sign beforehand that his prediction would come true. She had never heard of such a thing. She must have wondered, *Who is this man? How can he ask this? How can he make such a promise? Is this some cruel hoax by a hungry vagabond to gain my last bit of food? But . . . but what if he is truly a prophet of God?*

She had little time to ponder her decision. What a huge test of faith and obedience for the starving mother! Studying Elijah's face, she perceived an authority in him as foreign to her as his garb and a sincerity that would never take advantage of her. As impossible as it all seemed, her faith caught hold of the promise.

Going straight home, she got out her flour jar and oil bottle. She set aside a puny ration for her and her son, and used the rest to make Elijah a cake. After he enjoyed his little meal, she went home to make a dinky cake for her and her son to share. But what a surprise awaited her! Peering into her flour jar, she saw something that made her heart leap. There was a plentiful supply of flour inside! And her empty oil bottle had plenty of oil, too! After she got over her shock, she must have laughed joyfully as she fingered the fresh flour and let the oil trickle over her hand. Truly, her guest was a prophet of the true God!

The widow opened her humble home to Elijah, and he stayed there for over two years. During this otherwise bleak time, the three-some enjoyed a perpetual miracle not unlike that given the Israelites in the wilderness as they received a continual fresh supply of manna. Daily the widow baked bread from the contents of her never-empty containers. Each time she took from the supply, more was added to it. "So there was food every day for Elijah and for the woman and her family. For the jar of flour was not used up and the jug of oil did not run dry, in keeping with the word of the LORD spoken by Elijah" (1 Kings 17:15-16).

But the eyes of the LORD are on those who fear him, on those whose hope is in his unfailing love, to deliver them from death and keep them alive in famine.

PSALM 33:18-19

In opening her hand to Elijah, the widow had opened her heart to him—and to His God. Before, she had heard about Israel's God from afar, but now she knew He was real and cared for her. Yes, what a difference having God's prophet living under her roof had made. Her trials seemed far behind her.

One day, however, her peaceful world shattered. Another crisis, a disastrous one, broadsided her faith. Her son had become ill, and she had been tending him. As she watched him steadily grow worse, she no doubt prayed, believing that the loving God who so faithfully cared for their dietary needs would provide here, too. But suddenly the unspeakable happened. The boy drew a last breath and died. The angel of death had finally won.

Before the first miracle, when Elijah asked for bread, she had already given up thinking that she and her son could live. She'd had plenty of time for that crisis to develop; she'd had plenty of time to get used to the idea of dying. But this current crisis swept upon her when she was peaceful, contented, and praising the Lord's goodness. Having grown accustomed to her special place of privilege with God's prophet, it took her completely by surprise. She had feared her son's death in the bad time, but now he was actually dead in the good time. It made no sense!

The poor woman experienced unspeakable heartbreak as she wept before God. *Why, Lord? Why? Why did You let my son die? Why did You spare him just to let him die now? He's all I had. I'm all alone in the world. Why?* Now her son was gone, and she reckoned that God had abandoned her and that she would have no one to care for her in her old age. When Elijah walked in, she unleashed a torrent of grief at him: "What do you have against me, man of God?" she cried. "Did you come to remind me of my sin and kill my son?" (1 Kings 17:18).

Why did she blame Elijah? Since God had used him to bless her, she now concluded that God had used him to curse her. With a deepened awareness of her own sinfulness, especially after hearing that sin had caused the drought and famine, she assumed that God was judging her own secret sins. If her present sins were not enough to bring this disaster, she could probably think of plenty of past ones, most notably that she had formerly worshiped the detestable Sidonian god Baal.

But God was not punishing the widow—in fact, just the opposite. He actually had a further compensation for her generosity to His prophet. He had further lessons of faith and compassion for His prophet to learn, too. Elijah had lived a long while with the two and knew them well. His heart went out to this dear woman whom God had appointed to take such good care of him. He had grown to care deeply for her and wondered why God permitted such grief to befall her. He also had grown fond of the boy. The grief struck his heart, too.

"Give me your son," he said. While he was not sure exactly what to do, he knew God could do anything. He would cry fervently to Him. He would wrestle for a miracle and believe for it. Taking the lifeless body into his arms, he carried him upstairs to his living quarters and laid him on his bed. He then began to cry vehemently, "O LORD my God, have you brought tragedy also upon this widow I am staying with, by causing her son to die?" (1 Kings 17:20). Next, Elijah reminded Him that she still provided for him and that this was a personal concern to him, too. Finally he pointed out that He was the one in charge and therefore bore the responsibility.

Then Elijah stretched himself out over the body three times and cried, "O LORD my God, let this boy's life return to him!" Perhaps in stretching himself over the boy's body, he tried to breathe life into it and warm it with his own body heat. Whatever his exact approach was, God made it work! The Bible says, "The LORD heard Elijah's cry, and the boy's life returned to him, and he lived" (1 Kings 17:21-22).

Meanwhile downstairs the widow agonized as she heard Elijah's desperate cries to the Lord. Then the cries stopped. *What? Why did he stop praying? Do I hear voices . . . two voices . . . two happy voices?* She leaped to her feet, but before she could run up the steps, Elijah came down carrying her son. She could scarcely believe her eyes. Seeing her look of fear and amazement, Elijah exclaimed, "Look, your son is alive!" (1 Kings 17:23).

We can imagine that she scooped up her son in her arms, weeping and covering him with kisses. Her heart overflowed with joy and gratitude to God for this latest and most wondrous miracle. She had not expected Elijah to work this kind of miracle. It would be the prophet's only healing miracle—and what a great one it was! This is the first instance recorded in the Bible of someone being raised from the dead. How blessed this widow and her son were to receive such mercy.

She had believed in the Lord before, knowing Him as a miracle-worker who cared for her needs. This latest crisis had made her doubt, but now her doubts were fully resolved. She knew that Israel's God was the true God, that Elijah was His true prophet, that the faith he professed was the true faith, and that all Elijah had said about the Lord was true—He could resolve *any* crisis. Overflowing with renewed faith and absolute conviction, she joyously declared, "Now I know that you are a man of God and that the word of the LORD from your mouth is the truth" (1 Kings 17:24). How the Lord yearned to hear such a testimony from the nation of Israel! This was her moment of full surrender to the Lord, and she would worship and obey Him for the rest of her life.

Oh, what joy and laughter God had brought to that humble home in Zarephath! It must have been a sad day for the threesome when God called Elijah away to his own country to decree the drought's end. We never hear whether he saw the widow and her son again. While we never learn her name, nearly nine centuries later, her story deeply impressed our Lord Jesus Christ. Preaching in the synagogue at Nazareth, He selected her for an object lesson. The audience sat spellbound as they listened to his "gracious words" (Luke 4:22). But while He impressed them, they did not believe in Him. They were more interested in seeing signs than in receiving His message.

So Jesus told them, "Surely you will quote this proverb to me: 'Physician, heal yourself! Do here in your hometown what we have heard that you did in Capernaum.' I tell you the truth, no prophet is accepted in his hometown. I assure you that there were many widows in Israel in Elijah's time, when the sky was shut for three and a half years and there was a severe famine throughout the land. Yet Elijah was not sent to any of them, but to a widow in Zarephath in the region of Sidon" (Luke 4:23-26).

What was Jesus saying? He pointed to God's providential care for seeming nobodies—the lost, forgotten, ignored—but He was saying much more. This story was an early sign of God's love and compassion for Gentiles. As God had visited the widow, sending her His choicest prophet, God sent Christ to visit not only Jews but Gentiles with salvation. God is no respecter of persons with His grace; none has exclusive rights to His mercy.

It was bad enough that God used unclean birds—ravens—to feed His great prophet in the wilderness, but sending him to an unclean pagan woman for his care was too much for this Jewish crowd to stomach. Preferring to forget about the widow of Zarephath forever, they took Christ's reference to her as the slap in the face He meant it to be. They could not miss His intimation that they were like the unfaithful Jews of Elijah's time and that Gentiles could possess the blessings of God that the Jews had missed by their disobedience. More specifically, He was saying that Nazareth would reject Him, but Gentiles would accept Him.

Until then everyone had hung on His "gracious words." But so deep-seated was their prejudice against Gentiles, so despised was the land of Sidon, that they felt intensely offended and wanted His blood immediately. Driving Him from town, they took Him to a cliff, intending to hurl him over and bury his body with stones. That they did this despite the fact that they could not legally exercise capital punishment shows the ferocity of their rage. Nevertheless, Christ's hour had not come, and He walked away unharmed.

Later, perhaps still enamored with this story, Christ decided to visit the region Himself: "Leaving that place, Jesus withdrew to the region of Tyre and Sidon" (Matthew 15:21). Was Christ thinking of the widow of Zarephath when He announced, "Anyone who receives a prophet because he is a prophet will receive a prophet's reward" (Matthew 10:41)? She received a prophet and a prophet's reward. She had shared her last reserves with God's prophet and gotten back many times more—and with interest!

The widow of Zarephath thought she was preparing her last meal for her and her son. But she opened her hand, her home, and her heart to God's servant, and God blessed her for it. Just look at the blessings that came to this woman who, in the midst of her bitter crisis, chose to step out in faith and obedience to honor God's word to her:

She and her son were saved from starvation.

She was privileged to care for one of Israel's greatest prophets.

She and her son enjoyed Elijah's friendship and leadership for some two years.

She saw the daily miracle of God's provision for those years.

She witnessed her son's resurrection from the dead.

She came to genuine faith in the true and living God.

She is recognized in both Old and New Testaments and even cited by Jesus Christ as an example of God's love and grace toward the least, the last, and the lost. The blessings this Gentile woman received from the Lord stand in stark contrast to the deprivation experienced by Israel at the same time. Surely the writer of Hebrews had the widow of Zarephath in mind when he wrote, "Women received back their dead, raised to life again" (Hebrews 11:35).

And let's not fail to recognize her significance to God's purposes for Israel. God used her to strengthen Elijah's body and bolster his faith in preparation for his next assignment. And what an assignment it was! Traveling back to Samaria, he single-handedly confronted and overpowered the priests of Baal, a victory that brought all Israel back to recognizing the true and living God (1 Kings 18:1-46).

The days of the blameless are known to the LORD, and their inheritance will endure forever. In times of disaster they will not wither; in days of famine they will enjoy plenty. But the wicked will perish: The LORD's enemies will be like the beauty of the fields, they will vanish— vanish like smoke.

PSALM 37:18-20

LESSONS FOR OUR OWN HEARTS

You may be praising the Lord that you have never had a serious crisis. Most of us, however, know from painful experience that getting through this life without crises is nearly impossible. Perhaps you are presently struggling. Like the widow of Zarephath, you may even live in an area of drought. Maybe you are about to lose your farm; maybe you don't even know where your next meal will come from.

Or perhaps it is something else—your son is in jail, and this is his third strike. Your daughter tattooed her face, dyed her hair turquoise, and is moving to Hollywood. Your husband just got the boot six months away from retirement; you are about to declare bankruptcy; someone threw a rock through your window and lit a cross in your front yard; a tornado just destroyed your home; your life work just went up in flames; a loved one has a terminal illness; your ministry blew up in your face. Of course, we could expand this list ad infinitum since "man is born to trouble as surely as sparks fly upward" (Job 5:7).

The widow of Zarephath was tested to her limit. But you might be tempted to think, *Well, that was in the Bible; my crisis is in real life today.* Yet God wants to comfort you with this story of a real person who lived through a terrible crisis. He wants to teach you valuable lessons and impart priceless wisdom through it. Here are some key points to remember when in the midst of besieging crises.

Do Not Let Fear Overcome You

First, if we have not already figured it out, we should realize that Christians are not immune to life's crises. We must again note that ours is a fallen world where often the righteous suffer with the unrighteous. Elijah suffered along with everyone else for Ahab and Jezebel's sins. People all over Canaan suffered. We might hope that God will spare the good folk and let the wicked suffer, but we all live with the aftereffects of the Fall. We all feel the effects when evil rulers make wicked and senseless decisions. God's Word assures us: "No testing has overtaken you that is not common to everyone" (1 Corinthians 10:13 NRSV). *Everyone?* That means all of humanity— Christians and non-Christians alike.

We embrace a false gospel when we believe otherwise. It is hard to deny that sometimes Christians seem to go through *greater* crises than do unbelievers. Our Gospel is good news, not because we never go through tribulations—for "in the world *you have* tribulation" (John 16:33 RSV, italics added)—but because Christ is with us to see us through them. Therefore, we can trust Him and not cave in to fear.

You have a God who is greater than any trouble. He can solve any crisis. Just look at the seemingly forgotten little widow from Zarephath! She was just a pagan nobody living far from where godly folk might expect a divine visitation. Yet God visited this woman in crisis; she was a somebody to Him. He could have sent Elijah to the Jordan River for water and let the ravens feed him there, but he sent him a hundred miles to meet her instead. Since the Lord did not fail to hear her heart's cry, how much more will He hear yours, His beloved child.

Some sixty times God's Word reassures His people to "fear not." The widow heard it, and He says to you, too, "Fear not!" When climbing something high, you are told not to look down because fear can seize you. In looking up, you can keep moving upward beyond the reach of fear's grasping fingers. That is why we should fix our eyes upward, gazing into our heavenly Father's loving eyes. As soon as we let ourselves look down, our problems look greater than He is, and our hearts fill with doubt and fear. When we keep our eyes focused upward, bold faith rises in our hearts, and we believe God's promises. Arm yourself with plenty of "fear nots" from God's Word.

The widow of Zarephath looked beyond her physical realities. As she listened intently to Elijah's hope-laced words, faith rose in her heart to meet the challenge. Trusting God for a miracle, she fearlessly emptied her containers.

Years ago a friend was praying with me about a crisis in my life. Suddenly she looked up, startled, and said, "Why, Cheryl, I believe the Lord is showing me that He wants to give you a gift of faith." Well, that sounded great. I envisioned one day soon saying, "Mountains, be moved!" and seeing them immediately stand aside for me. But my friend added, "It will be a faith that leads you to see your empty cupboard and know God will provide." I was no longer impressed. I never wanted to see my cupboards bare like Old Mother Hubbard's; I never wanted to be tested in this way. I'm thankful that though we have been down to our last dollars a few times through the years, we have never been down to our last bite.

Nevertheless, I have read the testimonies of amazing saints who lived exactly this way, not for a minute or a day, but as a way of life.

George Muller never knew where the next day's food would come from or how he would house his constantly growing brood of orphans. But he just kept taking in more until he finally fed and housed 2,000 of them. Basilea Schlink began her Lutheran sisterhood in bombed-out Darmstadt, Germany, with no money for food, let alone the resources for their building project. However, provisions always came in, just enough for that day's need.

Perhaps your "empty cupboard" is in the spiritual rather than the material realm. If you are like me, sometimes the cupboard of your heart seems empty. You long for the Holy Spirit's presence, and He seems nowhere to be found. The devil seems to triumph over you, or fear intimidates you, forcing your vision downward to the swirling troubles below. At those times I have learned to look up and say, "God is for me! In Him I have no fear! In Him I have all the provision I need! His cupboards are full, and in Him my cupboards are full!"

Yes, dear friend, when you think you are going down for the last count, when all seems lost, God is still alive and on His throne. You can trust His resources; He has ample provision for you. Though your heart is crisis-stricken, you can still look through eyes of faith, not fear, and see your cupboards full. By faith the widow of Zarephath lived to see her jar and jug continuously refilled.

Trust God's Power to Restore

Do you feel stripped of your strength to go on? Are your jars and jugs empty, your cupboards bare? Has your present crisis made you decide that you have no future, that you are in so deep that there is no way out? Do you think your life has lost all rhyme and reason, that everything important to you is gone, that you have come to the end of your resources and the end of yourself?

Remember this: You are not alone. You may feel alone, as the widow did, but "the Lord is near" (Philippians 4:5). He loves you and will send you help from an unexpected corner. Prepare your heart to receive it and to act upon it. Little did the widow know that her deliverance was at hand. Right when things were at their worst, God sent help to restore her life. Indeed, He gives "beauty for ashes, the oil of

joy for mourning, the garment of praise for the spirit of heaviness"
(Isaiah 61:3 KJV).

Once at a conference I was watching an artist do a chalk drawing. He expertly drew a mountain lakeside scene in soft pastel hues.
When it seemed complete, he jolted us by taking a black piece of chalk
and wildly slashing the scene. He explained that we can go along
serenely, and then an ugly crisis suddenly sweeps in and slashes
across the beauty of our lives. With that same dark chalk, he turned
those ugly, violent marks on the landscape into lovely pine trees sil-
houetted against the lake. Once the scene was completed, those trees
seemed destined to be there all along. In fact, the scene's beauty
would have been greatly diminished without them.

Similarly, there is a story of a Far Eastern town famous for centuries for its exquisite pottery. Its tall urns, in particular, were strik-
ingly beautiful and admired the world over. As legend has it, when
each urn was finished, the artist smashed it. He then pieced it
together again with gold filigree, thus transforming it into a stunning
work of art. Until the vessel went through the breaking, it really was
not complete. So with us. We go through many tragic crises that leave
us feeling useless and ready for the trash heap. Yet a patient and loving divine hand takes our broken pieces and fashions us into a mas-
terpiece of infinite beauty.

---

*Though you have made me see troubles, many and bitter, you will
restore my life again; from the depths of the earth you will again bring
me up.*

PSALM 71:20

*And the God of all grace, who called you to his eternal glory in Christ,
after you have suffered a little while, will himself restore you and make
you strong, firm and steadfast.*

1 PETER 5:10

He restores my soul.

PSALM 23:3

Meet the Challenge of Giving

How difficult was it for the widow, all alone in the world except for a son who depended on her, to give her last food to a stranger? We can only imagine. Elijah's challenge to open wide her crisis-stricken heart and give unselfishly to him seemed wholly unreasonable. What she did not know was that the Lord had "commanded" her to share with Elijah, and if He had deemed her extreme poverty and sorrow an excuse not to obey, He would not have assigned her. How ironic that if she had not shared her last meal, it really would have been her last meal! Yet God knew her heart was willing, and He would make her able.

While sight saw the impossibilities and nothing but death, faith arose in her to believe for a blessing. Making the difficult choice to act on God's word to her, she denied herself and trusted the divine promise. What at the outset further deepened her terrible crisis—the act of giving—is what literally resolved her crisis. A cup of cold water given will not lose its reward (Matthew 10:42), and she gave more than a cup. First she went for the cup of water, but then she sacrificed her food. She proved daily that sharing her substance with others would not break her but would save her. God miraculously increased her flour and oil—for at least two years! How true for her that the Lord gives "oil to make the face shine, and bread to strengthen the human heart" (Psalm 104:15 NRSV).

The Lord has a command for us, too. It matters not whether we are in crisis or whether we are rich or poor. He says to us all, "Give, and it will be given to you. A good measure, pressed down, shaken together and running over, will be poured into your lap. For with the measure you use, it will be measured to you" (Luke 6:38).

God's rules for investing are so much different from the world's. Do you wish to see your flour and oil multiplied, your cupboards full, to receive your daily bread? It will come, not in storing, hoarding, and affording, but in sacrificially sharing. God may not ask you to share your last meal with a stranger, but He does want you to have a generous heart—even in the midst of crisis.

Some people do great things for God, proving that when they are weak, He is strong in them. Others let their trials hamstring them. They pull back from faith, becoming self-preoccupied and self-protective. But we can never find freedom in this way. Victory comes as we hear the divine command, disregard our own pain, and reach beyond ourselves in faith. As we exercise love, praising and thanking God and acting in compassion toward others, we find transforming grace for our lives. Satan tries to turn us inward, to focus on the pain and the injustice we suffer. Yet miracles are on the way when we can say, "Okay, I am in a dreadful crisis, but whether I live or die by it, I will glorify God in it."

Those who stand on God's promise can trust God's provision. They will do what He asks of them. They will empty themselves by giving to the dregs if need be. How heartening it was to hear stories of the already deeply impoverished Albanian Christians who filled their homes with Muslim refugees who had fled ethnic cleansing in Kosovo.

Your crisis is a test of faith. God allows such crises to test our hearts, to reveal what is really deep inside them. It tested the widow's faith greatly when she gave out of her extreme poverty. She was amazingly generous, and for it she saw miracle upon miracle. If she could give out of her crisis, you can too, dear one in crisis. You may feel you have nothing left to give, but God will provide you with something. Give out of your brokenness; give out of your poverty. Don't hold back. You will soon see miracles of God's providential care even amid your seemingly impossible crisis. You may feel forsaken by God, but, as with the widow of Zarephath, He may be commissioning you to your greatest service.

The next time you wonder whether you should guard your little or give it away when God asks, the next time you feel tempted to disregard the Spirit's prompting and instead hoard your resources, remember the widow. What would have become of her and her son had she refused God's call?

Don't Try to Go It Alone

Just as we must be willing to give to others, we should also receive from them. Isn't it actually easier sometimes to give than to receive? Our pride resists letting others know our need until, driven by desperation, we finally open up to them. While this book deals with individual hearts, we cannot overestimate the importance of the role of community in the Christian life. The independent, self-made person does not impress God so much as people helping one another through life's upheavals.

For God's miracle it took two people in our story to interact. God stopped sending ravens to feed Elijah and sent Him to live with the widow for reasons that enriched them both. When Elijah predicted that she would provide for him, she was certain she could not. But his faith encouraged her to have faith, too, and she went on to fulfill her God-ordained assignment.

This is how God most often works with His people today. He uses us in each other's lives to encourage us, to spur us on to faith and obedience, and to help provide solutions in times of crisis. Christ said He would build His church (Matthew 16:18), and Paul used the analogy of a human body to portray it. Collectively, this body of Christ is one unit with Christ as the head. As individual members of this body, we need each other and must work as an interdependent unit. In this way each individual is enriched and the entire body strengthened. If we isolate ourselves from the body, we cannot truly obey the scriptural admonitions to love one another (John 13:34), bear one another's burdens (Galatians 6:2), pray for each other (James 5:16), or suffer with each other (1 Corinthians 12:26). The Lord has specifically given us to each other, and we shine brightest as Christ's body when we help each other through life's crises.

I urge you to find others who will stand with you in times of need. The widow did not at first realize the resource she had in Elijah. She soon learned though. And Elijah, if he had chosen for himself, would never have thought to go to her for his care. Through our mutual love and support, God can provide for us in ways we would never expect.

Trust God's Purpose

Following her first crisis and miraculous deliverance, the widow may have thought all her trials were behind her. But a second and more devastating crisis unexpectedly rocked her life. The fact that her son experienced constant miracles did not spare him from life's other realities. He who had been fed miraculously for more than two years suddenly died. This second crisis seized the widow so ferociously that she forgot all the Lord's former mercies.

It is a bitter pill to swallow, but we can be in the path of duty, in the center of God's will, living righteously, have a very blessed and fruitful ministry, and even receive wondrous manifestations of grace, and yet still be hit by severe crises through no fault of our own. It seems senseless; it seems all wrong. But since we cannot understand the complexities of God's design, we have no choice but to trust Him. By believing that He will weave all our threads—even the dark crisis-threads—into something beautiful, we open ourselves to His handiwork in our lives. We let Him weave an eternal design of incalculable worth.

> *For our light and momentary troubles are achieving for us an eternal glory that far outweighs them all. So we fix our eyes not on what is seen, but on what is unseen. For what is seen is temporary, but what is unseen is eternal.*
>
> 2 CORINTHIANS 4:17-18

Someone has said, "So many calamities have been lost upon you if you have not yet learned how to suffer." Suffering purifies our nature. Wanting to test the genuineness of our faith, God allows us to suffer various crises, sometimes even excruciating ones. If we yield our hearts to Him, however, the tested faith that remains after the suffering has passed will be pure, genuine, and enduring.

After the widow came through her afflictions, look what happened to her crisis-stricken heart. It was healed. And look what happened to her faith. Did you notice how it skyrocketed? She had previously referred to the Lord as "the Lord *your* God." After her crises, she declared with joy, "Now I know that you are a man of God and that the word of the LORD from your mouth is the truth." Somehow serious trials produce great faith. The dreadful suffering she endured gave her faith to fulfill her life's purpose. If she had not been tested, she would never have experienced miracles, and she would never have testified with certainty to the truth. Her crises built a remarkable testimony for her.

But you may wonder how you will ever get through to the other side. You may feel that you live in a war zone, waiting for the next disastrous bomb to hit. You may wonder how you can ever find hope and security again when your life seems like a never-ending series of crises. At such times surrendering our hearts fully to God is critical. We can pray like this: "Lord, I don't understand You or Your ways, but I choose to trust Your love. I surrender all, Lord, to You." Such prayers will bring your heart peace.

Perhaps you find it difficult to surrender to God. If you do, meditate on the truth that God knows and loves you completely and perfectly, that He sent Christ to die just for you. Satan wants to blind you to the depth of God's love for you. He wants to make you angry, mistrustful, and rebellious so your heart will turn from God. But perfect love casts out fear, and standing in the knowledge of God's love forces Satan to lose his grip. What comfort we should take in knowing that even if we lose everything else in this life, we still have the love of God. With Jesus in our heart, we have the greatest treasure in the world, and nothing can rob us of Him.

For I am convinced that neither death nor life, neither angels nor demons, neither the present nor the future, nor any powers, neither height nor depth, nor anything else in all creation, will be able to separate us from the love of God that is in Christ Jesus our Lord.

ROMANS 8:38-39

Our troubles are never entirely over in this life. Seasons of crisis are normal and unavoidable. If you are presently suffering, it may be difficult for you to see where the nighttime of your experience will end and the morning begin. You have God's sure promise, however, that "weeping may remain for a night, but rejoicing comes in the morning" (Psalm 30:5). Trust Him. Live in the hope of the morning and sing of the soon-coming dawn. You will see the rising sun; the Lord will heal your crisis-stricken heart. Then you will know, indeed, that His grace proved sufficient for your need, that His love and compassion never failed you (see 2 Corinthians 12:9; Lamentations 3:22).

I will exalt you, O LORD, for you lifted me out of the depths and did not let my enemies gloat over me. O LORD my God, I called to you for help and you healed me. O LORD, you brought me up from the grave; you spared me from going down into the pit.

PSALM 30:1-3

Heart Check

1. Are you currently in a crisis?

2. Is God calling you to pour out your little handful of something? Do you fear that obeying God will deepen your crisis?

3. Do you have others standing with you during this time?

4. How has the Widow of Zarephath given you hope for your own situation?

5. Compose a prayer to God in response to this chapter's lessons.

5

THE DESPERATE HEART

GENESIS 16; 17; 21:1-21; 25:12; GALATIANS 4:21-31

SHOULD I GO THIS WAY? No, perhaps that's better. Dazed, confused, and reeling, the Egyptian woman stumbled on aimlessly yet determinedly under her precious burden. After a few more yards Hagar stopped. Her body taut with attention, her heart beating wildly, her eyes searching frantically, she scanned the rugged wilderness terrain. Nothing in any direction offered even the remotest hope.

She had spoken reassuringly to her distressed son, Ishmael. When his own strength failed, she had bowed under his weight and carried him. Now, with the hard fist of fear knotting her stomach, she stared into his pale, motionless face. *He's almost dead. Oh, God, he's almost dead! P-l-e-a-s-e, help us!*

Clueless about which way to turn next and buckling under her son's weight, she collapsed. *I'll rest just a moment. . . . Just a moment . . . that's all I need. . . . That's all I've got. . . . Just a moment.* As she sat there, a torrent of tears rained from her eyes—if only it would rain from heaven! Her blistered lips, bloated tongue, bone-dry throat, baking body, and befuddled brain blazoned her desperate need.

After a few moments, she rearranged her son's weight, drew a painfully deep breath, and threw all her strength into hoisting him again. But this time it was just too much for her. *I must get up; I must go on! I must find water!*

Hagar's heart pounded wildly as she tried hard to suppress the scream clawing at her throat. She kept struggling to get Ishmael to his feet—but it was no use. Sandwiched there between scorching sun and searing sand, she was out of water, out of strength, and . . . out of hope. Her nightmare had reached its tragic end. She was dying, and worse, her beloved son—all she had left in the world—was dying.

It's over; it's all over. Just like everyone else, even God has abandoned us. Unable to bear watching Ishmael's painful death, she pushed him under a scrub brush and crawled away. In a paroxysm of emotion—she could hold it in no longer—she threw her head back and screamed a guttural cry of terror. Sobbing, crying, wailing, she pleaded to heaven. No one but Ishmael seemed to hear, and he, too, wept bitterly beneath his bushy grave marker.

Hagar's was The Desperate Heart. Abandoned and terrified, she had no one to help her and her child in their greatest time of need. To look at her distraught face caked with dirt and sweat, you would never guess that a few days earlier her life was completely different. Then, feasting at a huge family celebration, she wore festive attire and looked stunning. Then her only worry for her son was his secondary rank in the family hierarchy.

But early the next morning she awakened to see her whole world blow up in her face. Abraham came to her tent with some food and a skin of water and gently but forcefully ordered her and Ishmael to leave. What? At the party she had glimpsed Sarah's disapproving look at Ishmael but had not sensed danger. Now she knew instinctively this thing was Sarah's doing. Sure, many years before she had done something to raise Sarah's ire, but she had repented. This time she felt betrayed.

Abraham's attitude shocked her most. Her home had been with him for thirty years! How could this righteous man send her and her son (who was his own flesh and blood) into the wilderness with only meager provisions and a weak platitude about God's will? Rejected and heartbroken, the unfortunate duo reluctantly had set out on foot from their home to search for a new life. God had given her a promise once, but now in her most desperate hour, He had evidently forsaken her, too.

How did Hagar get into this horrid predicament? Her story is inextricably linked to that of Abram and Sarai (Abraham and Sarah). Without them she would have no place in the biblical record. Yet through their turbulent relationship, the insignificant young woman would rise to become a major player in world history—the mother of Abram's first child, Ishmael, and, therefore, the "foundress" of the Ishmaelites and the Arab nations.

As impressive as this might sound, Hagar was a victim of her times. A mere slave-girl, Abram and Sarai obtained her for their household probably while in Egypt. Possibly Pharaoh gave her to the affluent nomads as part of a sizable gift (Genesis 12:16). She served uneventfully for some time as Sarai's maidservant. Legally she belonged to Abram and Sarai, and they were obliged to support and protect her.

Evidently Hagar's status did not allow her reproductive rights. But Abram needed an heir, and this is where she really enters the story. God intended to make Abram the father of a chosen people, a God-centered nation that He would bless and call His own, that would be a light and inspiration to the entire world. Concerning Abram's heir, God made significant promises: "I will make you into a great nation" (Genesis 12:2); "To your offspring I will give this land" (12:7); "A son coming from your own body will be your heir. . . . Look up at the heavens and count the stars—if indeed you can count them. . . . So shall your offspring be" (15:4-5); "To your descendants I give this land" (15:18).

But Sarai had been barren all her life. While their household of servants now numbered in the hundreds, what they wanted most, one heir, she had failed to produce. Waiting and waiting for the promise, they had hoped in vain for her to conceive. Sarai finally became desperate enough to take a drastic measure. Reasoning that God must have had another plan, she thought, *I must find another way.* She was certain that motherhood was humanly impossible, and so she devised a human scheme to work the humanly possible. It was a repugnant solution, but she could think of no other. She had not yet joined the ranks of those who "through faith and patience inherit what has been promised" (Hebrews 6:12).

Looking around at her servants, she wondered, *Hmm, which one?* Likely it only took her a moment to select Hagar. Sarai trusted her. Hagar had always been loyal and responsible in carrying out her tasks. She had earned a prominent position within the family circle, and the fact that she was young, healthy, and hopefully fertile made her suitable for this mission.

Sarai ran to Abram for her plan's approval. "The LORD has kept me from having children," she said. "Go, sleep with my maidservant; perhaps I can build a family through her"(Genesis 16:2). While Abram had always assumed that Sarai would be his child's mother, God had never said who the mother would be. Long years had come and gone, and here was a solution.

Could this be *the* solution? It probably seemed reasonable to Abram. He could think of many reasons beyond the obvious: *It was legal.* Sarai was entitled to do as she wished with her slaves. *It was customary.* At the time this practice was popularly sanctioned for obtaining children. Often a married woman unable to bear children was even required to give a female servant to her husband to produce heirs as her proxy. *It was good for Sarai.* Hagar was Sarai's personal property, and any offspring from her union with Abram would be considered Sarai's own. *It was fair to Hagar.* While still Sarai's servant, Hagar would receive new status as Abram's second wife. *It was righteous.* After all, this act would be done for no other reason than to fulfill the Lord's promise to Abram.

Well, at least this may have been Abram's perspective. That the promise had not been fulfilled put pressure on him to act. It seemed a good solution, so he agreed to it. Yet no matter how well-intentioned, Israel's future patriarch was detouring from faith and letting reason (and Sarai) guide him, not God.

Poor Hagar! What choice did she have in the matter? None. After securing Abram's permission, Sarai likely sat her down and explained, "Hagar, as you know, the Lord promised us an heir but failed to open my womb. I believe He wants you, my dear, to produce a child for us. I want you to sleep with Abram; he has already agreed. Surely this is the Lord's solution." End of discussion.

At first the thought of bedding down with her eighty-six-year-old master might have seemed shocking to young Hagar. Still, as previously stated, this would not be an entirely bad deal for her. A wife, if only a second wife, figured much more prominently than a maid. For the Scripture does say that "Sarai his *wife*" gave Hagar to Abram "to be his *wife*" (Genesis 16:3). The same Hebrew word identifies both women. Sarai was elevating Hagar from maidservant standing to that of Abram's wife.

So Abram slept with Hagar, and in a short time she came to her mistress with tidings of victory. "Guess what?" she may have said. "It's happened. I'm pregnant!" This was the exact news Sarai had longed to hear. What, then, was the unsettled feeling rising within her? Why could she not dote on her antidote?

Sarai had not understood it, but this news would bring a double-edged sword to her heart. *Hagar's pregnant . . . already?* Sarai had tried for some sixty years, but Hagar conceived immediately. Coping with her own failure would not be easy, but Sarai would do her best, keeping in mind that Hagar's child would be counted her own.

Abram must have rejoiced greatly. Surely the entire household, except perhaps Sarai, was thrilled. But however unselfish Abram and Sarai's motives may have been, and even Hagar's, trouble was bound to surface in their tents. Out of God's perfect will, they created what would become a chain of vexing conflicts. For God intended monogamous marriage, and polygamous ones in the biblical record never made for happy homes.

Their test had come as a matter of timing. Often the hardest thing to do is to wait for God's timing. Having lost patience with Him, they took matters in their own hands. But to Hagar this was not interference; it was God's divine will. Abram had feared having to make his head steward his legal heir, but thanks to her, God was finally answering his prayers. Pregnant with Abram's seed and thinking she carried the child of promise, she saw herself in a new light.

No longer a simple servant, she was important, more important—dare she think it?—even than Sarai!

She was only a secondary wife, but she looked down on Sarai. Compared with herself, her old mistress was a lightweight, no longer meriting respect. Hagar had succeeded, Sarai had failed; Hagar's star had risen, Sarai's had fallen. Bursting with contempt, her heart boasted, *I'm alive, I'm young, I'm fruitful, I'm blessed of God. Since I've been proved the better woman, I'll also prove the better wife and mother. I needn't obey Sarai any longer. I'm in the driver's seat now.*

God's Word says, "When she knew she was pregnant, she began to despise her mistress" (Genesis 16:4). But Sarai would only take so much provocation from this young upstart who strutted around before her. She stomped off to find Abram. As the elder and first wife, she still had rights, and she would use them. Hagar was still her property, and she would ruin her. But she was also furious with Abram. Perhaps he had not directly encouraged Hagar's attitude, but he had let it go unchecked. "You are responsible for the wrong I am suffering," she barked at him. "I put my servant in your arms, and now that she knows she is pregnant, she despises me. May the LORD judge between you and me" (Genesis 16:5). So bitter was she against Hagar that she refused to even say her name.

Hagar had presumed that in a dispute with Sarai, Abram would side with her, the bearer of his only child. She was wrong. Not wanting to enrage Sarai further, he, too, avoided saying Hagar's name. "Your servant is in your hands," he assured her. "Do with her whatever you think best" (Genesis 16:6).

This was exactly what Sarai hoped to hear from her husband. But behind her cries for justice, we see something else in her heart—vengeance. Blazing up to Hagar like a fire-breathing dragon, Sarai let the woman know that she was in charge. We do not know what she did to Hagar, but we can reasonably think that she had her beaten. The Hebrew word used here, *ànah*, means to afflict or humble. Whatever her method, it was harsh.

A person's pride will bring humiliation, but one who is lowly in spirit will obtain honor. . . . Under three things the earth trembles; under four it cannot bear up: a slave when he becomes king, and a fool when glutted with food; an unloved woman when she gets a husband, and a maid when she succeeds her mistress.

PROVERBS 29:23; 30:21-23 NRSV

Poor Hagar. She was riding high for a moment, but Sarai yanked her down and trounced on her. But was it not Sarai who instigated this problem? It was her idea to choose Hagar to bear a child for her husband.

Obviously, by now everyone wondered where they had gone wrong. They had all made serious errors in judgment: Sarai, with her finger-pointing; Abram, with his passivity; and Hagar, with her pride. Their arrangement—a human idea, not God's—had blown up in their faces.

Used, abused, and confused, Hagar fled to the wilderness. Her very name means "flight." In her mind her punishment did not match the crime, and she would run all the way back to Egypt before putting up with Sarai's mistreatment for another moment. She ran until she was far from home on the road to Shur, a wilderness caravan route.

She may have traveled for several days when she reached the vicinity of Kadesh. Having lived a relatively sheltered life, the farther into the inhospitable wilderness she had come, the tougher it had gotten. It was dawning on her that in her condition she might never make it to Egypt. She and her unborn child might die out there. Even if she did make it, a pregnant runaway slave would not be looked upon kindly anywhere. Still, going back seemed unthinkable. Exhausted, she came to a little roadside desert oasis and stopped to refresh herself. But lingering near the spring, and feeling desperate and alone, she wondered, *I don't know what to do. Which way should I turn?*

Suddenly an angel stood before her—the first angelic appearance in Scripture. "Hagar, servant of Sarai," he said. This salutation told her many comforting things: She was not alone in the wilderness; the Lord cared about her life; He knew her by name. Yet it also told her something else: The Lord still viewed her as Sarai's servant. This humbled her, reminding her that she was not where she belonged, that she had left home and duty without permission and was out of God's will. Sarai had done wrong, but Sarai's maid still belonged at home in her mistress's tent. But rather than correct her, the angel simply asked, "Where have you come from, and where are you going?" (Genesis 16:8).

Readily admitting her guilt, Hagar confessed, "I'm running away from my mistress Sarai."

He did not condemn her. Instead, he compassionately gave her a course of action, a way of deliverance: "Go back to your mistress and submit to her" (Genesis 16:9). *Go home and face Sarai?* What a discomforting thought! It would take courage; it would mean swallowing her pride, working on her attitude, apologizing—no matter how justified she felt.

Knowing that doing the right thing would not be easy for her, he added to his command a gracious promise. "I will so increase your descendants that they will be too numerous to count," he said. "You are now with child and you will have a son. You shall name him Ishmael, for the LORD has heard of your misery" (Genesis 16:10-11).

Did you hear that—"your descendants"? God did not see her as a mere womb for Sarai. In fact, in God's eyes this was not Sarai's child. Hagar would safely deliver a son. He would be her son, and she would even name him. Not only that, but her posterity would be "too numerous to count!"

Abram and Hagar's union had never been God's will, but since it had happened, He would not abandon her and her offspring. The child's name, Ishmael, means "God will hear." So God had heard her heart's cry and promised to keep hearing. Though her short-lived status had been stripped from her, Ishmael more than covered her loss. His name would ever remind her of her desert visitation, that the

God of Abram—not the gods of Egypt to which she had tried to return—had responded to her need.

The angel said of Ishmael, "He will be a wild donkey of a man; his hand will be against everyone and everyone's hand against him, and he will live in hostility toward all his brothers" (Genesis 16:12). While this description is one to make a mother cry, it did not seem to bother Hagar. Blessed with a promise remarkably like that given Abram, she was told that her son would found a great nation of people. Now knowing that her life mattered to God, nothing Egypt could offer compared. God's promise would enable her to surrender her heart and return home to accept the role God had prepared for her to play in history. No longer vying as a rival wife, she would resume her role as her mistress's submissive handmaiden.

Before turning to go home, Hagar showed evidence of another revelation given her. *The angel of the Lord* who spoke to her suddenly revealed Himself as *the Lord*. Filled with awe and wonder, she responded by giving Him a name previously not seen in Scripture, *El Roi*—"the God who *sees* me." He had seen her sins, He had seen her trials, He had seen her flight, and He had seen her sitting at the well. He could see everything she did and everywhere she went. He had even seen the desperate cry and sorrow of her heart and now saw its repentance. Seeing her with love and mercy, He gave her precious promises. She marveled, not only that God had seen her, but that she had seen God and lived to tell about it. "I have now seen the One who sees me," (Genesis 16:13) she said with awe.

The spring where Hagar met the Lord was called Beer Lahai Roi—"the well of the living God who sees me." Whether or not Hagar actually named the well, it was kept as a lasting memorial of her encounter with the awesome God who saw and heard and cared for her in the wilderness. It was there that the eyes of this pregnant, lonely, and fearful fugitive were opened to see that someone in this world, in fact the living God, loved *her*. For the rest of her life, every time she pronounced Ishmael's name, she would remember El Roi.

Hagar rejoined Abram and Sarai. She no doubt told them of her experience with God, and the three had a time of repentance and mutual forgiveness, resolving to live in harmony as best they knew how. When Hagar gave birth to her child, in obedience to her revelation, Abram named him Ishmael. What joy the eighty-six-year-old man must have felt over his first and only son. Through the ensuing years, Abram loved him dearly, affording him all the stature of his heir.

As time went on, Abram prospered financially, the land was at peace, and life was good. Hope of Abram and Sarai ever having a child together was all but forgotten. Ishmael was growing up, and they were convinced he was the child of promise. But one day, after thirteen years, the Lord paid Abram a startling visit, announcing: "I will make you very fruitful; I will make nations of you, and kings will come from you. I will establish my covenant as an everlasting covenant between me and you and your descendants after you for the generations to come, to be your God and the God of your descendants after you. The whole land of Canaan, where you are now an alien, I will give as an everlasting possession to you and your descendants after you; and I will be their God" (Genesis 17:6-8).

God went on to change his name to Abraham, meaning "the father of a multitude," and instituted the practice of circumcision as a symbol of their covenant. But what He said next came as a total shock to the old man: "As for Sarai your wife, you are no longer to call her Sarai; her name will be Sarah. I will bless her and will surely give you a son by her. I will bless her so that she will be the mother of nations; kings of peoples will come from her" (Genesis 17:15-16).

How did Abraham respond? First, he fell on his face laughing and said to himself, "Will a son be born to a man a hundred years old? Will Sarah bear a child at the age of ninety?" Then, realizing what this would mean for his son Ishmael, he pleaded for him to be the kingdom heir: "If only Ishmael might live under your blessing!" he cried (Genesis 17:17-18).

But the rightful heir to the redemptive covenant would come only through divine intervention. The Lord replied, "Yes, but your wife Sarah will bear you a son, and you will call him Isaac. I will establish my covenant with him as an everlasting covenant for his descendants after him." Then, confirming His promise to Hagar, He added, "And as for Ishmael, I have heard you: I will surely bless him; I will make him fruitful and will greatly increase his numbers. He will be the father of twelve rulers, and I will make him into a great nation. But my covenant I will establish with Isaac, whom Sarah will bear to you by this time next year" (Genesis 17:19-21). After this Abraham, Ishmael, and all the males in the household were circumcised together.

Just as God promised, Sarah conceived and bore Abraham his son Isaac. What had been humanly impossible, God had done through a restorative miracle—"Is anything too hard for the LORD?" (Genesis 18:14). What a thrilling time this was in the lives of Abraham and Sarah!

About three years later, little Isaac was weaned. The time of weaning, a significant milestone in any child's life, was marked with festivity. We can imagine that in Isaac's case the celebrating was par-ticularly great. The entire household of hundreds of servants and workers, along with lots of friends and neighbors, came together to see the wonderful miracle God had done for one-hundred-year-old Abraham and ninety-year-old Sarah.

Hagar and Ishmael, however, had been largely lost in the shuffle since Sarah's pregnancy. For so long Ishmael had been his father's only child, the apple of his eye, the heir-apparent. It was not his fault (or his mother's) that he had been born because of a temporary lapse of faith by Abraham and Sarah. Conceived in unbelief, he felt rejected and inferior to Isaac, the child of promise, whom faith had conceived.

It is not at all hard to understand why the young man might have had a problem over his much-celebrated little half-brother. On this day of festivity, Ishmael, now about sixteen years old, was ridiculing Isaac. Sarah saw Ishmael's mocking and knew this was no innocent jesting by a brother who loved his sibling. Ishmael was jealous. At once simmering old resentments, rivalries, and suspicions erupted in her heart; she wanted to be rid of Ishmael and his mother forever.

Intent on protecting her own son's interests, Sarah went straight to Abraham. By legal standards Ishmael was entitled to a share of the inheritance, but Sarah wanted Isaac to be the sole heir. Legally a slave woman's son could forgo his inheritance in exchange for his freedom, and Sarah would drive him to that freedom. "Get rid of that slave woman and her son," she said, "for that slave woman's son will never share in the inheritance with my son Isaac" (Genesis 21:10). Harsh words for a woman who had been her servant for so many years and a son whom her husband loved!

At first glance Sarah's reaction seems shallow, and it did show a weakness in her own character. Yet it underscored a fundamental division that in time would reveal the irreconcilability of the natural with the spiritual (Psalm 83:4-6; Galatians 4:29 and context). Sarah's eyes were open to the true nature of their clash; she knew what was at stake. Ishmael resented Isaac's privileged position and would never simply accept second place in the family. As only Isaac would receive the covenant promises, the relational conflicts between the two would just become more pronounced in time.

But Abraham was mortified! He *loved* Ishmael. Grieved and confused at Sarah's attitude, he didn't know what to do. How could he expel his own son? Shouldn't they all just get along as one happy family? So God stepped in and told him, "Do not be so distressed about the boy and your maidservant. Listen to whatever Sarah tells you, because it is through Isaac that your offspring will be reckoned. I will make the son of the maidservant into a nation also, because he is your offspring" (Genesis 21:12-13).

While Sarah's heart was not right toward Hagar and Ishmael, God had confirmed that she was acting in harmony with His plan. Abraham now understood the issues at stake and viewed the separation as crucial. There had to be a clear distinction between the two sons. The patriarchal line would run through Isaac, not Ishmael. God's assurances that He would not overlook Ishmael gave Abraham the inner resolve to send him away. But he must have taken God's instruction to *listen to whatever Sarah tells you* quite literally. He sent them out with nothing but what they could carry on their backs, without a servant, a camel, a goat, or even a lamb!

Sad to say, Abraham had been passive in this drama all along, and this greatly added to the conflicts. First, he had gone along with Sarah's ill-conceived plan for a child. Then when pregnant Hagar treated her contemptuously, he never noticed to correct the problem. Instead, it grew unchecked until Sarah exploded. Finally Sarah again was the one to detect trouble between Ishmael and Isaac. It took God Himself to get Abraham to take action, and when he finally did, it would seem impulsive and unfair.

Early the next morning Abraham took some food and a skin of water and set them on Hagar's shoulders. This is what Hagar was given after nearly thirty years of service, and she—"the slave woman"—not Ishmael, had to carry it. How could he send her out like this? Perhaps he thought they could easily make it to a nearby settlement. Archaeological findings show that there were many settlements in the area then. Still, whatever his thinking, this was an unfair way to treat one who had served them for so long, not to mention his own son. No doubt Sarah did not show up for the good-byes.

Hagar, once driven from Egypt, was now driven from the community of people she had known and served for most of her life. Earlier she had run away, but this time she was *sent*—despised, rejected, grieving, defenseless. So the two castoffs went their way into the wilderness of Beersheba. Evidently they became disoriented and roamed around until their provisions ran out. In desperate need of water, they searched frantically for a spring. Ishmael fainted first, perhaps because he gave his mother most of their water to drink. He fell to the ground, unable to go on.

Trying desperately to save him, Hagar supported his weight for a time. But she couldn't do this for long and shortly could go no farther. Finally parched and exhausted, she abandoned all hope. It was all she could do to push Ishmael under a shrub for a little shade from the cruel sun. This was the last service she could provide her beloved son. Desperately grieved, she thought, *I cannot watch the boy die* (Genesis 21:16). So she used her last ounce of strength and struggled to move a distance away. Then, with excruciating sorrow and anguish of heart, she wailed and prayed as she waited for death to come and claim them both. Apparently Ishmael, too, prayed and cried pathetically.

Oh, but had they both forgotten Ishmael's name? Did they forget that "God will hear"? In this same wilderness He had given her a promise many years earlier, but in her desperation she had lost faith in it. Nevertheless, the one who named the youth Ishmael before he was even born "*heard* the boy crying" (Genesis 21:17). An angelic voice from heaven broke through her mourning, calling to her, "What is the matter, Hagar? Do not be afraid; God has heard the boy crying as he lies there. Lift the boy up and take him by the hand, for I will make him into a great nation" (Genesis 21:17-18).

With the Lord there is "no variableness, neither shadow of turning" (James 1:17 KJV). He had not forsaken them in their time of desperation after all! They still remained under His protection! Hagar looked, and the God whom she had once called El Roi—"the God who sees me"—opened her own eyes to see. Not far from her she saw a well of water that she had missed before. A miracle! Leaping to her feet, she hurried over and refilled her water skin. What joy! What relief! They would live! Soon she and Ishmael were gratefully gulping down a cool, refreshing drink.

The eyes of the LORD *are on the righteous and his ears are attentive to their cry. . . . The righteous cry out, and the* LORD *hears them; he delivers them from all their troubles.*

PSALM 34:15, 17-18

Hagar had been an underdog and a victim of her times. But praise be to God—He *cares* for underdogs and outcasts. He took note of the lonely and forsaken figure out in the wilderness—not once but twice. He heard and answered her heart's desperate cry. Her life was not a mistake! He had a plan for her all along!

Rather than trying to go on to Egypt as she had before, Hagar remained in the wilderness of Paran. There God had met them and promised to provide for them, and there she chose to raise her son. Like a widow and an orphan, the two had ventured forth as outcasts. But God had not cast them away. He simply had another plan for them. Loving and caring for them, He gave them hope for their future.

"God was with the boy as he grew up" (Genesis 21:20). Ishmael provided for himself and his mother by becoming a skilled archer. He would be a brave man of conflict and conviction who could choose to use this innate strength either for God or against Him. He would be the one to decide. Whatever his choice, God had proved that He keeps His promises. Just as God had promised, Ishmael grew up, married, and became the father of a great nation.

In the New Testament, the apostle Paul saw in this story a spiritual meaning. He takes the conflict between Sarah/Isaac and Hagar/Ishmael and uses it allegorically to illustrate the ongoing conflict between grace and law, spirit and flesh. He parallels Hagar's literal slavery to the spiritual slavery caused by the Law given at Mount Sinai. He likens Hagar to the earthly city of Jerusalem of his day that bore children enslaved to the old covenant, who had not yet come to freedom in Christ. Those seeking salvation by legalistically trying to keep the Law are born of the flesh. Those, on the other hand, who share in God's promise are children of faith, like Isaac, and not in bondage to the Law. Born of the lawful wife of Abraham, the free woman, the Jerusalem that is above, they have found freedom in Christ and are the rightful heirs of His kingdom (see Galatians 4:21-31).

Ironically, Isaac eventually lived in Beer Lahai Roi by the well where the angel visited Hagar (Genesis 24:62). Evidently, some contact had been kept between the two families, and there was even some reconciliation. The last we hear of Ishmael, he and Isaac are together burying their father in a cave near Mamre (Genesis 25:9).

Hagar's children became desert nomads. Living in the harsh regions of the Sinai Desert, south of what would later become Israel, these proudly self-reliant people were rugged hunters and ruthless warriors who "lived in hostility toward all their brothers" (Genesis 25:18). As we know, Arab-Jewish hostility continues even to this day. Yet we can be assured that even today God loves the Arab nations. Hagar, their mother, stands in history as proof that God loves all people.

The poor and needy search for water, but there is none; their tongues are parched with thirst. But I the LORD will answer them; I, the God of Israel, will not forsake them. I will make rivers flow on barren heights, and springs within the valleys. I will turn the desert into pools of water, and the parched ground into springs.

ISAIAH 41:17-18

For he will deliver the needy who cry out, the afflicted who have no one to help. He will take pity on the weak and the needy and save the needy from death.

PSALM 72:12-13

LESSONS FOR OUR OWN HEARTS

Do you feel abandoned and sent out to a wilderness? Perhaps you are not down to your last gulp of water, wailing for your dying child on the hot scorching desert sand. But things may seem that bad to you. Sometimes life can cave in on us, leaving us desperately confused and needy. Still we can take heart, knowing that wherever we are and whatever we are going through, His promise extends to us.

What can be worse than the desperation a mother can feel for her child? I have briefly felt this myself. My daughter Hannah was twenty-one when she went on a short mission trip to Eastern Europe with a youth organization. I told her that if I were young and in her shoes, after the outreach I would take advantage of the opportunity and go on over to Western Europe and do some sightseeing. Clay had strong reservations about her going on this trip alone, and he told us so. But she liked the idea.

So Hannah toured Western Europe by rail and stayed in hostels. She was supposed to check in with us at an appointed time, and the call failed to come in. We became nervous. We were scheduled to leave on a trip of our own but postponed it. As the hours ticked by, we became increasingly alarmed. That night Clay sat up in an all-night prayer vigil. I tried hard to keep my wits about me but thought seriously of flying to Europe to rescue my child. But where would I begin? What country?

After a long and sleepless night, I was sure of the worst. I made every bargain with God I could think of. I pleaded, "Please, Lord, let my little girl live!" To make things worse, I was consumed with guilt. I had suggested this foolish thing—and everyone knew it. Well, the phone finally did ring, twenty-four hours late. "Hi, Mom and Dad!" came the bouncy voice. "I'm having a great time!" She had locked her calling card in a train station locker somewhere and figured we would know she was busy having the time of her life.

Another time Hannah's health spiraled downward. At the same time her boss at work persecuted her severely. She was determined to be a Christian witness and kept taking the abuse. Plagued with dizziness, blurred vision, and even fainting spells, I watched help-lessly as my precious daughter, who had barely missed a day of school growing up, suffered nobly with growing physical difficulties. Was her job killing her? Or was her trouble due to an automobile accident she had been in? For many months the problem persisted. She lost weight, was sick and weak.

With my mother-heart breaking, I literally believed I was wrestling for my daughter's life as I agonized in prayer for her. When a cardiologist did a tilt table test on which she fainted and her heart stopped beating, he put her on beta blocker medication and a strict health regimen. But El Roi did not forget us. He touched Hannah, and today she lives a normal life, free of medication.

Of course, there are many other kinds of desperation unrelated to loved ones, some sweeping in on us seemingly from nowhere and others plaguing us for what seems like forever. Many people live lives of ongoing "quiet desperation." I know a woman who spent many years desperately searching for the good life. But she, like Hagar, was a slave—a slave to sin, to the devil, to a shattered ego. It must have started very young. She was slow in school and slow to make friends. Life was hard for her, and she believed it was her fault. Still in grade school, she listed the reasons she should not have been born. "I'm dumb, skinny, shy, have stringy hair, bite my nails . . ." Fortunately, she was also cowardly. Sometimes standing on a hillside cliff, she tried to gather the courage to fling herself off the edge.

Junior high school came, and her desperate shyness drove her sometimes to eat lunch alone in a bathroom stall. Too ashamed to ask anyone how to open her locker, she awkwardly carried all her books and a violin to her classes for an entire school year. At school dances she stood on the sidelines, tormented and alone. When in a group of girls, she agonized over what to say. *Think of something cute. Act bubbly, carefree; laugh. Do it now!* But it just wouldn't come, so she quietly stayed in her shell. Report card time was the worst time of all; she was always terrified of failing.

High school came. She thought she was so skinny that she wore a coat to cover herself even in the southern California heat. All any-one could see of her was a sullen face, hair that never cooperated, and stockings that always sported a run or two. This backward young woman stared jealously at the popular girls who laughed and teased, who got good grades and boyfriends. She wondered why life was so easy for them. When she graduated—oh, what a relief!—she never bothered to buy a yearbook.

In junior college she was so depressed that she barely scraped along there. She tried to make life work for her, but, like Hagar, she was a slave. Her master, the devil, was dreadfully cruel and constantly abused her. Driving her failures home, this master convinced her of her worthlessness. She was his, both because she was sold to him, a helpless victim and outcast in life, and because she was a sinner receiving her just reward. Trying to escape her master's captivity, like Hagar, she fled. But whatever she tried just drove her deeper into the wilderness of despair. There she sat, parched, gasping, hopeless.

But El Roi saw her desperate heart. He had let her reach the end of herself. Little did she know that His Spirit had actively led her to the place where she would gratefully "draw water from the wells of salvation" (Isaiah 12:3). She never heard His voice from heaven as did

Hagar, but at the age of twenty-two she heard it no less: "Cheryl," He called, "I'm real. I love you, and I'm here for you. Come to Me."

Yes, I was that young woman, and the Lord graciously opened my eyes to see His spring of life-giving water. I drank; I was spared. Satan no longer had rights over me; I was free to go forward in life with new hope, new life, new direction. Oh, the tender mercy and love of our God—it is beyond compare! That, of course, was not my last struggle, but once you know El Roi is watching over you, you are never completely without hope again.

Desperate hearts. God took note of a young pagan woman, alone and desperate in the Arabian wilderness—twice. He took note of me when I was a modern-day young pagan woman lost and desperate in my wilderness. How much more will He rescue you, His beloved daughter?

You have shown your people desperate times. . . . But for those who fear you, you have raised a banner to be unfurled against the bow. . . . With God we will gain the victory, and he will trample down our enemies.

PSALM 60:3, 4, 12

Perhaps this is too much for you to receive right now. In light of your circumstances, you cannot imagine that God cares about you. You feel you have done everything right; you have even loved and served Him faithfully. Yet you feel the bitter sting of injustice, abuse, victimization. You have suffered losses until your heart cries desperately for relief. *It makes sense that unbelievers should suffer so*, you think. *But why me?* The lessons Hagar learned about God from her experiences can also give us fresh perspective and hope. Let's look at several of them.

God Cares

I think Hagar has gotten a bum rap. When I think of her, I don't see her as a mistake. I see God's grace and mercy extended to "the least of these" (Matthew 25:40). She may not have been as central a figure in His plan as were Abraham and Sarah, but God saw her as a person and cared about her. The angel of the Lord *found* her (Genesis 16:7) out in the wilderness. In other words, God went looking for her and proved that all was not lost and hopeless in her life. Later He did not let the two castaways die in the desert. His heart went out to them, and His heart continues to go out to the Hagars and Ishmaels of this world, the widows and orphans, the lost and rejected, the abused and desperate.

This is not a story about Hagar's merits. Whether she was good or bad had little bearing. She landed in the wilderness twice. One time she had sinned; the next time she had not. But God rescued her both times, showing us more about His character than hers. She did not deserve God's mercy—nor did Sarah, for that matter. Both women made errors in judgment; both were sinners. Yet God chose Sarah for a special call while still remaining loving and merciful to Hagar.

Just think, dear sister in Christ, how much God has blessed you. Look what He has done for you—He sent His Son to die for you! Through Christ's atoning blood, your sins are forgiven, and you are a child of God—a joint heir with Christ. You don't deserve such favor; His grace is a gift you cannot earn, but it is yours nonetheless. You are eternally significant to Him!

You may wonder, "If God so loves me, why am I in such desperate straits?" You cannot understand Him. Nor could Hagar. She was ousted and forsaken, sitting in the wilderness, her only child dying, and He asked her, "What is the matter?" Go figure! Wouldn't she feel like crying, "Don't you get it, Lord? Where have you been? We're dying out here, and you ask, 'What is the matter?'"

But things are not as out of control as they seem. God cares deeply. He proved it to Hagar, and He has proven it to you, too. He proved it first at Calvary, and He will keep proving it. He understands your pain; He understands your heartbreak; He understands what it is to suffer unjustly. He has been there before you. Scorned, ridiculed, plotted against, desperately praying in the garden, yielding to the

Father's will, betrayed, killed—yes, He understands your afflictions and cares deeply about you.

God Sees and Hears

Do you feel lost in your wilderness? Take heart. God saw Hagar and, in fact, never lost sight of her. He knew all the details of her comings and goings and even called her by name—"Hagar, servant of Sarai." He keeps proving His knowledge of and concern for those who feel cast off and forgotten. Amazed, Hagar called Him El Roi ("You are the God who sees me"). And God sees you, too. He takes note of your deep needs, has every hair on your head counted, and knows your every tear. "For the *eyes* of the LORD range throughout the earth to strengthen those whose hearts are fully committed to him" (2 Chronicles 16:9, italics added).

He also hears you. His ear is open to you, so don't ever give up praying. As Hagar sat desperate and alone, wondering what to do, the Lord heard her mother-heart's desperate cry. She couldn't bear to hear her child crying. Nor could God. Bringing wondrous news, the angel told her, "God has *heard* the boy crying as he lies there" (Genesis 21:17, italics added).

Our God is an all-seeing, all-hearing God, and His eyes and ears are open to us. He knows our need. When everyone else abandons us, and it seems no one cares whether we live or die, *He* does. Wherever we are, wherever we have strayed, wherever the enemy has mauled and dragged us, God's ear is open to our cry. We are never too far away for God to hear and rescue us. What hope this should give you!

In my alarm I said, "I am cut off from your sight!" Yet you heard my cry for mercy when I called to you for help.

PSALM 31:22

For the eyes of the Lord are on the righteous and his ears are attentive to their prayer.

1 PETER 3:12

God Promises

Do you need some bright hope, some shining vision, some radiant assurance? Do you need help and support? Have you looked lately to the promises of God's Word—that "living and active" manna for your soul? You will find your heart strengthened; you will find wisdom, instruction, encouragement, and revelation. No matter how bad things might seem, God has promises for you. Cling to them; they are there for *you*.

In deep distress Hagar watched helplessly as her son's life ebbed away. But God said those wonderfully reassuring words: "Do not be afraid." Why not? Because she had nothing to fear! As bad as things looked, God had already made her a promise that her son would live to be a great man. Hearing the promise again was a balm to the poor broken-spirited Egyptian who had forgotten the truth. It revived her faith and gave her strength to go on.

What has God promised you? He has given you marvelous promises, "very great and precious promises" (2 Peter 1:4).

God Guides and Provides

God may or may not send you an angel, but He has given you someone better, a Divine Counselor—the Holy Spirit. Have you looked to His presence, power, and guidance lately? No matter how desperate your situation, this third person of the Triune God is with you. David learned this truth and prayed, "Where can I go from your Spirit? Where can I flee from your presence? If I go up to the heavens, you are there; if I make my bed in the depths, you are there. If I rise on the wings of the dawn, if I settle on the far side of the sea, even there your hand will *guide me*, your right hand will hold me fast" (Psalm 139:7-10, italics added).

Hagar learned this, too. God had guidance for her desperate heart. The first time He sent her home to her mistress. The next time He directed her to a spring of water. He had guided her faithfully until the water was within reach, but with her eyes blinded by tears and swollen from weeping, she had at first missed it. It was there for her though—not just a cup but an entire well!

God has provided a well of "living water" for us (John 4:10; 7:38). Every other source on earth may dry up, but God's wellspring never runs dry. You may go on day after day anguishing over your life, blind to that well of grace from which you might draw. But look up. Let Him show it to you.

In view of these comforting realities, how should we respond?

Don't Rebel, but Surrender to God

God often lets us go into a wilderness and meets us there. Pregnant Hagar fled to the wilderness, away from the path of duty. She was there for her rebellion against Sarah, but God graciously intercepted her. If she had persisted on her rebellious course, she might have died there. The only way out of the wilderness was to fully surrender her stubborn heart to the Lord. That meant going back and submitting to Sarah.

What might surrendering mean for us? First, let us be clear about something: It would be foolish and cruel to think that every misfortune—every accident, sickness, grief, disaster—is God's punishment for some sin or disobedience. Many Christians treat their suffering friends in just this way, heaping guilt on them, telling them to try harder, to seek God more sincerely. Who needs Job's friends?

Still sometimes we do suffer for failures and unwise choices. A full surrender in this case would mean *repenting*—that is, facing the Lord's loving correction and responding as Hagar did. She repented. She humbled herself, went back to the place where she had left God's will, and made it right. She had a mistress, but we have a Master to whom we must submit. If He seems far away, check your heart for unconfessed sin that may have driven you to a wilderness place.

On the other hand, we may not have sinned at all. Life has dealt us a bitter blow, and we feel unjustly treated. The psalmist fumed at God over life's injustices: "When my soul was embittered, when I was pricked in heart, I was stupid and ignorant; I was like a brute beast toward you." But knowing that this attitude had gotten him nowhere, he surrendered his heart again, saying, "Whom have I in heaven but you? And there is nothing on earth that I desire other than you" (Psalm 73:21-22, 25 NRSV).

Don't Abandon Hope, but Trust God

God is the master of the "just in time." As with Hagar, He often seems to wait for the last moment. Just in time He leaps to our aid, showing us that all we had to do was keep our hope fixed on Him. Do you need a revelation of His love? Hope in Him; He will come just in time. Do you need wisdom? Hope in Him; He will come just in time. Do you need provision? Hope in Him; He will come just in time. Whatever your desperate need, God will come just in time.

In one of the most memorable sermons of my life—I heard it some twenty-five years ago—the preacher charged, "Don't doubt in the dark what God has shown you in the light." In her dark hour Hagar forgot God's promise, and we can easily do the same. Not only must we see God as sovereign in our doctrinal statements, but also in our hearts and lives. We must trust His sovereign care. He may not calm our storm. He may even choose to let our storm rage so He can calm *us* in the storm! How was it that Jesus could sleep peacefully on a boat in the midst of a raging sea? He knew who was in charge. He knew His destiny, and it was not to die in that storm.

You can let hope, like an anchor, keep you from despairing when life's storms hit. Realizing who you are in Christ, you can say with Paul, "If God is for us, who is against us?" (Romans 8:31). Will you say it? Do you believe that God is for you? It is easy to give a resounding "yes" when life is going your way. But can you still say it, can you still believe it, when forced to travel dark and desperate valleys? From personal experience, the apostle could assert that when we know God is for us, it does not matter who is against us. When we know God wants us, it does not matter who rejects us.

When things in your life are shaking loose, keep hoping in the unshakable God. Look to Him in His Word, in prayer, in your circumstances. The darkness will disperse as the Son rises in your heart. You can keep hope alive by testifying to the truth: "God is for me.

Saving and keeping me, He won't let me come to ruin in the wilderness. Neither Satan nor all the world nor even death itself can destroy me and my hope. My God is guiding me through the events of my life to bring me to a glorious finish."

May the God of hope fill you with all joy and peace as you trust in him, so that you may overflow with hope by the power of the Holy Spirit.

ROMANS 15:13

We have this hope as an anchor for the soul, firm and secure.

HEBREWS 6:19

Heart Check

1. In what ways can you relate to Hagar? Do you have a desperate heart?

2. How do you view God when in desperate circumstances? Is He your El Roi?

3. Have you fled when challenged with difficult responsibilities?

4. How can you better surrender to God and trust Him to bring you through your trials?

5. Compose a prayer to God in response to this chapter's lessons.

6

Leah

THE LOVELORN HEART

GENESIS 29—33; 34:1; 35:23, 26; 46:15, 18; 49:31; RUTH 4:11

HER DREAMS AND ILLUSIONS were shattered. The young virgin had lain quietly under the cover of darkness with her bridegroom, to consummate their marriage. She tried imagining that he really loved her, that his heart blazed with love for her alone. *Maybe it won't matter. After this night with me, he will realize that I satisfied him and will keep doing so. Yes, maybe he truly loves me.*

Dizzy with joy and excitement, he could not help but utter his true love's name. He likely whispered, "Ah, Rachel, I have waited so long. At last you are mine. I adore you." These words, however, would stab her heart. For her name was not Rachel—it was Leah. In his heart and mind Jacob made love, not to her, but to her sister on their wedding night. As he drifted to sleep, she lay awake, dreading the morning. *What if he hates me?* Finally she fell asleep, too.

Jacob awakened early, his eyes bright, his heart racing. Rolling over to gaze at his beloved bride—the one whom for seven years he had cherished, dreamed of, labored tirelessly for, and would have died for—he had the shock of his life. *What! Leah? How did Leah get in my bed? What's going on here? Where is Rachel? . . . Oh, no! It can't be! Not Leah!*

As the truth hit, Jacob leaped to his feet with a horrified shriek. Anguished and angry, he ran from the tent to find his father-in-law. *Laban has deceived me! How could he force this woman upon me that I don't love?* It was evil, it was cruel, it was the worst thing that had ever happened to him. Also it was too late—Leah was his wife.

Leah was crushed. Trying to make the best of the deception, she had surrendered her body, heart, and soul to her bridegroom, hoping against hope that he might somehow love her. Now, her hopes dashed, she knew she meant nothing to him. Thinking otherwise had been crazy. He had always loved Rachel—not her. How would she ever forget his horrified look as he rolled over and met her eyes? She wished she could turn the clock back, but she could not. She was Jacob's wife. Her future was determined. She must endure a married life without love. *Lord God, why did You let this happen to me? Didn't my father believe he could find me a husband without resorting to this?*

Weighing her options, she must have decided that the only feasible one was to make the most of the mess by being the best wife she could be. *Perhaps all is not lost after all. If I dedicate myself to love and serve him, perhaps I can still win his heart.*

After a while Jacob returned to his tent. Leah stared at him, wondering, *Is that a glimmer of happiness I detect in his eyes? Has he forgiven me? Will he try to love me?*

"I'll stay married to you," he announced, "but next week Rachel will be mine, too. I've agreed with your father to work another seven years for her hand." He might as well have struck her. She knew she had no hope now. She would have a marriage, but Rachel would have the husband. Jacob would gladly work fourteen years for her sister but would not have taken her for free.

Leah would never forget her wedding night, the night Jacob thought she was Rachel, the one night she experienced passionate love. Only occasionally would he sleep with Leah, but then for procreation, not love.

We call Leah's heart the Lovelorn Heart. For though she craved her husband's love, she was bereft of it. He is marked as the most devoted lover in the Bible, with a love that would stand firm through the tests of time, but this love did not extend to Leah. He kept his eyes and heart settled on Rachel, his first and only true love.

The rejection Leah felt on the first morning of her marriage would dog her for a lifetime. Alone night after night, she probably cried into her pillow, hoping that somehow, someday, Jacob might love her, too. *Will he ever love me—just a little?* Jacob's actions shouted no. In fact, her father did not love her, her husband did not love her, and her sister, viewing her as a threat, did not love her. Worse, not only was she unloved, but she was hated. She must live under that hatred year after year after year.

How did Leah get into this terrible predicament? To understand, we should first get to know Jacob. He and his brother Esau were rivals, even from the womb. As they "jostled each other" within Rebekah's womb, the Lord explained that she was carrying twins who would become two competing nations of people, the older brother serving the younger. When they were born, Esau came out first with Jacob behind him grasping his foot. Thus they named the younger Jacob, meaning "heel-holder" or "supplanter" (Genesis 25:22-26).

The boys grew up, and one day when Esau was famished, Jacob seized the advantage. Living up to his name, he convinced Esau to swap his birthright (a special honor given the eldest son) for a pot of lentil soup. Moreover, with his mother's help, Jacob deceived his father into giving him the patriarchal blessing of the firstborn. Esau, stripped of his inheritance, both in terms of wealth and leadership, furiously plotted to kill Jacob upon their father's death. Rebekah heard and had Jacob sent some four hundred miles from their home in Beersheba (in Canaan) to his uncle Laban in Haran (in Mesopotamia).

On the way he received his "Jacob's ladder" dream where God extended His covenant with Abraham to him, saying in part, "I will give you and your descendants the land on which you are lying. Your descendants will be like the dust of the earth, and you will spread out to the west and to the east, to the north and to the south. All peoples on earth will be blessed through you and your offspring" (Genesis 28:13-14).

Surely this talk of descendants made Jacob think about finding himself a wife. He was not getting any younger. Nor were Leah and Rachel, neither of whom had married. Possibly Laban, their father, had stood in the way, waiting for the right situation to play to his best advantage.

As youngsters, the two sisters probably had gotten along fine. Giggling together, as little girls do, they dreamed of love, marriage, and having babies of their own. As they grew older, though, Leah giggled less. For right before her eyes, her little sister blossomed into a stunning beauty. But the only description we have of Leah is of her eyes: "Leah had weak eyes" (Genesis 29:17). Perhaps she had poor eyesight, or her eyes were pale and dull when compared with her sister's lustrous, sparkling eyes. Yet the Hebrew word *rak* used here can also mean tender, soft, or delicate. So her eyes may have been very sensitive. Calling attention to them, however, suggests that her beauty lay only in her eyes, and that she was no match for Rachel who was "lovely in form, and beautiful" (Genesis 29:17).

When handsome Cousin Jacob showed up, a man they did not know existed, Rachel was the first relative he met. Homesick and exhausted, he broke down at meeting her, giving her a kiss of greeting and weeping aloud. Then he met Laban, who insisted on his moving in with the family.

Both women cast their eyes on Jacob. They both hoped; they both dreamed. But Jacob, having already proven himself a man with high aims in life, aimed high again. Never even noticing Leah, he fell head over heels in love with beautiful Rachel. He knew this was the woman for him, that God had chosen her, and that she would be the perfect mother for the nation God had promised to make of him.

To Laban's delight, Jacob made himself useful by helping in the family business, primarily overseeing the flocks. Jacob was happy, too; for Rachel was a shepherdess, and this kept her near him.

He had been there a month when Laban approached and said, "You are my own flesh and blood. . . . Just because you are a relative of mine, should you work for me for nothing? Tell me what your wages should be" (Genesis 29:14-15). He had noticed how quickly Jacob and Rachel's relationship had developed and knew Jacob's desire. He also knew his own leverage. For penniless Jacob could pay no bride price, a customary substantial marriage gift given by the groom or his family to the bride's family. So under the guise of generosity, Laban let Jacob name the terms, knowing he would get the bargain.

Sure enough, Jacob asked for Rachel's hand in marriage, making a generous offer: "I'll work for you seven years in return for your younger daughter Rachel" (Genesis 29:18). What a windfall for Laban! This was double a typical bride price. Plus, as Jacob's father-in-law, he would reap other advantages. Jacob would work hard for seven whole years and would doubtless have a substantial inheritance of his own one day. Thinking nothing of exploiting Jacob's love, Laban quickly agreed to the proposal. "It's better that I give her to you than to some other man," he said. "Stay here with me" (Genesis 29:19).

So Jacob served seven years as Laban's indentured servant to get Rachel for his wife, "but they seemed like only a few days to him because of his love for her" (Genesis 29:20). When his seven-year contract was up, he ran to Laban and said, "Give me my wife. My time is completed, and I want to lie with her" (Genesis 29:21).

Backslapping his soon-to-be son-in-law, Laban called Rachel. After congratulating the joyful couple, he invited many guests to a large wedding feast. But not even Jacob matched Laban in trickery. The area had a custom, one still practiced today. An older daughter must marry before a younger. Perhaps Laban originally had intended to find Leah a husband, or perhaps he had planned to deceive Jacob all along.

Whatever the case, while Jacob and the guests celebrated, Laban called his two daughters aside to launch a plan that would forever drive a wedge between them. He might have said something to the effect: "Rachel, go to your tent and stay there. You are not marrying Jacob tonight." Heartbroken, Rachel would have run sobbing to her tent. Then turning to Leah, he might have said, "Get yourself ready, for this wedding night is *yours*; I'm taking *you* to Jacob tonight."

How could they get away with such a scheme? Several factors would contribute to Jacob's inability to recognize the substitution. Such a feast provided much food and wine. Jacob, in high spirits, might have had enough wine to dull his senses. Also, customarily on the wedding night the bridegroom waited in his dark bedchamber until the father of the bride brought her to him. She would come silently and heavily veiled into the darkness and stay that way, even in the nuptial bed.

We can imagine that as Laban led his daughter to Jacob's tent that night, he gave her the only premarital counseling she would receive: "Don't let him know who you are until morning, or you'll ruin everything." When they got there, he passed her to Jacob, congratulated them, and blessed their marriage. Then, smiling, he disappeared into the night, leaving them alone.

Leah obeyed her father. Did her complicity with his plan mean she accepted her assignment willingly? We don't really know what went through her mind and heart. The moral environment in the home obviously was poor, but surely she knew the wrongness of this scheme. She may have felt jealousy toward her sister, but there is no reason to think that she would enjoy hurting her or Jacob. We do know that Leah loved Jacob and that till the day of her death, she wanted him to love her.

Jacob, deceiver of his own father, fell victim to deception. Jacob, supplanter of his own brother, fell victim to supplanting. How could he not notice the comparisons? Perhaps seeing that this was retribution for his own schemes softened his anger. He did not blow up at Leah but ran to the instigator. "What is this you have done to me?" he cried to Laban. "I served you for Rachel, didn't I? Why have you deceived me?" (Genesis 29:25).

Laban had his reasons. First, he needed a husband for Leah, and if given the choice, Jacob would not have consented. Laban thought it a safe bet that once Jacob married her, he would not disgrace her by tossing her out. Second, he wanted to solicit Jacob's services into the future. Jacob, energized by love, had prospered Laban by his tireless labor. To ensure Jacob's continued cheap labor, he would use any dishonest means—even both his daughters. To him the worst that could happen was that Jacob would refuse to work longer, and Laban would have to find Rachel another husband. If his plan worked though, he would double his original bargain.

Laban was ready for his son-in-law. "It is not our custom here to give the younger daughter in marriage before the older one," he explained. "Finish this daughter's bridal week; then we will give you the younger one also, in return for another seven years of work" (Genesis 29:26-27). In other words, after Leah's week was up— seven days of feasting for her marriage—Jacob could also have Rachel if he committed himself to serve another seven years.

Jacob agreed. For a second time shameless Laban had scored a windfall by exacting an enormous payment for love. Not only had he married off his least desirable daughter, but he had gained a total of fourteen years of labor from Jacob.

Poor Leah. Did she wonder if someone might have chosen and loved her for herself? She could never know. She was a pawn of her father and disregarded and unloved by her husband. This was hardly the bridal week of which she had dreamed. As she began her first days of marriage, she got the full picture. These would be the only days she would ever have her husband to herself. Lovesick and panting for Rachel, he would soon run to her arms and there stay. Sleeping with Leah had not cooled his passion for Rachel one bit. God's plan for marriage was monogamy, and this had been Jacob's plan, too. With a monogamous love for Rachel, he eagerly anticipated the end of Leah's week and the start of Rachel's.

So viewing his first marriage as more of an unfortunate interruption, Jacob finished his week with Leah and then took Rachel as his wife. Finally with his true love, he settled in to serving his father-in-law for another seven years.

Unfortunately, this arrangement would create much family tension, disunity, and rivalry. The sisters would engage in a long-standing ferocious contest. Still Jacob's heart would remain bound to Rachel and shut to Leah. Is it not interesting, then, that we never find any real evidence of Rachel so loving Jacob? Evidently more high-spirited and self-willed, commentator H. V. Morton even says of her, "Rachel remains one of those women with nothing to recommend her but beauty. . . . She is bitter, envious, quarrelsome and petulant. The full force of her hatred is directed against her sister, Leah" (quoted in *All the Women of the Bible* by Herbert Lockyer, Zondervan).

In contrast, Leah seemed more meek and submissive, more able to see the Lord as sovereign and to accept His purposes. In view of her suffering, it is not hard to imagine that she turned to Him for hope. Charmed by Rachel's outward beauty, Jacob ignored Leah's inward beauty. But God judges by another standard: "Man looks at the outward appearance, but the LORD looks at the heart" (1 Samuel 16:7). He saw in Leah a heart He alone appreciated, a precious heart, broken and lovelorn, reaching to Him for help. Just and compassionate, He defends the despised and downtrodden, especially unloved wives.

Rachel had nothing to fear from Leah in the beauty department, but God chose to bless Leah, not Rachel, in another significant area: "When the LORD *saw* that Leah was hated, he opened her womb: but Rachel was barren" (Genesis 29:31 KJV, italics added). Leah became pregnant and gave birth to a son. Repeatedly, at the births of her children, we will see her character—her faith in the Lord, her sense of gratitude and accountability to Him, and her earnest desire for Jacob's love. While he continued to wound her, the names she chose for her children neither criticized nor rebuked him.

She named her firstborn child Reuben, saying, "It is because the LORD has seen my misery. Surely my husband will love me now" (Genesis 29:32). The name sounds like the Hebrew for "the Lord has seen my misery" and means "See, a son!" Deeply grateful to the Lord, she perceived that He had noticed her anguish and graciously given her this son. Becoming hopeful, she thought, *Surely with this sign of God's favor, Jacob will find love in his heart for me.* But even at the birth of his first son, Jacob's heart failed to turn to Leah. Still the little boy named, "See, a son!" would always remind her that despite her afflictions, she could "see" proof of the Lord's love and compassion for her.

When Leah became pregnant a second time, her hope revived. But the pregnancy turned bittersweet as Jacob's heart remained unmoved. Bearing another son, she said, "Because the LORD heard that I am not loved (*hated* in the KJV), he gave me this one too" (Genesis 29:33). So she named him Simeon, a name meaning "heard." Learning to go to the Lord for love and approval, her prayer life had grown, and she believed He had given this son in answer to her prayers. At the first birth she claimed God had seen her, but with this one she claimed He had heard her. As Reuben would ever remind her that God saw her misery, Simeon would always remind her that God hears and answers prayer.

When Leah had a third son, her heart again swelled with hope. Feeling certain that Jacob would finally see God's favor on her life and love her, she said, "Now at last my husband will become attached to me, because I have borne him three sons." So she named him Levi (Genesis 29:34), a name meaning "attached" or "joined to."

With each new son Leah longed to see a difference in her marriage. Few women could be sadder than Leah as she named her first three sons. Staring proudly at her little boys, she wondered how, when Rachel's nest stayed empty, Jacob could find no room in his heart for her. Year by year her hopes for gaining his love grew weaker. Yet her faith in God grew stronger. She was coming to a place of acceptance where she could praise the Lord for her blessings whether or not Jacob ever loved her.

By the time Leah gave birth to her fourth son, preoccupation with the Lord had replaced preoccupation with her husband. Swinging from craving Jacob's love to rejoicing in God's love, she gave Him center stage in her heart and wholly looked to Him to satisfy her heart's craving. Before, she had acknowledged Him, but now her praises were higher and fuller than ever. "This time," she exclaimed, "I will praise the LORD" (Genesis 29:35). So she named her child Judah, meaning "praise."

After this, Leah stopped having children. She had given up the notion that Jacob could ever love her, and his use of her only for bearing children was hurtful and degrading. Still she showed great character by not returning insult for insult. Unlike Hagar with Sarah or Peninnah with Hannah, Leah did not become arrogant in her pregnancy, throwing it in her rival's face. Her sister envied her, and their relationship was touchy, but we do not detect sin in Leah's heart.

However, watching her sister blessed with four sons drove Rachel to despair. One day, deeply jealous, she hollered at Jacob,

"Give me children, or I'll die!" Obviously Jacob was not the problem here, and he angrily retorted, "Am I in the place of God, who has kept you from having children?" (Genesis 30:1-2).

Desperate, she offered him her maidservant Bilhah as a surrogate wife. "Sleep with her," she told him, "so that she can bear children for me and that through her I too can build a family" (Genesis 30:3). Like Sarah who gave her maid Hagar to Abraham, Rachel chose to employ a legal remedy. As a second-class wife, any child Bilhah might bear would legally be Rachel's.

So Jacob slept with Bilhah, and she became pregnant and bore him a son. Rachel said, "God has vindicated me; he has listened to my plea and given me a son" (Genesis 30:6). Therefore, she named the child Dan, meaning "he has vindicated" or "he has judged." As the sense of the word is one of avenging, requital, and executing judgment, we see here the intensity of Rachel's competitive spirit. She was certain that this child meant that God had taken her side, having judged between her and Leah.

While Leah had rested her need for love and approval in God, Rachel's competitive spirit drove her focus back to the struggle. She had watched cautiously as Rachel gave Bilhah to Jacob, and when Bilhah bore a second son for Rachel, Leah felt threatened, especially when she heard about the child's name. Rachel had named him Naphtali, meaning "my struggle," and had said, "I have had a great struggle with my sister, and I have won" (Genesis 30:8).

Rachel had seen herself winning on two fronts and named the two children accordingly. By the first name, Dan, she had won legally—God had judged in her favor. By the second name, Naphtali, she had won in war—God had let her triumph. Therefore, Leah leaped back into the child-producing contest, determined to stay ahead of Rachel. Leah prevailed upon Jacob to take her maidservant Zilpah to bear more sons in proxy for her. Zilpah also conceived.

Again focusing on what she had, not on what she lacked, Leah rejoiced at the child's birth, saying, "What good fortune!" (Genesis 30:11). She named him Gad, meaning "good fortune" or "a troop," possibly signifying that she gloried in her multitude of children.

Then Zilpah bore Jacob another son. Overjoyed, Leah exclaimed, "How happy I am! The women will call me happy" (Genesis 30:13). So she named the child Asher, meaning "happy."

Still Leah continued to live in a loveless marriage, and the contest with her sister would last most of her life. Her heart no doubt ached, and she fought hard to keep it centered in the Lord. An example of the daily strain in her relationships with Rachel and Jacob is seen when young Reuben gave his mother mandrake plants he had found while playing in a field. These plants, also called "love apples" and "May apples," produced an orange berrylike edible fruit. Perhaps because their roots resembled a human body, people in the ancient world highly regarded them for having medicinal and magical powers. Women used them as an aphrodisiac and to increase fertility.

Rachel would go to any length to see her barrenness cured, and when she heard about the mandrakes, she was intent on getting them. "Please give me some of your son's mandrakes," she pleaded with Leah (Genesis 30:14). Evidently it had been a long time since Leah had slept with Jacob, and since she had stopped bearing children, she had intended to keep the mandrakes for herself. So she objected: "Wasn't it enough that you took away my husband? Will you take my son's mandrakes too?" (Genesis 30:15).

But Rachel wanted those mandrakes, and she knew how to get them. "Very well," she said, "he can sleep with you tonight in return for your son's mandrakes." Enough said! Leah immediately forfeited the mandrakes.

As Jacob came in from the fields that evening, Leah went out to meet him. "You must sleep with me," she said. "I have hired you with my son's mandrakes." Leah, so overlooked and forgotten, was still willing to suffer humiliating abuse to be with her husband. Rachel never had to pay for Jacob, but Leah had to "hire" him to sleep with her that night.

Rachel's plan for overcoming her barrenness backfired though. Ironically, the wife who got the mandrakes did not get pregnant, but the one who parted with them did. Clearly, Leah had been praying for another child, and God heard her. He "listened to Leah" and she conceived and bore her fifth son. At his birth she said, "God has rewarded me for giving my maidservant to my husband" (Genesis 30:18). Considering herself compensated for having given Zilpah to Jacob and for hiring him in exchange for her mandrakes, she named the baby Issachar, meaning "my hire" or "there is recompense."

After this, Leah conceived and gave birth to her sixth son. "God has presented me with a precious gift," she exulted. "This time my husband will treat me with honor, because I have borne him six sons" (Genesis 30:20). Still, after so long, her heart reaches toward Jacob, but, accepting the reality of her situation, she has lowered her expectations. After the birth of her first child, she had announced, "Surely my husband will love me now." After the birth of the third, she said, "Now at last my husband will become attached to me." Now, no longer looking for love, she hopes only for honor.

Jacob had honored Rachel by laboring fourteen years for her, but God had honored Leah with six sons. Recognizing her brood of children as a "precious gift" from Him, she praised Him and named her little son, Zebulun, meaning "to exalt" or "to dwell," and possibly "to dwell exaltedly."

Sometime later Leah gave birth to a daughter and named her Dinah, meaning "justice" or "judgment." Then the Lord remembered Rachel. After she had been sufficiently humbled, He "listened to her and opened her womb." After so many years, she conceived and bore a son, saying, "God has taken away my disgrace" (Genesis 30:22-23).

How wonderful that we no longer detect the ugly competitive spirit that drove her earlier. Instead, like Leah, Rachel expressed gratitude to God for His blessing. Still, hoping for more children, she named her child Joseph, meaning "may God add." She said, "May the LORD add to me another son" (Genesis 30:24). Jacob felt more joy at Joseph's birth than he had over the sum of Leah's children. So again Leah felt the wounds go deep, this time not only for her but for her children.

Years later Jacob would suffer for the sibling rivalry his favoritism had wrought. Joseph's brothers, jealously selling him into slavery in

Egypt, would cause Jacob deep grief. The same Hebrew word used earlier for Jacob's hatred of Leah ("when the LORD saw that Leah was *hated*") is used for the attitude of Leah's sons toward Joseph ("they *hated* him all the more," Genesis 37:5, 8, italics added).

After his fourteen years of service ended, Laban and Jacob entered a business arrangement that over the years made Jacob wealthy at Laban's expense. The effectiveness of Jacob's labors on his own behalf had substantially reduced the inheritance of Laban's sons, and they and their father were jealous. The Lord told Jacob to return to Canaan, promising to be with him. So Jacob called Leah and Rachel out to the fields to plan their flight from the area. For the first time we see the two sisters unite. Not only had Laban constantly tried to cheat Jacob, but he had cheated them. With one voice, they said, "Do we still have any share in the inheritance of our father's estate? Does he not regard us as foreigners? Not only has he sold us, but he has used up what was paid for us. Surely all the wealth that God took away from our father belongs to us and our children. So do whatever God has told you" (Genesis 31:14-16).

A father generally set at least part of a bride price aside for his daughter. He either kept it as a type of trust fund for her in case her husband died or returned it to her as an indirect dowry. But Laban had, in effect, sold his daughters. Failing to pass his gain from Jacob's fourteen years' labor on to them, he treated them like "foreigners."

Thus, with their united support for taking the wealth Jacob had earned and leaving, they fled with everything they owned for the land of Canaan. When Laban overtook them, God warned him in a dream not to make trouble. So Jacob and Laban made a covenant of peace, and Jacob resumed the journey.

We find one final illustration of Jacob's partiality for Rachel. As they entered the Promised Land, Jacob feared his brother Esau, who had threatened his life twenty years earlier. When he heard that Esau was coming with four hundred men, he was terrified, especially for the mothers and children. Because of his special love for Rachel and Joseph, however, he put them at the rear of the caravan, the place of greatest safety. To everyone's relief Esau came in peace.

The caravan pushed on, but Rachel was pregnant and went into labor. She received what she asked for—another son—but not with the hoped for result. She had a terrible time during the delivery, and the midwife told her, "Don't be afraid, for you have another son." But she was dying, and breathing her last, she named her child Ben-Oni, meaning "son of my sorrow." Jacob changed his name to Benjamin, "son of my right hand" (Genesis 35:17-18).

What Rachel had most wanted in life spelled the end of her relationship with the man who loved her so dearly. He had loved her at first sight and had loved her until the end. To his great sorrow, he buried her along the way, some twelve miles north of Bethlehem.

As for Leah, we have no record of her last years after Rachel's death. Did Rachel's shadow still fall across her path? Or did Jacob and Leah finally come to enjoy a committed mutual love? We do not know. Leah did get to stand beside her husband as his number one wife. Perhaps they finally made some happy memories together, and his heart finally embraced her, but we do not know that.

We do know that in one very important sense, Leah did get her heart's desire. At the birth of her last son, Zebulun, she had hoped that Jacob would treat her with honor. Finally in death she got her wish. Shortly before his own death, Jacob told Joseph how he had buried Rachel near Bethlehem (Genesis 48:7). Then, calling his other sons together, he blessed them and requested that they bury him in the family's burial cave at Machpelah where he had buried Leah, their mother (Genesis 49:30-31). Thus, after her death Jacob honored Leah by placing her alongside the other two patriarchal couples—Abraham and Sarah, Isaac and Rebekah. She—not Rachel— would share the grave with her beloved Jacob.

Leah may not have been physically beautiful, but what she lacked in beauty, she made up for in faith and character. Despite her heartache, she rejoiced in her blessings. She was a loyal wife and a devoted mother, rich in faith and piety. It seems she was much better suited for her role as a mother of the tribes of Israel than was Rachel. While despised for much of her life, God brought beauty from the ashes of her incinerated dreams. He had the last word and exalted her.

Leah could not have imagined the importance of her life. The truth would unfold in passing centuries. She brought into the world six of twelve sons who would become the twelve tribes of Israel. From her, not Rachel, arose the royal Messianic and the priestly tribes in Israel. From her third son Levi sprang the tribe of Levi, from which came Aaron and the Levitical priesthood. From her fourth son Judah came the tribe of Judah, from which came Boaz, Jesse, David, and ultimately Jesus Christ. Indeed, God dramatically used Leah's life to bless all of humanity.

May the LORD make the woman who is coming into your home like Rachel and Leah, who together built up the house of Israel.

RUTH 4:11

LESSONS FOR OUR OWN HEARTS

Love is central to human existence. What sunshine is to poppies, love is to human hearts. Everyone thrives on it, and within every heart God places a hunger for it. Even beneath the hardest exterior beats the heart of one who needs love and appreciation. All over the world lovelorn hearts cry out, "Please love me!"

Yes, there is much pain in this world. The other night I was up praying at 1:00 A.M. I didn't know exactly why I was still up, but I was enjoying a sweet time with the Lord. Suddenly the phone rang. The twenty-six-year-old woman on the other end, someone dear to me, was sobbing. After a four-year relationship, the man in her life called it quits. Only two months before, they had started looking for wedding rings.

I well remembered the intense pain I suffered when my first boyfriend threw me over. I was sixteen years old. You might have called it puppy love, but I had been madly in love with the boy and was crushed. When the phone rang a few months later, and I heard his voice on the other end, I nearly had a heart attack. He merely asked for my friend's phone number, and his rejection stabbed me again like a knife. As painful as that and other experiences have been, I have never been locked in a tormenting marriage with a man who repeatedly proved he did not love me.

How many women in loveless marriages does Leah represent? Multitudes! With shattered hopes and shredded dreams, their families and their very lives are a shambles as they have been abandoned, cheated on, and abused. But even more often the other lover, the "Rachel" that controls their "Jacob" and leaves them lovelorn, is not another person at all. The rival instead might be a job, TV, alcohol, drugs, porn, sports, or hobbies—to which he has wedded himself.

A woman who suffers with a crushed and lovelorn heart may find well-meaning friends giving her laundry lists of unhelpful hints. Often a woman has already done all she can do. She has prayed, loved, listened, served, forgiven, honored, made herself more attractive, and studied the marriage-improvement books for one more key to success. At the end of her efforts, however, she realizes she cannot obtain the unobtainable. Exhausted with trying to be Superwoman, Miss Universe, and Martha Stewart rolled into one, she collapses in a heap under the weight of it all. No longer trying to pull out a victory, she simply wants some hope and healing. It will come not so much by fresh activity as by fresh perspective.

It may seem impossible to lovelorn hearts, but "in all things God works for the good of those who love him, who have been called according to his purpose" (Romans 8:28). As we look at Leah's life, how can we see this proved true? How does God work the heartbreak of the lovelorn for good?

He Reaffirms His Love

Leah could not win her husband's love. Every time she tried, she hit her head against the wall. Which way would she turn in her sorrow? Would she harden her heart or reach out for God to satisfy her need for love and approval? Such deprivation can either lead one to withdraw in bitterness or turn to God. Leah turned her heart to God.

The LORD is close to the brokenhearted and saves those who are crushed in spirit.

PSALM 34:18

He heals the brokenhearted and binds up their wounds.

PSALM 147:3

Most of us come to the Lord out of a felt need for Him. But when life gets easy, we are prone to grow complacent and lose our sense of dependency on Him. If life were always smooth, probably most would have little prayer life at all. We tend to coast along, content with a lukewarm, haphazard walk with God. But when things get stressful, we find ourselves spending much more time in earnest prayer.

Undoubtedly, Leah spent much time in prayer. Deprived of human love, desperately lonely, and needing hope, she learned to find solace in God. Her trials drove her to Him so He could reaffirm His love and commitment to her. When she needed a friend to talk to or a shoulder to cry on, her Lord became that Friend. He wants to prove Himself to you, too. When human love is beyond our reach, what a Friend we have in Jesus!

The Rachels of this world are loved by the Jacobs, and God loves them. But He shows special kindness to the Leahs, giving them tokens of His love and affection, letting them know that they are significant and even cherished. Yes, the Gospel is good news to the poor—to the disenfranchised, the downtrodden, those on the underside of life. "The Lord saw that Leah was unloved" and "He opened her womb," blessing her with six children. Each time she cradled a newborn baby, He reaffirmed anew His love for her.

I love the book of 1 John. In my Bible I count the word *love* or a form of it nearly fifty times in this short epistle, and I have circled them all. Once I read the entire book and wrote a fresh little meditation each day for a month. At the month's end my heart nearly burst with love for God. I would have cherished spending time with

John and listening to his stories of how God's love had come to so captivate his heart. This "apostle of love" recognized the profundity of God's love—that "God is love" (1 John 4:8, 16). He knew that all love begins and ends in God. In love God created us, sent Christ to rescue us, gave His Spirit to guide us, and will take us into His home to be with Him forever. Yes, forever! His love is unchanging, unceasing, unfailing, and unconditional. His very heart beats with love—not mushy sentimentality but deep, committed, self-sacrificing love. We may harbor doubt and unbelief in our heart and have a hard time knowing the comfort of His love, but His love still holds firm.

If only we could grasp the intensity of God's love for us! "How great is the love the Father has lavished on us," says John (1 John 3:1). He was an old man when he wrote this book. What carried him through the years? He tells us: "And so we know and *rely* on the love God has for us" (1 John 4:16). When the world is against us, when our husbands, boyfriends, children, parents, Christian brothers or sisters let us down, we can *rely* on God's love. Lovelorn hearts, to God you are precious, purchased at great price, beloved. Rely on His love.

A few days after I prayed with the young woman who called me at 1:00 A.M., she was still deeply distressed. But she told me, "The Lord has shown me that I need to put my hope in Him. I can't put my hope in winning my boyfriend back. Nor can I put my hope in finding someone else. It has to be Him; the Lord must be my hope." What a valuable lesson she is learning!

Hope . . . love . . . faith. Isn't it all words, lofty platitudes, and pretty truisms until we are forced to flee to Christ and discover for ourselves "how wide and long and high and deep is the love of Christ, and to know this love that surpasses knowledge" (Ephesians 3:18-19).

The Lord blessed Leah, and He wants to bless you, too. His Word charges, "keep yourselves in the love of God" (Jude 21 NRSV). Let your heartache and pain drive you back to Him so He can reaffirm His love to you. He calls, "Let Me comfort you. Let Me draw you close and hold you in My arms of love. Let Me be your heart's desire. I will be your all in all—your Father, your confidant, your closest friend, the one who loves you beyond words." He appeals, "Will you open your heart to Me? Will you allow My love to restore you? Will you enter a love relationship with Me that will satisfy your deepest soul?"

God loves us so much that He sent His Son to die for us. Christ has paid the price of what is unlovable in us, and now our names have been changed from "unloved" to "beloved." We cannot earn His love; He already loves us. We do not deserve His love; it is a gift of grace. Will you rest in His love, enjoy His love, immerse yourself in His love, let His perfect love cast out your fear?

"For your Maker is your husband—the LORD *Almighty is his name—the Holy One of Israel is your Redeemer; he is called the God of all the earth. The* LORD *will call you back as if you were a wife deserted and distressed in spirit—a wife who married young, only to be rejected," says your God.*

ISAIAH 54:5-6

How awesome is the Lover of our souls. Human love may break down and fail us, but His does not. He loves us unconditionally, unabatedly, unalterably. Having Him in our hearts is the greatest treasure, the highest privilege.

He Refines Our Character

When it seems that God has not answered our prayers, we get disappointed and even angry. But perhaps He did answer, and the answer was not what we were looking for. God in His sovereign love is able to work His purposes in us through our pain. Our hearts shout, "No, Lord! This is not how my life is supposed to be, so fix it!" But He often allows us to suffer so He can refine us, making us more like Christ. That is not to say that God wants us to be treated like Leah.

He does not want us stripped of all our feelings of value. Leah's story is no defense for letting someone despoil us of our dignity.

This third I will bring into the fire; I will refine them like silver and test them like gold. They will call on my name and I will answer them; I will say, 'They are my people,' and they will say, 'The LORD is our God.'"

ZECHARIAH 13:9

Nor does Leah's story convince us to stay in abusive relationships. But God has a way of honoring those who choose to honor Him by hanging in with a difficult relationship for Christ's sake. Their painful trials refine their hearts and enrich their characters, enabling them to become more Christlike and blessed with His nature and presence. Very often the conflicts even get resolved, providing a grand testimony to God's glory.

Living in a culture that craves instant gratification of every desire, we find it especially disconcerting to endure the refining *process*. Don't you just hate that word? Who wants to go through a process when we could just be done with it and move on? But often our adversities don't just blow over. They can be chronic and persistent, wearing us down, and the pain can go on and on.

A wounded spirit is a dangerous thing. When wounded, we want to kick back, returning evil for evil. We may hate that "other woman" or the heartless man who has caused us grief. But hatred is poison in the heart, and if we want a healthy heart, we must surrender our hurt, anger, and vindication to the Lord. We must even learn to forgive "seventy times seven" times. Someone has said that when you harbor bitterness, happiness will dock elsewhere.

As is often true, afflictions enriched Leah, and sorrows refined her. The refiner's fire she endured made her a pillar of strength and virtue. And God lets that same fire work in us, too. Amazingly, even Christ, while perfect in character, was somehow enriched through suffering (see Hebrews 5:8).

He Redirects Our Focus

A woman with a lovelorn heart has likely lost self-confidence and self-respect. Wanting to fix herself, she can search for renewed self-esteem in many ways. Leah might have tried to regain her self-esteem by working on her appearance. But she never could have improved herself enough to compete with Rachel.

Living in a culture today that puts such a premium on external beauty, this is exactly where many of us focus our effort. Of course, accentuating our external beauty in modest ways is not wrong, but we should not get wrapped up in external appearances. "Save yourselves from this corrupt generation" (Acts 2:40) that values a charming face and bubbly personality more than inner virtue. God's Word asserts, "Your beauty should not come from outward adornment.... Instead, it should be that of your inner self, the unfading beauty of a gentle and quiet spirit, which is of great worth in God's sight. For this is the way the holy women of the past who put their hope in God used to make themselves beautiful" (1 Peter 3:3-5).

Outward beauty, while praised for a while, can fade quickly. Developing the inner character of the heart, however, brings eternal and unfading glory. Do you want to make yourself more "attractive"? The first person in our lives we should want to attract is the Holy Spirit.

God wants to give you peace in who He made you to be. Leah would likely have spent her entire life in hopeless defeat had she kept looking to Jacob to fulfill her. She could have wasted her life cursing her limitations and blaming God for them. But she focused her efforts in another direction. She stopped bewailing and started availing. She went to God and took what He gave her. Not arguing, she accepted her weaknesses and embraced her strengths. She accepted herself because she knew God accepted her.

Lovelorn hearts can become self-justifying—"I did nothing to deserve this," or self-reproaching—"I did everything to deserve this." Both reactions have a wrong focus—us. Our self-esteem comes not from who we are and what we have or have not done but from *whose* we are and what He has done. He gives us true identity: "And God raised us up with Christ and seated us with him in the heavenly realms in Christ Jesus" (Ephesians 2:6). Focus on Him.

If you are looking for some hero to pop up from the pages of a romance novel to give your life meaning, good luck! It's fiction! The thrill, the passion, the drama that you so desire must be surrendered to—and found in—God. In naming her fourth son Judah ("praise"), Leah shifted her focus from what she lacked to what she possessed. With Jacob still crazy with love for Rachel, Leah saw no hope for change in that department. But *Leah* changed. Changing her focus to what she had as God's beloved daughter, she exchanged her lovelorn heart for a rejoicing heart.

Often we cannot change our circumstances or the hearts of others, but we can let God change and heal us. Letting God determine her significance, Leah found wholeness in the Lord. We might wonder why a woman with such a loving heart as hers could not find love herself. She did! She received the love of God and of her children. She gratefully raised her children and prepared them for the destinies God had for them. In the end her faithful life paid off for her. Jacob honored her by wanting to be buried beside her, and God worked miracles for the world through her.

Do you feel unloved, rejected, passed over, shelved, or forgotten? With Leah's first three sons, she kept striving for acceptance. But she suddenly awakened to the wealth God had given her and said, "This time I will praise the Lord." And this is where we find strength and healing, too—not in staying bound to our idealistic fantasies of what might have been, but in seeing what God has given us and being grateful. Leah should encourage us that one can carry tremendous burdens but, in surrendering them to the Lord, still be used as a channel of tremendous blessing.

It is so easy to stare from the outside at those who "have it all" and think we have nothing. *They must be so happy,* we think. But we cannot see the whole picture. Often things are not as they appear. Rachel, with her flawless beauty and her husband's undying devotion, had it all. Or did she? She, too, lived with heartache and disappointment and finally died in childbirth. Meanwhile Leah lived to raise her large and thriving brood.

The more we count our blessings, the more we see our sorrows melt, our hearts rise, and God's grace sufficient. What is your need, your disappointment, your heartbreak? Will you choose to look through your blinding tears and trust God's love, to see Him as ever-faithful and true, to surrender your sorrow and pain and let Him give you a reason to sing? Will you say, "This time I will praise the Lord?"

Heart Check

1. How do you identify with Leah's needs? How does her life encourage you?

2. How has the Lord proven His love to you?

3. Do you see ways that the Lord has worked deeper character in your life through your pain?

4. What pain and heartache can you give to the Lord now?

5. Compose a prayer to God in response to this chapter's lessons.

7

Elizabeth

THE DISAPPOINTED HEART

LUKE 1:5-80

"SURELY, YOU JEST, Zechariah! Did the lot really fall on you?" Elizabeth was incredulous. Her husband had never before been called to burn the incense at the temple. Now he stood before her trembling with joy, his eyes sparkling in a way she had not seen for as long as she could remember. Having suffered so much pain and disappointment in his life, he had needed a sign that God was with him. "Thank you, Lord!"

Yet, as wonderful as this was for Zechariah, Elizabeth's heart was suddenly stricken with an old wound. This special blessing expressed none of the Lord's favor toward her. Through a lifetime of dedicated service to the Lord, she had tried to bury the sad disappointment that would not die. Now seeing her dear husband's dancing eyes, she could not escape thinking of how those wonderful eyes had for so long reflected sorrow because of her.

Five words concerning this couple reveal a world of heartbreak: "But they had no children" (Luke 1:7). Constantly, year after year they had prayed and yearned for a child, but Elizabeth simply could not conceive. The hope that once blazed in her heart had grown dimmer and dimmer until it finally flickered out. Now they were old folks, seemingly much too old for children. Pushing back tears and sighing deeply, she thought, *Yes, the Lord has done a good thing for Zechariah today.*

We call Elizabeth's heart The Disappointed Heart. She had long believed the sacred promises such as: "Delight yourself in the LORD and he will give you the desires of your heart" (Psalm 37:4). But especially she had looked to God's covenant promise: "He will love you and bless you and increase your numbers. He will bless the fruit of your womb. . . . You will be blessed more than any other people; none of your men or women will be childless" (Deuteronomy 7:13-14). Yet her heart's cry never got answered; it seemed that God had forgotten His promise when it came to her.

Elizabeth and Zechariah had served God faithfully. Unlike the religious leaders whom Jesus would later label hypocrites, this couple was not simply outwardly religious, going through the motions of obeying God's laws. On the contrary, they genuinely loved God, following not just the letter of the Law but following Him from their hearts. Elizabeth was in her own right a woman of admirable faith and piety. She had gladly obeyed all the Lord's commands, neglecting nothing He required of her.

But, oh, the heartache! In light of her devotion, her barrenness was even more painful. Her malady meant multiplied sorrow for several reasons. First, her culture considered childlessness a disaster and even a curse from God. With the Law sometimes considering it a judgment for sin, many people naturally assumed the worst. Jewish teachers even urged men to divorce a barren wife so they could marry someone else who could bear children. Zechariah had kept Elizabeth, but she felt useless to him. Forced to bear this huge stigma, she no doubt experienced derision from those who did not recognize her piety. And not only was her barrenness a social disaster, but it often forecast economic ruin. With no heirs to care for the couple in old age, they would have no financial security.

Added to these social and economic calamities, Elizabeth bore the pain of being a "daughter of Aaron." (Aaron was Israel's first High Priest.) While priests could marry any pure Israelite, marrying a woman with Elizabeth's pedigree was considered a special blessing. She came from a long line of Aaronic priests. Her very name derived from Elisheba, Aaron's wife. When Zechariah, also an Aaronic priest, married her, he thought he could do no better. Here was a woman not only of the right lineage but one who also sincerely loved the Lord and planned to devote her life to preserving Aaron's holy ordinances and raising sons to follow in their father's footsteps.

How disappointingly different life had turned out. The stricken couple would have no little ones to cherish—no grandchildren, no one to carry on their priestly line. Elizabeth felt she had let down not only her husband but her entire family as well. How often throughout the years had she cried, "Why me, Lord? What have I done wrong? Why have You withheld Your blessing from me?"

Although God generally promised that there should be no barrenness among His faithful people, He still allowed exceptions to the rule. Sometimes He had a special purpose. An extraordinary conception and birth to a previously barren woman glorified Him and brought great blessing to His people. So had it been with Sarah, Rachel, Rebekah, and Hannah. While Elizabeth could not know it, this was true also of her. Therefore, countering any misconceptions arising from conventional wisdom, Luke's Gospel attests that Elizabeth's childlessness was not God's judgment on her or Zechariah: "Both of them were upright in the sight of God, observing all the Lord's commandments and regulations blamelessly" (Luke 1:6).

They searched for some divine explanation for their affliction, but God gave them no answers. Forced to trust Him, they continued to love Him with all their strength and never succumbed to grumbling and rebellion. In fact, they seemed largely to have worked through their pain, resigning themselves to God's sovereign and unsearchable ways.

As a Jewish priest, Zechariah managed temple affairs. At this time there were as many as twenty thousand priests in Israel to serve in only one temple. They served on a rotating basis. From the time of David, priests were organized into twenty-four divisions (1 Chronicles 24:7-19), each division on duty twice a year for a week. The time came for Zechariah's division (that of Abijah) to report for duty.

While priests were to be supported by tithes, the unfair policies of the priestly aristocracy, not to mention high taxes, made it hard on poorer priests. Thus many spent their two-week term of service in Jerusalem and lived elsewhere, taking on secular vocations. Tradition says that Zechariah and Elizabeth resided in the village of Ain Karem in Judah's hill country, about four and a half miles west of Jerusalem. With no son to support him in his old age, he likely still worked a small farm or did other labor there in the hills.

When Zechariah went to the temple for his week of service, Elizabeth probably accompanied him. Being a devout Jew, she would not want to miss this special opportunity to worship the Lord in the temple Court of Women.

At least eight hundred priests were in each division, far too many to perform the given temple functions. Thus they chose specific tasks by lot, including burning the incense—something done twice daily in the Holy Place. A supreme honor, no priest could perform this duty more than once in his lifetime, and some never got the opportunity.

We can imagine Zechariah excitedly entering the Court of Women one day during his week of service. Finding Elizabeth, he told her that the lot had fallen to him to offer the incense. Did he realize that this was no chance toss of the dice, that God had a specific reason for choosing him at that time? Indeed, as wonderful as this event was for him personally, a far greater event was unfolding simultaneously in heaven. In fact, all heaven stood on tiptoe. This day God would finally unveil His cosmic plan for the ages. The final countdown had begun for His Son to descend from heaven and physically come to earth. The high-ranking angel Gabriel had already descended and waited in the Holy Place to make the first glad announcement.

A large crowd of worshipers watched as Zechariah reverently approached the entrance of the Holy Place. He had dreamed of this, his life's most important moment, from his youth. Normally the rite took a short time to complete. The priest would cast incense on the altar, pray, prostrate himself, and then exit. The people outside in the court would see the rising smoke—symbolizing their prayers ascending to God's throne—and they would pray. The priest would reappear to bless them: "The LORD bless you and keep you" (Numbers 6:24), he would say. Then the people would depart.

As Zechariah entered the Holy Place, he felt a heaviness in the air. God was there! Awestruck, he carefully burned the incense and began his priestly prayer, interceding for Israel and asking God to send Israel's Messiah. Did he tack on a personal petition of his own? "Lord, my standing here is a miracle. Perhaps, then, if You don't mind, how about another one? How about a son?" Whether he prayed this that day or not, we don't know, and it doesn't matter. God remembered the innumerable prayers of many years and was about to answer them with a mind-boggling yes.

Suddenly Zechariah had the fright of his life! A brilliant angel appeared, standing in the center of the room beside the altar of incense. No vague vision or dream—this creature was real! Zechariah was "gripped with fear" (Luke 1:12). The angel said, "Do not be afraid, Zechariah; your prayer has been heard. Your wife Elizabeth will bear you a son, and you are to give him the name John" (Luke 1:13).

So often when it appears that God has no interest whatever in an issue, that He has completely killed it, and we have finally given up all hope, He surprises us. How did Zechariah respond to this wonderful surprise? It was too extraordinary for him to believe. Would God really remove their shame . . . now? How could it be? He thought of a small, laughing son tearing through their infinitely quiet house. *Impossible,* he thought.

The angel, not omniscient, could not read Zechariah's doubting mind. He was eager to give the stupefied old man surpassingly glorious news, the news that his personal blessing would become a blessing to Israel and to the entire world. The Messiah was about to come, but first His prophet must prepare His way. "He will be a joy and delight to you," the angel continued, "and many will rejoice because of his birth, for he will be great in the sight of the Lord. He is never to take wine or other fermented drink, and he will be filled with the Holy Spirit even from birth. Many of the people of Israel will he bring back to the Lord their God. And he will go on before the Lord, in the spirit and power of Elijah, to turn the hearts of the fathers to their children and the disobedient to the wisdom of the righteous— to make ready a people prepared for the Lord" (Luke 1:14-17).

Even coming from the mouth of a splendid angel, this was too much for Zechariah. It was just too good to be true. So what did he do? Daring to question the angel's word, he asked for a sign. "How can I be sure of this?" he asked. "I am an old man and my wife is well along in years" (Luke 1:18).

Oops. Really big mistake! The angel—not just any angel, mind you—was not at all pleased. "I am Gabriel!" he thundered. "I stand in the presence of God, and I have been sent to speak to you and to tell you this good news. And now you will be silent and not able to speak until the day this happens, because you did not believe my words, which will come true at their proper time" (Luke 1:19-20).

Zechariah got his sign all right. Instantly he was struck speechless for his unbelief—not that he was dying to speak after that gaffe. Gabriel departed, and Zechariah tried to compose himself enough to go out and meet the waiting crowd in the court. Meanwhile since priests normally emerged right after lighting the incense, the crowd became troubled. Had Zechariah been disrespectful so that God had to strike him dead? Did something else go wrong? If his offering had failed, the standing of their prayers was also in jeopardy. So everyone just stood there, not knowing what to do.

Finally Zechariah shakily stumbled out, not looking at all like the honorable priest who had marched reverently into the Holy Place. In fact, he was beside himself. Looking pale and disoriented, he could not say a syllable but kept waving his arms and making signs to the people. Naturally they concluded that something highly unusual had occurred, perhaps a vision.

What a shock for Elizabeth when she finally got her husband alone, and he scrawled these words, "Y-o-u w-i-l-l b-e-a-r a s-o-n." Sure enough, she conceived, and great was the old couple's rejoicing. Unlike most other boys in Israel, their long-awaited son would have a unique calling. As herald of Messiah's kingdom, he would usher in His appearing. Exulting in the Lord, Elizabeth cried, "The Lord has done this for me. In these days he has shown his favor and taken away my disgrace among the people" (Luke 1:25).

Rather than publicizing her good news, she hid herself for five months, probably devoting herself to praising God and seeking to understand His will for her promised son's life. She surely must have wondered, "If my son's destiny is to prepare the way for the Messiah, where is the Messiah? How will He be revealed?" She had no doubt fervently prayed for His appearing, and now in this solitary time of seeking God, she received further revelation.

In Elizabeth's sixth month of pregnancy, the Lord sent the angel Gabriel on another grand errand. This time he visited Elizabeth's relative, Mary, a young virgin in the town of Nazareth. He announced to her that she would conceive and bear a son whom she must call Jesus. Her son, the Messiah, would be called the Son of God. When she asked how this could be since she was a virgin, he replied, "The Holy Spirit will come upon you, and the power of the Most High will overshadow you. So the holy one to be born will be called the Son of God." Then to verify the truth of his claims, he offered her a sign, saying, "Even Elizabeth your relative is going to have a child in her old age, and she who was said to be barren is in her sixth month. For nothing is impossible with God" (Luke 1:35-37).

Indeed, Gabriel pointed to an extraordinary sign. While Mary had not asked for one, having believed his word, he wanted to support her faith. If old Elizabeth, whom all knew to be barren, could be six months pregnant, God could even make Mary, a virgin, pregnant by a creative miracle. As Gabriel had intended, she quickly got her things together and hurried off to the hill country to visit Elizabeth.

As it was a three- to five-day journey, Mary probably hooked up with a caravan heading that way. When she arrived at Elizabeth's home, what a joyous faith-boosting scene awaited her! Prepared by the Holy Spirit beforehand, Elizabeth was ready for Mary. As the young woman walked into her door and gave a friendly greeting,

Elizabeth's unborn child immediately responded. Already under the Holy Spirit's influence, he leaped inside her. This did not alarm Elizabeth, for she recognized her child's movement for what it was—a joyous response to the holy Christ Child that Mary carried within her.

Elizabeth's child, appointed to herald the coming Messiah, already had begun his ministry, leaping for joy as if welcoming Him. This was no natural prenatal occurrence but a supernatural one. The Holy Spirit moved the one whom He would fill from birth to rejoice over the Holy One whom He had conceived. Years later Christ's presence would again stir him. Pointing Christ out to a crowd of seekers, he would shout, "Look, the Lamb of God!" (John 1:35).

Elizabeth, filled with prophetic inspiration from the Holy Spirit, immediately exploded with praise: "Blessed are you among women, and blessed is the child you will bear! But why am I so favored, that the mother of my Lord should come to me? As soon as the sound of your greeting reached my ears, the baby in my womb leaped for joy. Blessed is she who has believed that what the Lord has said to her will be accomplished!" (Luke 1:42-45).

The formerly barren woman, once so full of disappointment, now abounded with confident hope and expectation. Not only the mother of Christ's forerunner, she had the distinction of being the first person to rejoice in Mary's blessed calling and to confess faith in Christ. Her astonishing confirmation of Gabriel's promise must have greatly strengthened Mary's faith in her own special calling. From personal experience her elder relative *knew* God could do *anything*.

We should recognize here the absence of all rivalry in Elizabeth's heart. While she was pregnant with her own long-awaited child, she still might have envied Mary, whose son would be even greater than her own. Yet we see no boasting or self-exaltation or jealousy on her part. As her child had already acknowledged the superior greatness of Jesus, now she immediately recognized the younger woman as her superior, calling her "the mother of my Lord" and "blessed among women." She was overjoyed that this honored young woman would pay her a visit.

Elizabeth's Spirit-anointed prophetic response prompted Mary to bring forth her own prophetic song of praise: "My soul glorifies the Lord and my spirit rejoices in God my Savior, for he has been mindful of the humble state of his servant. From now on all generations will call me blessed, for the Mighty One has done great things for me—holy is his name" (Luke 1:46-49).

Clearly, this was no ordinary exchange between two ordinary women, one young and one old. No, this was a conversation between two uniquely blessed women—one, the mother of the one chosen to prepare the way of the Lord and the other, the mother of the Lord Himself!

For three happy months, Elizabeth enjoyed the privilege of hosting Mary. Although they were at least half a century apart in age, they had a common bond, both being pregnant by a divine miracle and awaiting the births of children with central roles in God's eternal plan to redeem humanity. Mary would have much to face when she got home. She needed encouragement and guidance, someone to pray with her who understood her condition. We can imagine during this period that Elizabeth had much godly advice for the young virgin. In the shelter of her home, the Holy Spirit bound these two hearts together in awe and worship, in hope and purpose. Talking about the great things God had done for each of them, praising His name together, what a rich sisterhood they shared! Mary must have been a great help to Elizabeth, this being her first pregnancy experience and at an advanced age at that. She stayed until the birth of Elizabeth's child and then went home.

At her child's birth, Elizabeth's heart swelled with joy. All her friends and neighbors heard how the Lord had shown her great mercy and came rejoicing and praising God with her. The birth of any baby boy was a big event, and Jewish tradition suggests that guests assembled every night at a family's home from the boy's birth to his circumcision.

On the eighth day, at least ten people had to be present for a cir-

cumcision ceremony. This would be a joyful occasion as they celebrated the child's becoming part of God's covenant people. In that
this birth was extraordinary and of widespread interest, a great number of folk gathered for the circumcision and the naming of the child.
Undoubtedly, everyone noticed the new mother's radiance coming
from a heart filled with gratitude to God. Meanwhile poor Zechariah
still couldn't speak. Even so, he beamed, too, as he scooped up his
new son in his arms.

Family lines and family names were important to the Jews. They
often named children for their fathers or grandfathers. Here everyone was certain the only son of old Zechariah would carry his name.
As they excitedly began to call the baby by this name, Elizabeth's voice
rose above their buzz. "No!" she announced. "He is to be called
John" (Luke 1:60).

This was a stunning development, too much for the crowd to
fathom. They complained that not only was this not the father's name
but that no one in the entire family line had this name. When
Elizabeth refused to cave in to their pressure, they turned to
Zechariah, for he had the ultimate say. But only one person had the
rights in this special case. God had already named the child John,
meaning "Jehovah is a gracious giver." And what name could be more
fitting?

Zechariah handed his son back to his wife and asked for a writing tablet. To everyone's amazement, he scribbled, "His name is
John" (Luke 1:63). As if this was not shocking enough, instantly, after
more than nine months of silence, Zechariah's tongue was loosed.
Filled with the Holy Spirit, he praised God in a prophetic song, often
called *the Benedictus*:

> Praise be to the Lord, the God of Israel, because he has come
> and has redeemed his people. He has raised up a horn of salva-
> tion for us in the house of his servant David (as he said through
> his holy prophets of long ago). . . . And you, my child, will be
> called a prophet of the Most High; for you will go on before the
> Lord to prepare the way for him, to give his people the knowl-

edge of salvation through the forgiveness of their sins, because of the tender mercy of our God, by which the rising sun will come to us from heaven to shine on those living in darkness and in the shadow of death, to guide our feet into the path of peace. (Luke 1:68-70, 76-79)

All the Old Testament prophecies were coming true. The Messiah would come in Elizabeth's lifetime, and her son, the prophet of the Highest, would pave the way! What a joyful moment for Elizabeth. God had healed her disappointed heart. He had removed her barrenness and taken away her reproach. As the angel had foretold, many rejoiced with her at her son's birth. With her jubilant husband standing beside her as she cradled her son in her arms, she was fulfilled in every respect.

Meanwhile news spread like wildfire: "The neighbors were all filled with awe, and throughout the hill country of Judea people were talking about all these things. Everyone who heard this wondered about it, asking, 'What then is this child going to be?' For the Lord's hand was with him" (Luke 1:65-66).

John the Baptist would play a mighty role in history, and Elizabeth would play a substantial role in shaping him. The preparation for his future ministry called for dedicated and prayerful instruction on her part. She left an indelible imprint upon his life. Surely her lovely, humble spirit influenced him. For, like his mother, who had rejoiced to give deference to Mary, John would gladly acknowledge Christ, saying, "He must become greater; I must become less" (John 3:30). Jesus Christ would acknowledge John, too, saying, "I tell you the truth: Among those born of women there has not risen anyone greater than John the Baptist" (Matthew 11:11).

With this godly foundation, John moved to the desert where God would directly nurture and prepare him for his mighty ministry. Was Elizabeth still alive to see her son march off into the desert to find his destiny? We do not know. What we do know is that this godly woman, who lived an exemplary life, played a significant role in history. Her name endures as a favorite for queens and women in all walks of life in the world today.

He settles the barren woman in her home as a happy mother of children. Praise the LORD.

PSALM 113:9

LESSONS FOR OUR OWN HEARTS

We all have disappointments in life. My first big one as a new Christian came when I entered a drawing for a new car. I needed one badly and was sure this was God's provision for me. Yet, shock of shocks, my name was not announced as the big winner. In fact, I didn't even get the cheap camera! I wondered where I had failed. Did I have sin in my life or not enough faith? I soon learned that God simply will not allow Himself to be a slot machine whose arm I can pull down whenever I want life to work my way. What a sad discovery it was for me to find that my solutions were not necessarily His solutions. Going on to learn a lifetime of lessons about God's wisdom and sovereignty, I experienced many joys in life but also bitter disappointments.

Think about Elizabeth's godly life. In God's eyes she served Him blamelessly. Yet she still suffered terrible disappointment. God ordained for her to walk a difficult road, living with the heartbreak of barrenness. Why? Because He was planning a greater blessing for her. But seeing her childlessness continue and her age advance, how could she look for anything hopeful on the horizon? How could she detect any good purpose for her suffering? How could she know that God wanted a miraculous birth for her son, the Lord's great prophet? Surely she gave up all hope of ever having a child of her own to love.

This should encourage us to know that one can be in the path of complete obedience and on the way to true and lasting joy and yet meet with many disillusioning trials and disappointments along the way. Painful afflictions do not mean that God has forgotten us!

Mary McLeod Bethune experienced bitter disappointment. The daughter of former slaves, she picked cotton until attending a mission school to which she daily walked five miles. At age twelve her heart responded to a call for missionaries to Africa. She worked hard and won scholarships to seminary and later to Moody Bible Institute, which was then a school of missions. She was Moody's first African-American student.

After graduating, however, the door slammed in her face. There were no missions openings for African-Americans. Her rejection came as a shattering disappointment. But giving her broken dreams to God, she taught at a mission school, served in jail and rescue mission ministries, and counseled hurting slum-dwellers. Later she opened a school for poor black children financed by sales of her homemade pies. It would become a prominent college and she a highly respected educator.

A leading black woman of the twentieth century, Mary was a woman of many firsts. Four American presidents appointed her to various government posts related to child welfare, housing, employment, education, and, surprisingly, national defense. She even directed a federal agency, the Division of Negro Affairs, and received an honorary doctorate from a white southern college. Serving in many national organizations and receiving numerous commendations here and abroad, she left a remarkable legacy of interracial cooperation.

Today Mary's portrait hangs in her native South Carolina's capitol; her statue graces Lincoln Park in Washington, D.C.; her Bethune-Cookman College boasts over 1,700 students. Of her earlier disappointment, she said, "Africans in America needed Christ and school just as much as Negroes in Africa. . . . My life work lay not in Africa but in my own country." In retrospect we see clearly God's sovereign hand in keeping Mary McLeod Bethune here in America.

Kings will be your foster fathers, and their queens your nursing mothers. They will bow down before you with their faces to the ground; they will lick the dust at your feet. Then you will know that I am the LORD; those who hope in me will not be disappointed.

ISAIAH 49:23

Almost no one could have suffered a more crushing disappointment than a woman I met recently, Renee Bondi. She is beautiful and a fabulous singer—oh, to have gifts like hers! She sang lovely words of faith: "Lord, I know my life is in Your hands; my heart is in Your keeping. . . . I'm never without hope, not when my future is with You. . . . I trust You, Lord. . . ."

These are not flimsy little phrases to Renee, for she is a quadriplegic. One night two months before her wedding date, in a freak accident she fell out of bed and broke her neck. After five years of adjusting to her condition, her sister had an accident that left her a paraplegic. Talk about disappointment with God! Says Renee, "For the first time in my life, I was mad, screaming, yelling, cussing like a sailor, and yes—at God." She stewed in her disappointment until she surrendered it to the Lord. Still, amid swirling emotions she had to tell Him, " I surrender . . . I surrender . . . I surrender."

Then one day she woke up with peace in her heart. "You did it, Lord!" she exulted. "This is the peace that passes understanding!" Why Renee has had to endure this suffering, only God knows. But by His grace she is a victor—more than a conqueror—in whom I easily saw Christ's radiance. If you go to her website (www.reneebondi.com), you will see that her music CD entitled "Surrender to Your Love" is said to reflect "the triumph and peace Renee has experienced from surrendering her life to Jesus Christ." Triumph indeed! Her schedule is full of speaking and singing engagements. She has a devoted husband and gave birth to a healthy baby boy. Her sister also ministers with her at times and works as a dental hygienist from her wheelchair.

Renee agrees that we can voice our disappointment and distress to God, but we must not let our hearts turn from following Him. We might feel like it, but we have to admit with Peter, "Lord, to whom shall we go? You have the words of eternal life. We believe and know that you are the Holy One of God" (John 6:68-69).

Do you suffer from a disappointed heart? A tragedy or an injustice you experienced may have caused your disappointment. Perhaps someone was disloyal, betrayed you, gave you a "Judas kiss." Perhaps your own wrong choices or sin damaged you; or maybe you have tried to serve God, and all your efforts seem fruitless. Perhaps, as with Elizabeth, despite doing everything right, your dearest prayers have gone unanswered—year after year after year! You are disappointed with yourself, disappointed with the world, and disappointed with God. You cry, "Why, God, did you fail to prevent my pain?"

If left unresolved, your disappointment, whether big or little, can fester and evolve till it becomes a gargantuan heart problem. How then can you find hope and healing for your heart?

Trust God's Love for You

The first step is to resolve in your heart to trust God and His infinite love. If you are a believer and have opened your heart to Christ, then you need to see yourself as the apple of His eye. You are a precious daughter of the King. He knows the details of your life, hears your cries of disappointment, and understands your pain. He cares! His heart hurts with you and even sheds tears with you. Why has He allowed your pain? He alone knows. You can trust, however, that He loves you, has your best interests at heart, works all things for good, and that you will not be ultimately disappointed.

They cried to you and were saved; in you they trusted and were not disappointed.

PSALM 22:5

Commit Your Life to the Lord

When you choose to trust Him, you learn the art of committal. When we think of commitment to Christ, we often see it as our sacred pledge of faithfulness to Him. He can count on us to be there for Him. But what does the Scripture mean when it says, "Into your hands I *commit* my spirit" (Psalm 31:5), "*Commit* your way to the LORD" (Psalm 37:5), or "So then, those who suffer according to God's will should *commit* themselves to their faithful Creator" (1 Peter 4:19)? Now we see another kind of commitment, one that does not mean Christ trusts us but that we trust Christ. To *commit* in this sense means we entrust our-selves to Him; we pass on to Him everything in our life, including our disappointments. Can you commit yourself to Christ? Will you let Him handle your disappointment? Will you let Him carry the burden that has weighed you down? Will you let it go?

Elizabeth could do nothing to fix her situation. She could not visit a fertility clinic or draw upon a sperm bank. She couldn't turn back the ravages of time; she could do nothing at all. She had to decide that the heartbreak and disappointment she suffered over her barrenness would likely never be resolved through having children. She needed to give "her" solution to God, leaving it in His hands.

After many years of disappointment, she surrendered her hopes and expectations to God and perhaps found joy in another form of motherhood. Perhaps she became a mother in Israel to the poor, the hurting, or others who suffered life's disappointments. What if she had spent her life instead in whining self-pity and regret over what might have been? What if she had kept trying to shape her life to fit the fantasy of how it ought to be? Then God would not have judged her blameless in His sight. No, she committed her disappointment to God and got on with her life.

Let Go of Your Own Expectations

After the Civil War had ended, Robert E. Lee had wise advice for a disappointed woman whom he visited. As she pointed out a once-lovely oak tree in her yard that invading armies had left seriously marred, she asked bitterly, "What should I do?" He quickly replied, "Cut it down and forget it." That is what we should do with our dis-appointment. As painful as it may be, if we hold on to it and nurse it, we will never experience victory. We must also let go of the source of the disappointment, the dream we so earnestly clung to. We need to cut these things down and forget them.

But you might ask, "How can I let go of my expectations, my dreams?" It seems that letting them go will spell death to your very soul. Perhaps it *will* mean a death of sorts, but God does not expect you to do it yourself. He wants to help you. He wants you to offer your disappointment to Him so that His divine scalpel can remove its bitterness from your heart. Then, rather than staying rooted in your painful past, you can experience new life. You can find the freedom to go forward and to finally begin to dream again.

Will you, by a decisive act of your will, let go of your struggle to make your dream come true? Will you surrender your pain, your expectations, your disappointment to the Lord? Will you let Him change you? Will you stop demanding Him to fit into your plans, to solve your disappointment your way? God may have another way to satisfy your heart. Will you let Him satisfy you with His plan, give you contentment in His purpose? Will you adjust your dreams to reality and receive new dreams for your future? Will you pray, worship, and trust Him to deal with your disappointment, no matter how distressing it might be? This is the path of healing for a disappointed heart, the way to find satisfaction.

Sometimes Elizabeth could not help but wonder if she did not measure up spiritually, if she had somehow displeased God. Sometimes she experienced humiliation, defeat, and even feelings of hopelessness. Yet, committing her life to God, she spent time worshiping Him, learning His truths, better understanding His character. Finding satisfaction in His friendship, she gained an increasing ability to trust Him, to glorify Him, to be blameless in His sight, and to receive a miracle.

You, too, can have a satisfied life, even without the realization of your dream. You can find your satisfaction in Him as, day after day clinging to Him and to His promises, you gain light and strength to carry on with your life. Once you are free, God just may surprise you. As with Elizabeth, He just may come back around and give you the very thing for which you originally asked.

And hope does not disappoint us, because God has poured out his love into our hearts by the Holy Spirit, whom he has given us.

ROMANS 5:5

The name of Elizabeth's son John means "God is a gracious giver." In hindsight how easily Elizabeth might have shouted, "Amen!" During the long years when God withheld her heart's desire though, it would have been much more difficult. Yet God did not just suddenly become faithful. He was and is eternally faithful. We need to believe it. He *is* a gracious giver; He is a gracious giver to *you*. Believe that He fulfills His promises, even when it seems that He may never do so. Wait patiently for the Lord to solve your impossible situations. At the proper time, in the proper way, He will do it.

All those years of disappointment did not allow Elizabeth to know her own significance. Yet God favored this special daughter and intended to bless her all along. Right when she was too old, right when she seemed completely dried up, He gave her the most important assignment of her life, proving that the condition of the heart, not the age of the body, counts most with Him. He had sovereignly waited to work in her impossible circumstance to fulfill the Messianic prophecies. At the appointed hour for unveiling His miracle, notwithstanding her age or any other barrier, He gave her a son uniquely gifted in history.

When you are tempted to believe that God's promise to you is impossible; when you feel shelved, useless, and fruitless; when you think that your life has been spent in vain; when you see no way for God to pull out good from your disappointing circumstance, remember Elizabeth. Be encouraged; have hope. Commit your heart to Christ and trust Him. Like the incense that Zechariah burned in the Holy Place, the offerings of your life ascend as a sweet fragrance to God's throne. He loves and appreciates you. He will heal your disappointed heart and satisfy your soul, "For nothing is impossible with God" (Luke 1:37).

Heart Check

1. What has God shown you about your heart through this chapter?

2. What are some of your disappointments in life? Have you committed them to God?

3. Can you see things God has taught you through your disappointments?

4. In what ways can you find encouragement from Elizabeth's story?

5. Compose a prayer to God in response to this chapter's lessons.

8

Bathsheba

THE EXPLOITED HEART

2 SAMUEL 11; 12:1-25; 1 KINGS 1:11-31; 2:13-25; 1 CHRONICLES 3:5

GOD! OH, GOD, what can I do? The distressed woman paced back and forth, wringing her hands and sobbing her heart out. *What will become of me? What if Uriah finds out? What if the neighbors hear? I don't want to be stoned to death. Oh, God, forgive me. Help me! HELP ME!* She felt very much alone as she tried desperately to think of a solution. None came. *If only I had refused! I should have . . . as if I really had a choice! He's the king after all!*

She would never forget that fateful night. We can well imagine it. It was late when her servant answered the knock at the door. He returned with a fearful look. "It's a member of the palace guard . . . and he wants you!" Trembling, she went to greet the guard.

"The king requests your presence at once!" he said.

"What? What would the king want with *me?* Is something wrong? Has something happened to Uriah?" He gave no reply. So obeying the summons, she went out into the night and was ushered inside the royal palace.

Taken to the king's personal chamber, she waited for a few moments. Then he entered the room—David, her king! She nearly gasped to think that she stood in the presence of Israel's great king. Terrified, she knelt before him and said, "You called, my lord?"

He waved his servants out of the room. Then he said gently, "I'm sorry if I've inconvenienced you. I know it's late. Thank you for coming. . . . Here, have a seat. Hmm, Bathsheba—a lovely name for a lovely woman. I—I . . . Well, let me come right to the point. I really do think you are beautiful, and I . . . When I saw you, I couldn't take my eyes off you; I knew I had to have you." The king knew how to get what he wanted. When it came to women, he did not have to beg. Caressing her cheek, he continued, "I must have you. You'll be serving your king; you'll be serving your country. I *must* have you . . . *now*. You do understand, don't you?"

As she stared at David, her hero and mighty king, she felt small and fragile. Merely a woman, she was among the lowliest of his subjects. She could not have resisted the will of her king had she tried. A king got whatever he wanted, especially where a woman was involved. Startled and confused, she wondered, *Is this the conduct that befits my king?* After all, this was David, the man of God; David, the paragon of virtue; David, who brought the Ark to Jerusalem and danced before the Lord with all his heart; David, whom the whole kingdom adored; David, the legendary champion and crusader for the Lord's honor; David, zealous to execute justice in Israel; David, exalted over Saul for having a heart after God's own heart. Yes, this was David! It made no sense, but it did not have to. She consented.

We call Bathsheba's heart The Exploited Heart. She had been a good and virtuous wife, a woman of sterling reputation until David, consumed with sinful passion, drew her into his wickedness. She was young and powerless; he was the middle-aged and mighty king. Using his powerful leverage, he corrupted her, treating her like an object to take and use as he willed, not as a person with dignity. Doubtless, no one in the world could have prevailed upon her to commit this sin against her devoted husband and against her God but David himself.

Weeks passed, and she realized she had a big problem. Anguished and not knowing what else to do, she sent David a message. The nation was at war with the Ammonites, and he was in his war room studying reports when a guard entered and said, "I told him you were busy, but a servant of one named Bathsheba insists he has a message you will want to see."

David immediately sat up. "Send him in."

His guard ushered the servant in to deliver the message to the king's hand. Curious, David unsealed and read it. It was short, only three words in length, but the news could not have packed a more devastating wallop: "I am pregnant."

He tried to look calm as he nodded his head and said, "Tell your mistress that I'll look into the matter." He tucked the note away and pretended to go back to work. But this was serious, very serious. The crime of adultery carried a death penalty.

How did David and Bathsheba get into this mess? It was springtime, "the time when kings go off to war" (2 Samuel 11:1). But David had sent Joab, his military commander, to lead his army against the Ammonites while he stayed back at the palace. Sometimes kings stayed home, and with the Ammonite capital a mere forty miles from Jerusalem, David could easily run the war effort from his palace. So he had sent his army off to fight a war that they would ultimately win. Yes, external enemies would fall, but an internal enemy, one in his own soul, would topple mighty King David. For he had a male weakness particularly common to those who, unlike Job, fail to make a covenant with their eyes (Job 31:1).

One evening David felt restless. He got out of bed and went up to the palace roof to enjoy the refreshing evening air. If only he had brought his harp to play the Lord some psalms. Perhaps he did, but as he looked out over the Kidron Valley, Satan enticed him. Scanning the dwellings below, something caught David's eye. *What . . . what have we here?* He stopped abruptly to take a closer look. Staring hard, a tingling thrill raced through him. For it was a woman, a beautiful woman— no, a sensational woman—and she was bathing! He should have turned at once and fled the temptation, but he did not. Feasting his eyes in the privacy of his roof, his heart filled with reckless passion.

Bathsheba was not taking a bath for her enjoyment. This was a required ritual bath that Jewish women had to take to purify themselves after their menstrual period. While she was not entirely discreet, she was innocent, no less. She may have bathed with a window open or on the flat roof of her house or in a garden bath. Whichever it was, she thought herself out of view and cannot be accused of intentionally causing trouble. Surely she would have been horrified had she known that any man viewed her nakedness, especially her king.

After her bath the onlooker may have watched as she gently rubbed her body with olive oil as was commonly done. By then he had forgotten his responsibility, his integrity, the Lord, the Scriptures, and even what sin was. Knowing what the bath meant, that she had just purified herself, he was intent on enjoying the object of his lust—that night.

He tore down from the roof and sent for a servant to find out about her. The servant reported, "Isn't this Bathsheba, the daughter of Eliam and the wife of Uriah the Hittite?" (2 Samuel 11:3). Hearing her marital status did nothing to dampen the fire he felt. Uriah was a loyal member of an elite inner circle of David's soldiers, his "mighty men" (1 Chronicles 11:41), someone David must have known personally. Knowing that Uriah was away at war, David felt safe and sent his men to fetch her. So while Uriah was hazarding his life on the battlefield for the honor of David and his kingdom, David was at home exploiting his wife.

Was Bathsheba a willing participant? Could she have refused him? Commentators differ. Some think she was a deliberate accomplice; others think she was a victim. Those critical of her point to Queen Vashti who refused to cooperate when her husband would have demeaned her. They also point to Abigail who had the wisdom to persuade David from his destructive course. They do not take into account, however, that Vashti was a queen and that Abigail faced David when he was young and not yet king. They also do not remember that even the patriarch's wife, Sarah, had been taken into the harems of two kings, Abimelech and Pharaoh, and escaped violation only by God's intervention.

It seems more appropriate to give Bathsheba the benefit of the doubt, to consider her a woman who was exploited and sinned against rather than the sinner in this story. Scripture nowhere treats her as a guilty party. We might be inclined to defend David simply because he is our spiritual hero, but this David whom we all love had grown spiritually lax and physically self-indulgent as spiritual leaders sometimes do. He let his sinful nature rule him, abused his position, and exploited this young woman. He put her in a very difficult position, and to assign blame to her only further abuses her. She knew that adultery was wrong, but refusing her king could be even deadlier. Whether she submitted because she feared his power and greatness, or trusted his goodness, or was just overwhelmed in his presence, she was far more a victim in this incident than an intentional sinner.

If Bathsheba had missed it before, however, she soon realized that going to bed with David had been a terrible mistake. The seventh commandment forbids a married person to have sexual relations with someone who is not his or her spouse. The Law condemned to death anyone who engaged in adultery. Worse, she was pregnant, and since she had just finished her period before going to David, she knew he was responsible for her pregnancy. Uriah had been gone too long for anyone to believe the child she carried was his, so there was no way to hide the affair. So she sent the message to David, making no demand, for she had no rights. She did hope, however, that the mighty and merciful king of Israel would know what she should do to prevent a scandal that might end in her death.

When David heard of the pregnancy, he feared, too. Uriah, so bravely fighting for his king and country, would be justifiably enraged and also deeply wounded by this betrayal of his wife and king. Man of honor that he was, Uriah might have his wife executed and even lead an insurrection against David. Unchecked sin finds a way to compound itself, and what David had done to Bathsheba would not compare with what he would do to her husband.

While Uriah's name means "Yahweh is my light," he was not a pure-bred Jew but a naturalized foreigner, a Hittite convert. Perhaps David rationalized that though he was a good soldier, he was but a Gentile and weaker in his allegiance. Concocting a scheme, David sent word to Joab, "Send me Uriah the Hittite" (2 Samuel 11:6). So Uriah came in from the battlefield to meet David.

At the palace David asked Uriah about the war, but his real motive was to get him home to sleep with his wife so he would believe the child was his own. "Go down to your house and wash your feet," he said (2 Samuel 11:8). So Uriah left, and David sent a gift after him, probably a fine meal for him to enjoy with Bathsheba. But that night Uriah stayed at the palace entrance and slept with the king's guards.

Next morning David summoned him and asked, "Why didn't you go home?" (2 Samuel 11:10). What he failed to grasp was that Uriah was an honorable man, much more than himself, with praiseworthy devotion to Israel's God and to military decorum. "As surely as you live," he vowed, "I will not do such a thing!" (2 Samuel 11:11). Consecrated to duty, he refused to sleep with his wife while the Ark of the Covenant, his commanding officer, and his fellow soldiers camped in open fields.

What a noble man the king had in his service! Uriah denied himself lawful pleasures that David had indulged in unlawfully. His commitment should have cut David to the heart, but too greatly hardened, David tried another ploy. Inviting Uriah to dinner, he made him drunk in hopes that he would forget his vow and either stagger on home or be carried. But Uriah proved to be a better man intoxicated than David was sober. Refusing to go near his home, he slept with the palace guards again.

Uriah's only vulnerability was that he trusted his king. When David could not coax him to violate his conscience, he felt he must dispose of him. With blinded eyes, hardened heart, and seared conscience, the man whose heart convicted him for cutting off a corner of Saul's garment plotted to kill his own fiercely loyal servant. How tragic that such an innocent, valiant, faithful, and honorable man, who would fight and die *for* his king, must die *by* his king.

David wrote a letter to Joab—one whom he knew lacked qualms when it came to treachery and murder—and sent it with Uriah. It said, "Put Uriah in the frontline where the fighting is fiercest. Then withdraw from him so he will be struck down and die" (2 Samuel 11:15). Can you imagine it? David ordered Uriah back to the front, carrying in his hand his own death warrant! How far "the sweet psalmist of Israel" (2 Samuel 23:1 KJV) had sunk.

To carry out the plot, Joab sent some of his soldiers, including Uriah, close to the defenders' city wall where archers could shoot at them. As a result, others died with Uriah. David, however, felt no remorse. He had now compounded his adultery with conspiracy and murder.

When Bathsheba heard that her husband had died, she mourned for him. How deeply she grieved, we do not know. While she must have truly mourned, she was surely relieved that Uriah had never learned of his king's betrayal and the result she carried in her womb. After she had spent the minimum number of days required for mourning, David married her so the adultery might not be discovered. It is quite probable that she knew nothing of the plot against Uriah.

Months passed, and a son was born. By this time David felt confident his crime had gone undiscovered. But what made him think that the Lord had missed it? At any stage along the way, David could have repented, but he had only grown more callous and indifferent to his sin.

Such behavior was common among pagan rulers, but Israel's king was not a pagan ruler. He was a servant of the true and living God. Sorely displeased, the Lord sent Nathan the prophet to him. Nathan presented what seemed to be a judicial matter for the king to resolve between a rich man with large flocks and a poor man with one little ewe lamb. The poor man and his family had raised the lamb and loved it dearly, but the rich man had seized it and prepared it for his guest's meal.

As the nation's chief judge, the king was responsible to administer justice on behalf of the poor and oppressed. Hearing of this cruel injustice infuriated David, and he rendered a swift verdict. "As surely as the LORD lives," he declared, "the man who did this deserves to die! He must pay for that lamb four times over, because he did such a thing and had no pity" (2 Samuel 12:5-6).

Nathan's previous message to David had predicted unlimited divine favor (2 Samuel 7:8-16), so he did not suspect that this was really a clever parable to get him to condemn himself. He had no idea that he was the story's villain; that Uriah was the man with one very dear lamb; that unlike David, he had no wandering eye and was fully committed to his wife. David, who had multiple wives, had seized Uriah's wife for his own, thinking in his heart, *I am the king of Israel. Uriah serves at my pleasure, and what belongs to him is mine.*

Suddenly Nathan shouted at David, "You are the man!" Then he declared, "This is what the LORD, the God of Israel, says: 'I anointed you king over Israel. . . . Why did you despise the word of the LORD by doing what is evil in his eyes? You struck down Uriah the Hittite with the sword and took his wife to be your own. You killed him with the sword of the Ammonites." Then, pronouncing God's judgment, Nathan predicted, "Now, therefore, the sword shall never depart from your house, because you despised me and took the wife of Uriah the Hittite to be your own"(2 Samuel 12:7, 9-10).

Nathan's words pierced David's heart. To his credit he did not make excuses, rationalize, or justify his sin but wholeheartedly repented on the spot. "I have sinned against the LORD," he cried.

He should have died for his sin, both by the law and by his own verdict. Instead Nathan said, "The LORD has taken away your sin. You are not going to die. But because by doing this you have made the enemies of the LORD show utter contempt, the son born to you will die" (2 Samuel 12:13-14).

With remorse for his monstrous sin, David wrote: "Have mercy on me, O God, according to your unfailing love; according to your great compassion blot out my transgressions. Wash away all my iniquity and cleanse me from my sin. For I know my transgressions, and my sin is always before me. . . . Create in me a pure heart, O God, and renew a steadfast spirit within me. Do not cast me from your presence or take your Holy Spirit from me. . . . Save me from bloodguilt, O God. . . . The sacrifices of God are a broken spirit; a broken and contrite heart, O God, you will not despise" (Psalm 51:1-3, 10-11, 14, 17).

Still the consequences of David's sin remained irreversible. Ultimately, all of Nathan's predictions would find their fulfillment. David and Bathsheba's child became ill. David pleaded to God and fasted for his life, but their son died. And this was just the beginning of David's woes. Most of his latter family life would be marred by events precipitated by his adultery.

And what of Bathsheba? Let us not forget that Nathan portrayed her as the innocent and helpless ewe lamb, stolen from her master and victimized by a more powerful man. The chain of events in her life must have left her devastated. She had suffered unfaithfulness to her husband, an unwanted pregnancy, fear of discovery of her pregnancy, the death of her husband, and the death of her child. David was guilty of the crime, but she paid the penalty along with him.

Nevertheless, their hearts melded together in their common grief. Their marriage had displeased the Lord, but He never commanded them to separate. David's repentance, though long in coming, was full and genuine, and he loved Bathsheba. That he so repented and continued to love her can only mean that he saw her as an innocent victim. She had not enticed him, but he had abused her. If she were at all guilty, she obviously repented and was restored along with David, or he, so deeply convicted, would not have continued to love, respect, and honor her.

God restored the joy of David's salvation, and he comforted his wife with the comfort he had received. He slept with her, and she conceived and gave birth to another son. They called him Solomon, meaning "peaceful." They knew that God had removed their stigma and given him as a gift, a sign that they were now at peace with Him. Remarkably, the record says of this child, "The LORD loved him" (2 Samuel 12:24). And lest the couple fear that God might strike this son as He had their first, God sent word through Nathan to nickname him Jedidiah—meaning, "beloved of the Lord." The Lord knew there would be no other stain on David's record: "For David had done what was right in the eyes of the LORD and had not failed to keep any of the LORD's commands all the days of his life—except in the case of Uriah the Hittite" (1 Kings 15:5).

Years went by, and David neared the end of the golden years of his reign. The kingdom was unified and God-centered, but when he was seventy years old, his health deteriorated seriously. Here we see the full extent of Bathsheba's restoration. No longer do we find a weak and exploited woman. Rather she has risen to a prominent place in the royal court and is now a mover and shaker in kingdom affairs.

David's fourth son Adonijah (by his wife Haggith) was the oldest surviving royal son. He would have been the logical choice to succeed David as king but for the fact that Bathsheba had secured from David a promise—her son Solomon would succeed him on the throne. But David's memory was failing, and he either forgot his promise or had failed to follow up on it. By delaying the naming of Solomon as his successor, he opened the door for political insurgence.

Adonijah knew he was not David's first choice and waited for the right time to seize the throne. One day, without David's knowledge, he began his campaign. His plan seemed promising, especially when Joab and Abiathar the priest defected to him. He invited all his brothers but Solomon and all the prominent royal officials but David's most trusted advisers to a coronation feast. He intended to put to death those whom he had not invited.

Nathan the prophet (one whom Adonijah avoided) knew Adonijah was neither David's nor God's choice for the throne (1 Kings 1:17, 30; 1 Chronicles 22:9-10), and he knew something must be done quickly to stop him. He went straight to the one whom he viewed most likely to intervene against the imminent coup—Bathsheba. Nathan, who had so vehemently denounced David and Bathsheba's union, was now her friend and ally. He cooperated with her to save their lives and see Solomon advanced to the throne. Evidently, she had won his utmost respect, and he had hers, too, as one of her sons bore his name.

Nathan urged her to go in to David and remind him of his promise and inform him of Adonijah's action. Her approach to the crisis would show immense wisdom, discretion, grace, and foresight. As she entered the king's chamber, a young woman named Abishag attended the weak and frail king. Bathsheba bowed before him, and he asked, "What is it that you want?" Explaining the day's events and reminding him of his oath to her, she urged him to act immediately. Then Nathan arrived to confirm her report, and she left to await the outcome.

David came to life; he was still the king, and he took charge. "Call in Bathsheba," he commanded. So she returned, and he pledged to her: "As surely as the LORD lives, who has delivered me out of every trouble, I will surely carry out today what I swore to you by the LORD, the God of Israel: Solomon your son shall be king after me, and he will sit on my throne in my place." Again she bowed low and replied, "May my lord King David live forever!" (1 Kings 1:28-31).

Acting quickly, David commanded his chief priests Zadok and Benaiah, along with Nathan, to have his servants set Solomon on the king's mule and lead him to Gihon, a sacred water source near Jerusalem. Nathan and Zadok were to anoint him there as Israel's next king and lead him back to Jerusalem to sit on the throne.

Bathsheba would not have missed this for anything. As the full regiment of David's royal guard ushered Solomon down to Gihon, it must have been the happiest day of her life. Crowds of people followed the procession. When they arrived, the royal guard stood in formation, ready for the ceremony to begin. Her heart no doubt raced as she watched her son standing among Zadok, Nathan, and Benaiah. Zadok took the oil and poured it over Solomon, the trumpet sounded, and all the people started shouting jubilantly, "Long live King Solomon! Long live King Solomon!"

Bathsheba's eyes could not have been dry as she joined the joyful chorus. The rejoicing and flute-playing was so loud as they led their newly anointed king back to Jerusalem that it seemed "the ground shook with the sound" (1 Kings 1:40). Adonijah's mutiny collapsed, and Solomon, who could have had him executed as a rival, instead forgave him and commanded him to go home and refrain from further attempts on the throne.

Largely because of Bathsheba's intervention, Solomon succeeded his father. David had other wives, but it was Bathsheba to whom he had made a promise; it was Bathsheba to whom he had hearkened; it was Bathsheba's son who succeeded him. He must have loved her and placed great confidence in her.

We can imagine that as the queen mother, Bathsheba became even more influential in the royal palace. This position commanded deep respect. One day Adonijah went to her with a request. Many years had passed since her early exploitation, and she was about to fall prey again, this time for her good-natured gullibility. Little did she know that he still coveted the throne. She asked, "Do you come peacefully?" He replied that he had, and she took his word for it. Then he asked for one small favor: "Please ask King Solomon—he will not refuse you— to give me Abishag the Shunammite as my wife."

Adonijah did not really care about Abishag. As the young woman who had cared for David in his old age and who was considered part of David's royal harem, she had some standing. Adonijah wanted her because this would move him closer to the throne.

"Very well," Bathsheba replied naively, "I will speak to the king for you." So she went to Solomon. When he saw her, he stood and then bowed down to her. Reseating himself on his throne, he had a second throne brought for her so she could sit at his right hand, a place of honor and authority.

"I have one small request to make of you," she said. "Do not refuse me."

"Make it, my mother," he replied. "I will not refuse you."

So she said, "Let Abishag the Shunammite be given in marriage to your brother Adonijah." She had believed the best, but Solomon saw through the scheme. This was another attempt to seize his throne! Wise Solomon esteemed his mother greatly and would have done anything for her but this.

"Why do you request Abishag the Shunammite for Adonijah? You might as well request the kingdom for him—after all, he is my older brother. . . ." Adonijah was executed that day, and Solomon firmly established his throne.

Four sons were born to David and Bathsheba—Solomon, Shimea, Shobab, and Nathan (1 Chronicles 3:5). But David had other wives, too, and his large family was unruly. Nathan's early prediction kept bearing itself out as David suffered repeated family crises. Somehow amid much hatred, subversion, and treachery, however, Solomon came through unscathed. Surely his mother had a positive influence on his life. Having lost her child born in adultery, she lived on to train her beloved Solomon in godliness, thus preparing him for his destiny as Israel's wisest and wealthiest king.

Despite the terrible sin and calamity that introduced her to the royal family, Bathsheba had gone on to walk in the love, grace, and fear of the Lord. She rose from her tragedy to become the link between Israel's two most famous kings, David and Solomon. She was a faithful wife and confidante to Israel's greatest king, the beloved mother of the wisest, and a woman whom Nathan the prophet respected. When King Solomon later strayed into sexual sin, his mother, remembering the consequences of David's sin with her, must have trembled.

David's adultery with Bathsheba could have ended the family line through which God intended to bring the Messiah. But God, in His mercy and sovereignty, redeemed their mistakes and brought good from these. Amazingly, the lineage of Jesus, the Messiah, comes down from David and Bathsheba through their son Solomon. Permitted to be in the messianic lineage, the New Testament refers to Bathsheba in Christ's genealogy as "Uriah's wife" (Matthew 1:6). The woman who began as an exploited young victim of a king's lust rose to influence all of history. "Oh, the depth of the riches of the wisdom and knowledge of God! How unsearchable his judgments, and his paths beyond tracing out!" (Romans 11:33).

LESSONS FOR OUR OWN HEARTS

Exploit is a powerful word. As a noun it can denote a heroic use of power. Turn it into a verb, however, and it denotes an unscrupulous use of power for taking advantage of others. Sad to say, this sinful world teems with powerful people who exploit the weak and disadvantaged for their own sinful purposes. Whenever a powerful man takes advantage of a woman sexually, there is sexual exploitation— whether that man is a president with a starry-eyed intern, a boss with a secretary, a rock star with a groupie, a drill instructor with a recruit, a professor with his student, or a king with his subject.

Was Bathsheba faultless? Probably not, but that is beside the point. David, one of the world's most powerful men, used his power to take advantage of a weak and vulnerable woman. Even if she were *completely* innocent, she still had significant issues to deal with. That fateful night changed her life forever. She could never go back and relive it. She could never reclaim her dead husband, her dead baby, or her unmarred life. Fortunately, David repented and comforted her in her distress. We can be sure he apologized with all his heart for bringing this multiplied tragedy upon her. We can also assume that he assured her of his love for her and that God, in His great love and mercy, would not abandon her.

Yet so many exploited and abused women receive no apology, reassurance, or sympathy—not from the perpetrators or from their communities. It can be a cruel world for the exploited, especially in a society that so often blames its victims. If we can live in denial, believing that a victim invited, consented to, or enjoyed the abuse, then the world seems a safer place. The victim is not really a victim, and we do not really need to deal seriously with the issue. That is why eight out of nine rape victims refrain from reporting assaults against them—they know they will not be taken seriously. And note: Statistically one in four women can expect to be raped or molested (from "The worst sexual sin: sexual violence and the church" by Christine Gudorf, *Christian Century*, January 6, 1993, pp. 19-21).

Think, then, of the rampant incidents of sexual harassment and other forms of exploitation. When the army instituted a hot line for anonymously reporting sexual discrimination, harassment, or assault, over four thousand calls were logged in the first nine days! An alarming 7-12 percent of therapists admit to engaging in behavior intended to arouse or satisfy their own desires. Doctors, lawyers, and even ministers have nearly the same rate of misconduct, and the effects can be devastating: Up to 90 percent of victims are emotionally, psychologically, and spiritually damaged—some severely. The sexually exploited can fear other relationships; hate or mistrust men; feel worthless, guilty, ashamed, or depressed; be promiscuous; have trouble relating to God. Often victims, fearing exposure for their own sake, their family's sake, or even the guilty person's sake, carry their mistreatment as a heavy, shameful, and secret burden. Facing our issues, we must allow the Lord to access our pain and let Him deal with it. He never tells us to suppress and hide our feelings but to bring them to Him.

While we can only touch lightly on the needs of those damaged by some form of sexual exploitation, there are two keys to healing, both related to forgiveness.

Extend Forgiveness

Bathsheba obviously needed to forgive David, and particularly so if she had been aware of David's direct involvement in Uriah's death. She may have needed to deal with bitterness directed toward God if she blamed Him for letting her be exploited. But perhaps she also had to forgive herself. Forgive herself? David had seduced her and perhaps deceived and even coerced her. Whichever, she would still tend to blame herself for bathing in the wrong place at the wrong time and for cooperating with his advances. Sometimes forgiving ourselves can be the most difficult of all.

Forgiveness is vital to restoration. Has someone exploited or abused you? If you keep brooding over past injustices, you let the one who hurt you keep on ruining your life. Hasn't he done enough already? If you keep wasting your emotional, spiritual, and even physical energy on your grievance, you cannot be useful to God, your family, your church, or your vocation. Satan loves to see it! He wants to make your heart a graveyard of painful memories where the ghosts never die. But it's your choice.

Once someone so wounded me that I seethed with bitterness. If I had possessed faith to move mountains, I would have dropped one on that person's head. Knowing I had to forgive, I told the Lord, "Okay, Lord, I forgive, but I hope you will squash that insect!" I just knew that if I released my bitterness to Him, He would smash my enemy for me. Instead He flashed me a picture of Jesus agonizing on the cross, crying, "Father, forgive them" (Luke 23:34). Instantly I saw what forgiveness means. Christ's forgiveness is a total kind that even invites the Father's blessing on those who abuse Him.

Did Christ approve of what His murderers did? Of course not! And in forgiving, we in no way approve of what they did to us. We just cancel the debt they owe us. As God's children, He wants us to think and act as He does. So He commands us: "Bless those who curse you, pray for those who abuse you" (Luke 6:28 NRSV). We may not feel forgiving, but it is more a matter of our heart and will. When we can forgive from our heart and even pray for our abuser, then we will finally be free to get on with our life.

Receive Forgiveness

We must also be willing to *receive* forgiveness. Through Christ God forgives us from the moment we turn in humble repentance to Him. But until we receive it, we cannot enjoy its liberating benefits. If one who was sexually mistreated felt any pleasure in it—this is often the case with victims of sexual abuse—they sometimes feel guilty and confused. Such inner conflicts make it hard to accept forgiveness because they take the blame. Why is it that so often the innocent victim carries guilt while the guilty victimizer protests his innocence? That's not right! We must let God remove the false guilt from us. Yes, there is a difference between true and false guilt. If you did sin, bring it to the Lord right now and humbly ask for His forgiveness. Then by faith in His promise (1 John 1:9), *receive* it. *Renounce* your guilt because it is no longer yours: "You were bought at a price" (1 Corinthians 6:20; 7:23).

Can you see what happened with Bathsheba? She lived with no stigma, no scarlet letter. She did not become a victim of her past. Her misfortune did not rule and ruin her life. She accepted grace for whatever part she played and went on to become a great and godly influence. Don't let an ungodly obsession with your past block what God has for you today. Give your past, your painful memories, and your regrets to God. Reclaim your life!

For those so blessed to have never been hurt sexually, may I sound a warning? Be on guard! Jesus warns us: "See, I am sending you out like sheep into the midst of wolves; so be wise as serpents and innocent as doves" (Matthew 10:16 NRSV). In other words, this

Scripture shouts, "Don't be stupid!" Wisdom is a gift from God, and we are responsible for how we use it. We should pray for wisdom and constantly seek it so that we will escape sinful entanglements and exploitation. We are particularly at risk when we feel insecure, hungry for attention, or when we are going through some trauma.

I was a twenty-eight-year-old wife and mother who felt distraught over many things in my church and my life. Finally I made an appointment with the senior pastor. Some women in the church whom he counseled idolized him. It concerned me that they were quite troubled, rabidly loyal, possessive of his time, and never seemed to improve. As I entered his office, he sat me down on the couch and closed the door. As I tearfully spilled out my woes, he listened sympathetically. Then drawing near me on the couch, he said gently, "Cheryl, I see that I have neglected you, and I want that to change."

For an instant I felt hope, but then alarms went off in me; everything felt weird and wrong; I felt unsafe. Shaken, I excused myself and retreated out the door. *What was that all about?* I wondered. *Was there something wrong with me, or was it him?* That was the last time I was alone with him. Sometime later it became known that he had exploited a number of women sexually, having devised many strange "inner healing" techniques such as caressing women's breasts to affirm their femininity. What a guy!

I am so grateful that I did not succumb to what would have spelled disaster. I did not need my pastor or counselor or "friend" to affirm my femininity, nor do you. Some women, it seems, are so easily exploited. They go from one disaster to another, perhaps because they lost their self-esteem or perhaps because they never had it. They see themselves as "damaged goods" and feel worthless and dirty inside. That is *not* God's point of view. We need to see ourselves the way He sees us and measure our value by His standard, not the world's. He loves us. To Him, we are precious gems—not junk. Like any loving parent, His heart longs for our best. Whatever our past, He forgives, cleanses, and redeems.

Our God is amazing! His willingness to forgive and His power to restore are absolutely beyond our comprehension. And no story in the Bible demonstrates this more clearly than that of David and Bathsheba. Just think about this. God in His love and mercy completely forgave them their sins and restored them to fellowship with Himself. Beyond that, He acknowledged their marriage covenant, though begun in adultery and made possible by murder. He blessed their marriage with a beautiful son, Solomon, following the death of their firstborn, and then chose Solomon to be the king of His people Israel. He blessed Solomon with such wisdom and honor and wealth that the entire world was astounded. And finally the most amazing of all: God chose to have His own Son, Jesus Christ, born in the lineage of David and Bathsheba through Solomon.

Imagine that! If God were willing to forgive and forget the sins and mistakes of David and Bathsheba, then how willing is He to forgive and forget *your* sins and mistakes? If He could so completely restore *their* lives and turn *their* tragedies into triumphs, just think how He can transform *your* tragedies when you turn them and yourself over to Him. "Amazing grace, how sweet the sound, that saved a wretch like me; I once was lost but now am found, was blind but now I see." Praise God!

You may still be asking, "Why, God? Why must we suffer so much pain?" Part of God's justice involves letting a sinful world that rebels against His righteousness suffer the effects of its depravity. Ultimately, at the final judgment the guilty will receive their due reward. For, "though the mills of God grind slowly, yet they grind exceeding small" ("Retribution" by Friedrich von Logau).

Meanwhile God offers amazing grace, mercy, and restoration to this world's victims. Let me tell you about my friend Diana. One day when she was a youngster, her grandfather—a deacon and head usher in their church—molested her. From then on she lived with fear. She explains:

> I never told my husband until after we had been married fourteen years, and he couldn't understand the devastating effects I suffered. When I joined a Christian support group for sexually abused women called Women of Courage, it was the hardest and

best thing that ever happened to me. The women understood. It was like we all had death inside that we couldn't wash away. We talked about our experience. Learning to trust again, we questioned God and confessed our anger without feeling like He would zap us. We let Him lovingly restore the person who had been killed in us.

We learned the difference between shame and guilt. Guilt is where you did something wrong, and you feel guilty for it. Shame is different. When my grandfather abused me, he was 100 percent guilty, but I felt the shame. But it was not my fault! I did not ask for it. I even ran. All my life I had shame, but now, like a child who trusts her father, I am learning to run into His everlasting arms of love. You see, that child, when she was abused, locked herself inside a steel shell and couldn't come out. She didn't know she did it; she didn't mean to; it just happened. Only pure love could rescue her—and He did!

As Diana's grandfather lay dying, he seemed to squeeze her hand slightly when she told him she loved and forgave him. Today Diana serves in our church's ministry to women with similar needs. It would be good for every church to develop such programs. God has hope for you too, beloved sister in Christ. Let Him head your heart.

Heart Check

1. Can you in some way relate to Bathsheba? Has your heart been damaged by sexual exploitation?

2. How have you seen God's restoring power, either in your own life or in the life of a friend?

3. How might friends or ministries help with the healing process?

4. What is the most important principle you can apply to your life from Bathsheba's example?

5. Compose a prayer to God in response to this chapter's lessons.

9

The Woman Caught in Adultery

THE GUILT-LADEN HEART

JOHN 8:2-11

"I'M SORRY. I'M *SO* SORRY. I made a mistake. I have no excuse. Please, be merciful! *Pleeeeease!*" Her cries fell on deaf ears. The morality police had been out in force, scanning the area for the perfect victim. Now they had her, and mercy was the furthest thing from their minds. Rushing her along the dusty Jerusalem street, they pushed, pulled, and cruelly jerked at her. So righteous did these religious leaders think themselves that even touching her meant defilement to them. But so intent on their purpose were they that nothing else mattered.

. . . in wrath remember mercy.

HABAKKUK 3:2

She knew she would die. The Law of Moses demanded it, and she deserved it. Guilt and dread both whirled inside her as she thought, *Oh, God, what have I done? What was I thinking? What a fool I've been! I don't want to die.*

To her surprise, instead of taking her outside town to a cliff to throw her off and then pummel her with stones, they turned toward the temple. *Where are they taking me?* Little did she know that she was not their first priority. They had an all-important stop to make first.

Meanwhile Jesus of Nazareth, believed by some to be the Messiah, was seated in the temple courtyard teaching a large crowd of people. Suddenly everyone heard a scuffle. A group of men, teachers of the law and Pharisees, forced their way through the crowd, angrily dragging with them a crying, disheveled, partially clad woman. Her arms were bruised, her toes stubbed, her heart crushed with guilt and shame. Shoving her up to the front of the gawking crowd, they made her stand before Jesus. All eyes were on the pathetic creature.

Her whole body shook uncontrollably, and her terror-stricken eyes glanced up only for a second, long enough to make a quick appraisal of her Judge. His eyes met hers in that moment, and she regretted it. For she felt His holiness and her vileness. Quickly dropping her gaze to the ground, she stared hard. She could not bear meeting those eyes again. *He will condemn me. I deserve it. I'm guilty . . . guilty . . . guilty.*

We call this woman's heart The Guilt-laden Heart, for she was an adulteress caught in the very act. They had yanked her from her paramour's bed early that morning, and she knew she had no excuse and no defense. By her disgraceful behavior, she had committed a terrible sin, not only against her husband but against a holy God. (This story is not in the most ancient manuscripts of John's gospel. It was likely passed on through oral tradition from early times. Many third-century Christian writers referred to it, and later it was included in a sixth-century manuscript of John. It was added to later versions because it was judged an authentic story consistent with Christ's compassionate ministry.)

There was obviously more going on here than meets the eye. Things had been heating up between Jesus and the religious establishment, and they despised Him. Not only had He offended them by healing people on the Sabbath, but He had also blasphemed, making Himself God's equal (John 5:16-18). Ever since, they had been hunting for some way to trip Him up in order to destroy Him.

Just a few days before, during the Feast of Tabernacles (or Booths), a week-long annual festival, these men had twice tried to seize Jesus. Both attempts failed, however, "because his time had not yet come" (John 7:30, 44). Even the temple guards faltered in their effort to arrest Him because "No one ever spoke the way this man does" (John 7:46). Furious and frustrated, the religious authorities looked for another way to trap Him.

Evidently the previous night had been the last night of the festival, and the celebratory atmosphere of joyful feasting provided many opportunities for sin. The crowds of pilgrims packed together in Jerusalem had camped all week in flimsy makeshift "booths." In these cramped quarters with thin walls, finding their subject may not have been hard for the religious authorities.

Jesus had spent the night at the Mount of Olives and gotten up that morning before dawn to return to the temple. He knew His enemies wanted to get Him, but He also knew that many people would be there early before leaving Jerusalem to return home. When they saw Him, a large crowd gathered around Him, so He sat down—as was the custom of masters and teachers—and began His morning teaching.

That is when the religious leaders barged up with the woman. Pretending to need help with a real dilemma, they put this woman on trial before Jesus and forced Him to play the judge. They were the prosecutors, and the whole crowd were courtroom observers. Although they tried to feign respect, their faces and their tone betrayed their derision. "Teacher," they said, "this woman was caught in the act of adultery. In the Law Moses commanded us to stone such women" (John 8:4-5).

They were right. The seventh commandment forbids sexual relations outside of marriage (Exodus 20:14; Deuteronomy 5:18; Leviticus 18:20). The Law of Moses even condemned both partners in adultery to death (Leviticus 20:10; Deuteronomy 22:22). This death sentence extended even to those who were betrothed (Deuteronomy 22:23-24). Whether married or betrothed, this woman had committed a serious and indefensible offense against God's command and covenant.

Jesus had repeatedly called the scribes and Pharisees "hypocrites," and here again their hypocrisy betrayed them. They seemed so concerned for justice, but where was the woman's partner in crime—the man? Her illegal act required a male counterpart. The Jewish leaders, self-righteous champions of the Law that they were, had actually disregarded the Law by singling her out for punishment.

This was only the tip of the iceberg of their hypocrisy. It wasn't that they truly hated adultery or genuinely regarded godliness. Their primary motive was not bringing this woman to justice for her crime but using her to entrap Jesus, their real target. If they could publicly discredit Him, their plan to kill Him might just work. If they could get Him to condemn Himself by running afoul of the Law, either religious or civil, they could proceed with a formal charge.

So they asked Him, "Now what do *you* say?" (John 8:5). In other words, "Do you agree with Moses or not?" Their intent was clear to Jesus. If He were who He claimed to be, it would be His solemn duty to honor the Mosaic Law. If He evaded the issue, He would disregard the Law by condoning her sin. If He acquitted her, they would accuse Him of disaffirming the Law. Calling Him an enemy of Moses, they would condemn Him as a lawbreaker and a fraud. He who claimed to fulfill the Law (Matthew 5:17) would have cast it off in deference to one whom it justly condemned. Not only would He be a friend of sinners, they would paint Him as a friend of sin, a sinner Himself. His supporters in the crowd were still defenders of Moses and surely would revolt against Him.

If, on the other hand, He condemned the woman by upholding the Mosaic Law, they would go report Him to the Roman governor (their civil authority) for challenging Roman law. While Jewish law mandated the woman's execution, Rome had removed capital jurisdiction from the Jews, and only Roman authority could try and execute her. His enemies itched to accuse Jesus to the Romans. Moreover, if He condemned the woman, after having befriended such people, they could accuse Him of being inconsistent: "He advocates mercy toward sinners, but look what He did to this woman!"

So what would Jesus do? It seemed the perfect trap. Only the day before He had defended His choice to heal on the Sabbath and told the people to "stop judging by mere appearances, and make a right judgment" (John 7:24). Well! Now they had Him! They had caught this woman in the act of adultery, and there was no appearance about it. The truth stood before Jesus, unmasked, uncovered, unveiled.

The teacher who always had plenty to say seemed now to have nothing to say. He didn't look ruffled; He just seemed uninterested in playing their game. Jesus, in His mercy and compassion, had no desire to hurl stones at this heap of broken humanity before Him. The Great Physician's purpose was not to condemn and destroy but to mend broken hearts and lives. To everyone's surprise, He stooped down and began to write in the dirt with His finger.

What on earth was He doing? He may have been expressing His disregard and aversion to this type of mock trial. Casting contempt on their tactics, He answered the prosecutors with deafening silence, a silence that set their teeth on edge, a silence that spoke more forcefully than anything He could have said. He left them standing there before Him staring blankly at Him and at each other.

The woman must have thought His behavior boded ill for her. *Why doesn't He say something? What is He thinking? The more He thinks, the more He will side with them.* Her soul screamed for mercy, but her guilt told her it was no use. Filled with remorse, she kept crying in despair, knowing it would all be over soon.

The men packed in tighter to see what Jesus was writing. Did He write their names (Jeremiah 17:13)? Did He list their sins—hatred, self-righteousness, greed, etc. (Matthew 23:13-34)? Did He record some Scripture such as: "You shall not covet your neighbor's wife" (Exodus 20:17)? This, too, constituted adultery (Matthew 5:28) and would declare them all guilty. Or was He merely passing time? As they waited, tension mounted. The only sound during that suspended moment was the woman's pitiful whimpering. Stunned, the accusers had never before seen Jesus act in this way and were completely unprepared for it. *What? Nothing to say?* Despite His unwillingness to play their game, they would in no way let Him off their hook. *He must give us a verdict—or else!*

Obviously it was not the woman but Jesus who was on trial here. The quintessential tempter and accuser, the devil, had enticed them to tempt and accuse the Lord. They were *His* accusers. Wanting to pin Him to the wall, they began peppering Him with questions, perhaps like these: "Don't you, the man with the answers, have one for us now?" "Shall we obey the Law or not?" "Surely you agree that we should stone her." "You don't want sin to run rampant, do you?" "Tell us the truth now—do you speak for God?" Did they have Him thoroughly confused, up against the ropes? No, He just kept writing in the dirt.

For the poor woman these were hair-raising, pulse-pounding, terrifying minutes. With guilt and shame boring a hole through her heart, she wondered, *Why doesn't He answer them? Why doesn't He just get it over with and condemn me?* But the difference between Jesus and her accusers was that while their hearts were full of bitterness and murder, His heart was filled with love and mercy.

The tension reached a flash point. Suddenly Jesus stood up and stared at them. Everyone fell quiet, knowing the moment of truth had come. "If any one of you is without sin, let him be the first to throw a stone at her," he declared.

What? They could not believe their ears. He had not answered their questions at all! They looked around, frustrated and speechless, wanting to execute justice but unable to. The Law, they knew only too well, normally required that the witnesses to a crime cast the first stones at the convicted. In serving as executioners, the witnesses would feel the full responsibility for their accusation. If proven to be false witnesses, they would pay the same penalty they hoped to inflict on their victim (Deuteronomy 17:6-7; 19:19).

It appears that Jesus had determined "for judgment to begin with the family of God"—those claiming to represent God (1 Peter 4:17). His brief answer was a clear indictment against them. He was asking them to examine their own consciences: "Are you ready to throw the first stone?" "Do you really have a right to bring charges against this woman?" "Are your hearts and motives truly pure?" Though fully clothed, the accusers felt naked before the one whose penetrating gaze pierced to their deepest souls. They were not the moral paragons they pretended to be. Consistent with His command to remove the beam from one's own eye before removing a speck from someone else's (Matthew 7:3-5), Jesus said nothing about the woman's sin. Pointing rather to their sin, He turned the challenge back on them.

By one short stunning sentence, he shamed and convicted not her, but them. By passing no sentence, He guarded His own reputation. They had no basis for accusing Him to Roman authorities. He appeared to agree with Moses that she deserved to be stoned, so they could not accuse Him of disregarding Jewish law. By charging those without sin to cast the first stone, He had exposed self-righteous hypocrisy and emphasized the importance of showing mercy, forgiveness, and compassion. Jesus could have cast the first stone, but He refused. His purposes were redemptive, not destructive.

Leaving His words to perform their task, Jesus again stooped down and began to write in the dirt. Confounded and dumbfounded, His opponents stared at Him with looks of anger, confusion, and amazement.

Jesus knew their hearts, and they knew it. While thanking God that they were not like this sinful woman, they had blinded themselves to the wickedness in their own hearts. Jesus had referred to them as "the blind leading the blind," and so they were. They needed to know what was in their hearts, to see their own wretched standing before God. Not only intending to bring the adulteress to repentance by showing her mercy, He also intended to bring her accusers to repentance by showing them their sin. The issue was no longer how *He* would decide but how *they* would decide. He had successfully driven a stake of conviction through their hypocritical hearts. Saying nothing further, He refused even to look up at them again, leaving them to appraise their own hearts.

They began to squirm. Seeing their own sins, they were humbled. Their desire to punish the woman dissipated. Now who was silent? The accusers had become the accused, the prosecutors, the prosecuted. They thought they would get the moral victory, but Christ had instead.

How the tables had turned! After accusing Christ publicly, they feared He might accuse them publicly. He had shown them their filthy hearts. Would He now expose them to the crowd? They quietly began to slink away. The oldest men were first to leave. Perhaps they were the greatest offenders, or perhaps they more easily recognized their own sins than did the zealous young men, the quickest to pass judgment. Whatever, they walked away from the only one with the power to cleanse their corrupt hearts. Their guilt would remain (John 9:41).

The shocked woman couldn't believe her eyes. One by one, those hard, cruel, and pitiless faces melted away. Finally left trembling by herself, she wondered what Jesus would do with her. She was as guilty as her accusers had said, and she might have been tempted to make a quick getaway while Jesus was occupied with writing in the dirt. But to Him they had brought her for judgment, and before Him she stayed, waiting for her Judge's decision.

Jesus had neither exonerated nor condemned her, and she no doubt wondered, *What should I do now? What does He want of me?* He had spared her but for what reason? To condemn her Himself? Waiting before Him, she felt the weight of her guilt, but strangely she also felt a sense of hope and relief well up in her heart.

Jesus stood up for a second time. He knew her accusers had left. He surveyed the area and then fixed His eyes on her, asking, "Woman, where are they?" (John 8:10). This was the first time anyone had asked her to speak a word, and she didn't know how to answer. She was afraid, but she forced her eyes up to His. Immediately she detected that He did not look at her with revulsion as the others had, but with mercy. She no longer felt threatened. On the contrary, she felt safe. "Has no one condemned you?" He asked.

Her trial had ended in a mistrial. The prosecution's witnesses had been discredited, and they dismissed themselves. She simply replied, "No one, sir" (John 8:11).

"Then neither do I condemn you," Jesus responded. "Go now and leave your life of sin" (John 8:11). He did not say this softly but with force, and she felt its potency. Yes, He had ordered her release, and she was free to go. But she would depart with a challenge and a choice to make. Would she return to her old way of living as she pleased? He wouldn't stop her. But giving her the freedom to choose didn't mean that He condoned her sin or that it didn't matter to Him. He knew more than anyone else the seriousness of sin and the price He would pay to break its destructive power.

In letting her go, He gave her a second chance, the opportunity to repent and follow Him. Her past mattered, but He offered her a future. She had broken both God's law and her commitment to her husband. That mattered. Sin always matters to Jesus. But having come to seek and save the lost, He would not waste this opportunity to show mercy and call her to repentance. In releasing her, He offered her forgiveness, a new life lived in the light of God's grace. This was no cheap grace but a costly one. He clearly expected her to "leave her life of sin" and begin as a faithful follower of God. Sometime earlier in this same place, He had told an invalid whom He healed, "See, you are well again. Stop sinning or something worse may happen to you" (John 5:14). Likewise, He called the woman to stop sinning, presenting her with a choice of life or death.

She must have wondered, *Can it be? Is He really saying I can go home?* The crowd had not dispersed. No doubt they were spellbound by what they had observed. They had watched the accusers leave without argument. Now everyone watched, flabbergasted, as the woman stumbled past them to leave the temple grounds. She had a lot to think about; they all did.

What became of this woman? We don't know. It would be incredibly foolish of her to come so close to death and go back and risk it again. Surely her traumatic experience left an indelible mark in her soul. Her experience of Christ's mercy and tenderness in the face of her own sinfulness must have left an even deeper mark. Her guilt-laden heart had been healed and her sins forgiven. Wouldn't she henceforth offer her life to God? We trust so.

Her sin would still have consequences, but soon Christ would take the guilt from her completely. Bearing her guilt in His own body on the cross, He would wash her heart clean and cure her guilt-laden heart for all eternity.

As far as the east is from the west, so far has he removed our transgressions from us.

PSALM 103:12

But he was pierced for our transgressions, he was crushed for our iniquities; the punishment that brought us peace was upon him, and by his wounds we are healed.

ISAIAH 53:5

LESSONS FOR OUR OWN HEARTS

In the last chapter we saw a woman who was sexually exploited. We have just seen a woman here, however, who chose her own path of sexual sin. She had willfully violated God's law, and she deserved punishment. What a terrifying disaster she had brought upon herself. Her private sin became a public scandal as she stood before the crowd in her "valley of the shadow of death."

Her accusers imagined that Jesus had no escape from their trap; He had no right to show mercy and grace to an adulteress. But this was not the first time Jesus had dealt with a sinful woman. On at least two prior occasions, He had extended grace to guilty women—the Samaritan woman at the well and the sinful woman who came to Him at the house of Simon the Pharisee. In all of these encounters Jesus consistently demonstrated compassion and mercy toward sinners. He treated each woman redemptively, looking for her restoration, not her ruin. And He treats us *all* redemptively! God gave Moses the Law, but God in flesh chooses mercy, for "mercy triumphs over judgment!" (James 2:13).

When your heart suffers the ravages of guilt, here are some things to remember:

We Are Guilty

Did Christ wink at the woman's sin? In no way. He felt compassion and even sympathy for the weakness that drove her to her crime. But He despises sin, and He would never condone sinful behavior (Matthew 15:19). In our age of false mercy, however, many react at even the concept of sin, particularly as it describes consensual sexual behavior. "Live and let live. Who are *you* to judge?"

But sinners *should* feel guilty. It is in their best interest to feel convicted for their sins, because then they can repent and call upon God's mercy and grace. The adulteress was forced to deal with the full weight of her sin, and acknowledging her need of grace and forgiveness was not hard for her to do.

Yet those hurling the accusations were guilty, too. Their self-righteousness, however, blinded them to their own sinfulness. When we point our index finger at someone else, we should see the three fingers pointing back at us—a reminder of things in our own lives that are not what they should be. This calls for humility, even at times when God may need us to minister to others ensnared in willful sin—"for *all* have sinned and fall short of the glory of God" (Romans 3:23).

Whether we stand with the woman or with her accusers, whether we feel guilty or not, we are all guilty before God and deserve His judgment. We may defensively protest our innocence, but He in whom "there is no darkness at all" (1 John 1:5) knows our hearts and has all the facts. Before Him our self-righteous pretenses will quickly be exposed, resulting in utter disgrace and humiliation.

Catching a glimpse of a TV interview with a celebrity who has been in and out of every sordid behavior, I was amazed to hear her say that she had never felt guilty—nor would she let herself. Too bad. Whether or not she feels guilty is irrelevant. Her guilt before God is a fact, and she desperately needs to seek His deliverance before it's too late. Siding with her, many in our culture might consider any guilt feelings self-destructive. But again if we are guilty, we *should* feel guilty. The great problem today is that, lacking reverence for God, we do not let ourselves be accountable for our guilt toward Him.

False guilt can come when we give heed to condemnation even after receiving Christ's forgiveness. This is very damaging and not of God. But true guilt is healthy, even a gift from God. He gave us consciences for a reason, and true guilt feelings mean that our consciences are awakened, not "seared as with a hot iron" (1 Timothy 4:2). The guilt we have over our sinful condition is the starting place for genuine repentance. Playing a crucial role in our salvation, guilty feelings make us conscious of our sinfulness, drive us from our sinful self-reliance to trust in Christ, and keep us on "the straight and narrow."

God Has Great News for Us

Christ sent the Holy Spirit to "convict the world of guilt in regard to sin and righteousness and judgment" (John 16:8). He defers imposing sentences on sinners to allow His Spirit ample opportunity to do His convicting work. The great news for us is that while we cannot stand up and defend ourselves in God's courtroom, Jesus Christ offered himself as a guilt offering in our defense (Isaiah 53:10). We were captive to sin and death, but He gave His life to free us. His blood meets the full demand for justice, wielding a deathblow to the guilt and sin that so offends God's holiness and severs our relationship with Him. Praise the Lord for His atoning sacrifice that paid for our sins in full measure. Through Christ we find pardon, our relationship with God is restored, and we receive eternal life. How sad that many think God delights in condemning people when He sent His Son not to condemn but to save.

> *For God did not send his Son into the world to condemn the world, but to save the world through him.*
>
> JOHN 3:17

But we must repent of our sins. Christ extended grace to the woman, but He never told her, "Everything is okay now. You're forgiven. Now you just go back to living however you want to live, and everything will turn out all right." No, His compassionate grace was accompanied by a strong call to repentance. His offer of grace was free, but unless she repented, she would not experience the benefits of grace. Rather, she would incur more guilt and ultimate judgment. She had an eternal choice to make—repent or perish (Luke 13:3, 5). Each of us must make that choice.

Christ is the perfect balance of justice and mercy, grace and truth. He knows everything about us but cares more about what we might become than what we have been. Never condoning sin, He consistently calls us to repent and follow Him. Repentance is where our old life leaves off and our new life begins. When we truly repent and trust Him for salvation, He declares us "not guilty." Taking our guilt, He no longer sees "sinner" but "saint" written across our heart. We are "born again." The old person we were is buried, and we begin a new life, clean and free. When God forgives, He truly forgives!

Though your sins are like scarlet, they shall be as white as snow; though they are red as crimson, they shall be like wool.

ISAIAH 1:18

You will again have compassion on us; you will tread our sins under-foot and hurl all our iniquities into the depths of the sea.

MICAH 7:19

We Must Release Our Guilt

Some people feel so guilt-ridden about their pre-Christian past that they cannot fully accept God's grace. They come to Christ for salvation but keep repenting over and over for sins long forgiven. Plagued by guilt and feeling that God has not forgiven or accepted them, they run to the altar repeatedly, crying to be saved. One of my relatives had asked Jesus into her heart so many times that she lost count. She just could not believe she was forgiven. One day, however, she finally reached out in faith and truly believed. If we sincerely repent, we can rest assured that He forgives and forgets our former sins. He wants us to *know* He has saved us. He wants us to go forward in our lives with new purpose and perspective—all things made new.

One young woman whom Clay and I counseled had been a heroin addict prior to becoming a Christian and had supported her habit through prostitution. As a Christian, she could intellectually acknowledge that Christ died for her sins, but she still felt guilty. One day as we counseled her, Clay convinced her that Jesus had taken her guilt, that He paid for it on the cross, that it was rightfully His, and, consequently, it was a sin for her to hold on to it. As we prayed together, she renounced this false guilt and experienced the full release of God's forgiveness and grace. After that, an infection related to her past activities, one for which she had received eight years of treatments, suddenly disappeared! She was spiritually *and* physically healed by the power of Christ's atoning blood.

Another young woman we met had had an abortion prior to becoming a Christian. Since then she had come to Christ and married a prominent Christian lawyer. For some reason Clay asked her if she had any children. She burst into tears. She had tried unsuccessfully to have a child but kept having miscarriages. She told us it was because God was judging her for her abortion. God had already forgiven her sin, but in not forgiving herself, she had been unable to experience release from this sin and its consequences in her life. We led her in a prayer to renounce her false guilt and to receive God's forgiveness.

Two months later we heard she was pregnant, and seven months after that, she became the mother of a baby boy. Both young women had confessed and repented of their sins, but self-condemnation had kept them from receiving the full provision of God's grace. Finally they both learned that "if the Son sets you free, you will be free indeed" (John 8:36).

The apostle Paul had to deal with tremendous guilt when He

came to Christ. He had tried to wipe out Christianity, and by his own admission he was a "blasphemer and a persecutor and a violent man" (1 Timothy 1:13) and "the worst of sinners" (1 Timothy 1:16). As a Christian, he no doubt remembered many faces of those he had tried to ruin. Yet knowing that Christ had forgiven him, he refused to dwell in the past.

Some of us, too, would do nearly anything to change our past. We can make restitution where possible, but beyond that, we must simply accept God's forgiveness and go on. Our hope is in Christ, and we must let go of what we once were and eagerly look to what He is making us to be. Listen to how Paul deals with his past: "But one thing I do: Forgetting what is behind and straining toward what is ahead, I press on toward the goal to win the prize" (Philippians 3:13-14). He had good reason to forget what was behind him, and so do we. If you still kick yourself for things for which God has forgiven you, stop, and get on with serving God.

Still, in our human frailty, we sometimes sin as Christians. When the Holy Spirit convicts us of our sin, we can feel a terrible sense of guilt. The question is, where will we go from there? We should gratefully receive His conviction as an act of His grace, not of condemnation. He wants us to confess and repent of our sins, receive His forgiveness, leave our guilt behind, and go forward with a clean slate (1 John 1:9). He does not convict us to beat us up with guilt but to restore us to fellowship with Him.

Some professing Christians seem to take God's grace so lightly that they repeatedly fall into sin with barely a thought. But others struggle under a perpetually oppressive load of guilt that blocks the channel of God's grace. Their cry is that of the psalmist: "My guilt has overwhelmed me like a burden too heavy to bear" (Psalm 38:4). Christ wants us to know that if we confess our sin and trust Him to forgive us, that He does forgive us, and we have no right or reason to carry the guilt any longer. He has taken it and nailed it to the cross.

My dear children, I write this to you so that you will not sin. But if anybody does sin, we have one who speaks to the Father in our defense—Jesus Christ, the Righteous One.

1 JOHN 2:1

Let us draw near to God with a sincere heart in full assurance of faith, having our hearts sprinkled to cleanse us from a guilty conscience and having our bodies washed with pure water.

HEBREWS 10:22

We should never let the devil browbeat us into thinking and feeling that God has rejected us. Our enemy tries incessantly to undermine our confidence in our position in Christ by exposing our weaknesses and inconsistencies. With heaping condemnation, he reminds us of all our past sins and failures. But God's Word defeats the accusations of this "accuser" of God's people (Revelation 12:10). When he throws our sins in our face, we can throw the truth in his. Here's the truth: *"There is now no condemnation for those who are in Christ Jesus"* (Romans 8:1). Christ's Gospel silences the devil's accusations. He may drag us before the judgment bench and call for a guilty verdict, but he has no right to drag us anywhere, and he has no right to reopen our case. We stand our ground against his accusations, not because of our own goodness but because of Christ's provision of grace on the cross of Calvary.

We Should Approach the Throne of Grace

I had to learn this the hard way. As a youngster, I never felt I matched up to what anybody expected of me—not my parents, not God, not even myself. When I came to the Lord, I was so happy to know that God loved and accepted me. Suddenly I was the somebody I had always wanted to be. I was His child; I was special. With the characteristic zeal of a young Christian, I spent every waking hour witnessing, serving, worshiping, and reading His Word. I was "on fire" for Jesus and did everything I could to please Him.

That's where I got into trouble—with pleasing Him. I had come to the Lord by grace because I did not "measure up," but now since He had done so much for me, I thought He expected me to measure up and be perfect. But strive as I might, I saw the glaring inconsistencies in my life and screamed, "Who will rescue me from this body of death?" (Romans 7:24).

Becoming a perfect Christian proved increasingly illusive. Despite my striving, I dealt with constant feelings of inadequacy, failure, condemnation, and rejection. My heart became so guilt-laden that a cloud of gloom enshrouded me. One day Clay said, "Okay, I want you to think of ten good things about yourself. What's number one?" I could not think of a single good thing about me, and I resented his making me try. But he persisted and even brought in a friend to help. Together they thought of ten good things for me: 1. You picked a good husband (Clay beamed); 2. You have a good heart; 3. You're committed to the church; 4. You want to try; 5. You love the Lord; 6. You are steadfast; 7. You are redeemed, cleansed, sanctified by the blood of Jesus; 8. You are a good writer; 9. You're a good wife and mother; 10. You're a good discerning minister. I rejected every one of them.

One year had been a particularly bad one. Experiencing little victory but much guilt and condemnation, I had done a lot of introspective "navel gazing," trying to figure out where I had gone wrong. It seemed to me I was under God's curse, or, at the very least, He was either angry or exasperated with me. "I know God loves me," I lamented, "but He can't stand me." I just knew that God ducked out of His throne room when He saw me pray. "Oh no!" He would say. "It's that whiner again; tell her I'm out!"

The new year was coming, and I was sick of my miserable existence. I decided, "I've had enough of this. I'm going to fast, pray, and find God or die." So I began a "Daniel fast" on January 1. Daniel had fasted for three weeks, humbling himself, not eating meat or choice food. So I would do likewise and get up early each morning and spend a solid hour in worship, Bible meditation, and prayer.

One morning the Lord led me to the book of Esther. I noticed that Esther approached the king's throne fearfully because anyone approaching the king (her husband) uninvited might be put to death. She explained to Mordecai, "The only exception to this is for the king to extend the gold scepter to him and spare his life" (Esther 4:11). It had been a month since the king had called for her, and she feared the worst if she went to him uninvited. But saying, "If I perish, I perish," she went ahead and approached him. To her great relief, he was pleased to receive her and gladly extended his scepter to her.

I knew God's promise about coming boldly to His throne of grace but had been unable to apply it to my life. As I pondered Esther, however, the Holy Spirit convinced my heart that I had a King of kings unlike that earthly king. Not wanting me to ever become insecure about my standing with Him, my King has given me an open invitation to come join Him in His throne room. In fact, He never wants me to leave! Ever wanting me near Him, my King extends His scepter to me as soon as I approach. Not only does He wait for me to come and touch it, but He even invites me to sit with Him—yes, I'm seated with Christ in the heavenly realms (Ephesians 2:6).

I suddenly saw that the guilt and condemnation so weighing my heart down was from the devil. In my mind's eye I marched boldly to that throne of grace and reached out and touched my King's extended scepter—what I called the scepter of approval and acceptance. Hope filled my heart as I took hold of this truth.

After this, I went to the throne of grace repeatedly. But the transformation of my way of thinking did not take place overnight. So accustomed was I to accepting the devil's "guilt trips" that I wrote out a little confession something like this: "I am God's beloved daughter, a child of the King. He delights in my coming to Him; He waits for my visit. He does not disapprove of me. In fact, He always holds out His scepter to me. I cast aside guilt and unworthiness; I refuse to accept them any longer. I reach out and touch the scepter; I receive God's grace and approach His throne boldly. Praise You, Father, for loving me!"

I carried my confession in my pocket during the day and pulled it out to read whenever accusing thoughts returned. Whenever I did stumble into some sin, I confessed it and took it to the throne of grace. Whenever the devil accused me and made me feel worthless, I took that to the throne of grace, too. This new perspective literally changed my life. At the throne of grace, tormenting feelings of guilt and failure always evaporate, leaving me with a clear conscience and the joy of the Lord.

Let us then approach the throne of grace with confidence, so that we may receive mercy and find grace to help us in our time of need.

HEBREWS 4:16

Do you have unresolved guilt in your heart? Has the devil used people, circumstances, or your own guilty conscience to pummel you, making you feel like a despicable creature? Then, dear sister with a guilt-laden heart, it is time to silence those accusing voices that tell you that you are a terrible excuse for a Christian, that the throne of grace is not for you. The devil has barged into God's throne room and accused you. He has worn your heavenly Father's heart out with his accusations against you. It grieves the Lord that you have endured these accusations and let a guilt-laden heart keep you away from Him and His abundant provision.

The Lord wants you to stop shrinking back. He wants you to realize that the father of lies has no right or authority to stand before God's throne accusing you when Christ has absolved you. The throne room is not for him, and the scepter is not held out to him. The throne room is *yours*, and your King holds His scepter out to *you*. Refuse any longer to hand your enemy an advantage over you by failing to go boldly to the throne of grace. Leave your guilt at the cross, give your heart afresh to the Lord, command your accuser to leave, and march boldly up and receive the truth that sets you free. Yes, touch the extended scepter! When you do this, the Lord will invite you to come join Him where He is seated so that you can begin to "reign in life" (Romans 5:17).

The woman caught in adultery did not need to go home that day with a guilt-laden heart. Weighed down beneath a load of guilt and condemnation, she might have felt inclined to finish what the religious leaders had begun. But Christ had refused to condemn her, showing her mercy instead. She had looked for love in all the wrong places but had finally met the true source of love, the one who loved her purely and perfectly, who did not saddle her heart with guilt, who gave her an opportunity to repent and follow Him in a path of wholeness, purity, and joyful obedience. When we come to Jesus with our guilt, He never fails to say, "Neither do I condemn you; go and sin no more."

Therefore, since we have been justified through faith, we have peace with God through our Lord Jesus Christ, through whom we have gained access by faith into this grace in which we now stand.

ROMANS 5:1-2

. . . this is the true grace of God. Stand fast in it.

1 PETER 5:12

Heart Check

1. As you examine your heart, do you see ways in which your heart has been guilt-laden?

2. How might the Holy Spirit be leading you into freedom?

3. What steps can you take to preserve your freedom in Christ?

4. What lessons can you apply to your life from the story of the woman caught in adultery?

5. Compose a prayer to God in response to this chapter's lessons.

10

The Widow of Nain

THE GRIEVING HEART

LUKE 7:11-17

THE PROCESSION HAD JUST come through the city gate on its way toward that dreadful, odious place. Leading the way was an infinitely sorrowful woman with faltering steps. She had never dreamed of her son riding in this type of parade. But there he was, following close behind her on this dark—no, black—day, his precious body lying cold and lifeless on a funeral bier borne by four pallbearers.

With torn garment, she trudged slowly along in the funeral procession, sobbing her heart out—clear and eloquent testimony to the fact that this had been someone very dear to her. It was not her first trip to the cemetery. She had already preceded another bier down this road—that of her late husband. Anguish coursed through her being. The nightmare this time was beyond anything she could have imagined. How she had loved her son! He was her only son, her joy, her very life since her husband's death. To make matters worse, his death was untimely; he was but a youth! She tried not to question, but she couldn't help it. *Why, God? You already took my husband. Why now my son? Aren't You a friend of widows? How can I survive?*

Her heart ached so intensely that she thought she might die. She wanted to. Could any catastrophe result in deeper feelings of abandonment and deprivation? The spirit of death had stamped through her family, and he might as well take her, too. He seemed to stalk her, tempting, taunting, convincing her that her life was over. Under his sway, her cry was, *It's hopeless. Take me, too!*

Had her pain come as a sudden and shattering trauma, an accident perhaps? Or had it come from some chronic and protracted agony? Whichever, a thunderbolt of grief had jagged through her heart. Her son had not been dead long now, for customs dictated that a body be washed, anointed, wrapped, mourned over, and buried within a day. This offered her no time to adjust to her new reality.

The family was responsible to prepare the body for prompt burial, and no doubt her neighbors had helped her with the loathsome task. Every thought of it plunged her deeper into grief. She relived it a thousand times and could still feel the cold skin that so shortly before had been warm. Praying desperately, she had strained to detect some sign of life, but her beloved son, once so bright with promise, was now a breathless, unresponsive corpse.

If only she could hear him laugh or sing or even express anger again. *This can't be; it just can't be. I've got to wake up from this nightmare.* She staggered on, knowing that every step brought her closer to the place where she must see her dear son put into the ground and out of her life forever. She would have to turn and go home—but to what? She could not bear the thought.

We call her broken and tortured heart The Grieving Heart. She had lost her future; she had lost her hope. Her son was all she had for support—her family, her joy, her life. This was death at its worst. In her culture women had few opportunities to earn a living. Totally dependent on men, widowhood put them at great risk, often exposing them to fraud and exploitation. Widows in those days had no financial safety nets or legal rights. They could not even receive an inheritance. After her husband died, therefore, the widow could be grateful still to have a son to care for her. As the new "man of the house," he supported his mother, working hard to keep the home together for them.

But now one of life's greatest desolations had befallen her. Since she was past childbearing age, remarriage was not an option. Unless relatives decided to take her in, she had no one to care for her in old age. Destitute, she would be reduced to begging for the rest of her life! Not only this, but with no male heir, the family line would be cut off in Israel.

Try not to think about it, she told herself. *Just get past the funeral—then worry about the future.* Nevertheless, since the business of living meant a fate worse than death, she would feel like flinging herself into the grave with her son once they got to the site.

Jesus Christ meanwhile had just journeyed twenty-five miles from the Galilean town of Capernaum where He had healed the centurion's servant. His ministry was in full bloom, and He and His disciples were surrounded by a large crowd. Going up the road toward Nain (modern Nein), they must have been enjoying the sights. Nain stood on the northwest slope of Mt. Moreh (modern Jebel ed-Duhy) overlooking the beautiful plain of Esdraelon. Perhaps this was the reason the town's name meant "lovely." This day, however, was anything but lovely for the people of Nain.

It was a small town, and it seemed everyone had turned out for the funeral. Honoring the dead was important in Jewish culture. Social obligation dictated that people drop whatever they were doing and join a funeral procession as it passed by. The large crowd accompanying the widow shows that people felt deep sympathy for her tragedy. For death to strike the only son of a widow was considered a shattering blow.

Mourners in Jewish culture expressed their grief demonstratively. As the procession moved toward the burial site, some worked themselves into a near emotional frenzy. All expressed their grief aloud, weeping, wailing, and beating their breasts. A family of means would hire a group of professional mourners to assure an orderly and ritually correct ceremony. While this woman could not afford much, she probably still had a few since custom dictated that even the poor must "hire not less than two flutes and one wailing woman" (Ketuboth 4:4, *Tyndale NT Commentary, Gospel of Luke,* p. 140).

The widow was leaving, followed by a large crowd, as Jesus was arriving, followed by a large crowd. Two crowds, two processions, two amazingly different contextual realities were on a collision course. One manifested death, the other life; one was on its way to a grave, the other to glory; one was filled with grief and despair, the other with joy and expectation. So what would happen in this encounter?

From some distance Jesus and His crowd could hear the cacophony of shrieking voices coming toward them. They knew it was a funeral procession leaving Nain for a burial place. As the two crowds neared each other, Jesus could see the open bier (a long plat-form) and the enshrouded body. He also saw the bereaved woman looking as if she might die any second. At the front of their respec-tive crowds, she and Jesus would be the first to meet. As He came toward her, she stared blankly, perhaps wondering if He would join her procession.

Jesus was no doubt tired and needed to rest. But this grieving woman was just the type of person He had come to help. Distressed women always stirred His heart, and He felt special concern for wid-ows. Sometimes He even sharply denounced their oppressors (Mark 12:40; Luke 20:47). When He saw her, He felt her heartache and agony; her tears were too much for Him to bear.

Perhaps His own mother was widowed by now, and He had wit-nessed her grief. But here was a case of compounded grief. While the mourners would all return to their homes and enjoy their families, this widow would return to emptiness. Stirred to the depths of His being and overflowing with compassion, "his heart went out to her" (Luke 7:13). The Greek word used here, *splanchnizomai*, is an intense word for describing sympathy. Suggesting a deep yearning compas-sion, it impels one to action and is also used of the father's compas-sion as he ran to meet his prodigal son (Luke 15:20).

Jesus had to do something. Would He offer her His deep con-dolences? Would He reach out and touch her, making her heart strong? Would He give her some hope-filled word of encourage-ment? Would He join ranks and wail with her? The Lord of life would do none of these things. Striding up with jaw firm, muscles tight, and heart burning, He broke up this procession of mourning, knocked the crown of gloom off the poor, grieving mother's head, and replaced it with a "crown of beauty" (Isaiah 61:3).

He said to her, "Don't cry" (Luke 7:13). Her swollen eyes stared with amazement at Him. She had expected some verbal condolence. *Who is this who tells me not to cry?* Those nearby stood dumfounded, wondering, *What kind of person would tell this woman who has lost her only son, who is a widow, and has lost everything in this world, "Don't cry?"*

Even a fool would know that it never comforts people in grief to tell them to cheer up. Telling this grieving woman not to cry would seem insensitive, even cruel, under normal circumstances. But these were not normal circumstances. She had just met Jesus, the Christ, the Son of the living God! He and He alone could give her a reason to stop her mourning. He, and only He, had the power to dry her tears. His simple words—"Don't cry"—were pregnant with comfort, hope, and promise.

No one had asked Him for help, but turning from the widow, He approached the bier carrying the stiff and straight corpse—Oh, how the Lord hated death!—and reached out to touch it. It was no gingerly touch, for the Greek word used here means to "lay hold" or "fasten oneself to." He grabbed hold of the bier so firmly that the pallbearers stopped the procession in its tracks.

The cacophony of wailing voices immediately died; a hush fell over everyone. They all knew something unusual was taking place, for Jesus did what religious leaders never did. First, He interrupted a funeral, a flagrant violation of Jewish law and custom. Second, He touched a bier carrying a corpse, exposing Himself to the severest form of ritual uncleanness in Judaism (Numbers 19:16). Only those closest to the deceased would intentionally expose themselves to such impurity. But Jesus completely ignored the ceremonial laws concerning defilement.

What the people did not yet know was that when facing human need, Jesus never worried about religious trifles or social conventions. In fact, with Him the influence always went the other direction. Nothing could make Him unclean; instead, He made the unclean clean again.

Compassion was regularly the motive of Jesus' miracles, and while He had not yet raised anyone from the dead at this point in His ministry, He intended to challenge death now. Defying the natural laws that held the young man lifeless, He who is "the Resurrection and the Life" spoke directly and with authority to the corpse: "Young man, I say to you, get up!" (Luke 7:14). In the words "*I* say to you," He declared His supreme authority. He was the one who told Moses, "I am." He was God the Son incarnate, and with divine power to match His words, He proved it.

Before the crowd of mourners could scold Christ for tastelessly raising false hopes for the widow and her dead son, there was a moving of the Spirit. Before they could rebuke Him for defiling Himself, and before they could doubt and laugh at His words, a *miracle* took place. The Spirit of life challenged the spirit of death, and death moved over. Immediately, the lifeless heart started beating, the stagnant blood began flowing, the cold body regained warmth and color, and the departed spirit returned. The young man who had been dead sat straight up.

You will grieve, but your grief will turn to joy.

JOHN 16:20

If the pallbearers had not already put down the bier, we can imagine that they would have dropped it! This was the shock of everyone's lives. They stood frozen, staring at the unfolding scene. Then, to everyone's further amazement, the young man spoke. He was one of the few to cross the river of death and come back to tell about it. Don't we wonder what he had to say?

Perhaps he said something like this: "Mom! What happened? I thought I was dying. I *did* die! But then I heard a voice shake my entire being awake. It commanded me to get up, and I couldn't help it—I got up! Now, please get these grave clothes off me and get me some real clothes. Tell the mourners they can go home and ask the funeral director for a refund. Tell the gravedigger that I'm not coming. I'm going home! I'm alive! Praise the Lord!"

Undoubtedly, Jesus felt the joy of that moment. Perhaps with His own heart rejoicing, He led the widow to her son and clasped their two hands together. What joy must have filled their hearts! We can only imagine the scene. The widow and her son embracing, weeping, laughing, and praising Jesus together. They were ready to begin life anew, filled with gratitude toward the one who had given them back their lives.

Jesus did not tell the young man to come follow Him as He could have. Instead, Jesus gave the widow back her son to provide for her. In restoring her son, He wasn't trying to gain a follower. He wasn't trying to make a scene or prove a point. Compassion had spontaneously moved His heart to perform a miracle of mercy for the widow's comfort and blessing.

Awe and wonder fell on everyone who witnessed this wondrous event. What manner of man could, with one mighty command, reach across the netherworld's dark threshold to extricate a departed spirit from death's firm jaws? Jesus Christ had more than proved Himself. Not only was He the Lord of life, but He was also the Lord over death.

Knowing that this amazing miracle could only be attributable to divine power, everyone praised and glorified God for graciously visiting them. "A great prophet has appeared among us," they said. "God has come to help his people" (Luke 7:16). Knowing their Bible stories, they remembered the great Old Testament prophets Elijah and Elisha who both gave dead boys back to their mothers alive. The raising of one even took place a few miles from Nain in Shunem.

While their understanding was incomplete, their conclusion that Jesus was a great prophet was true. But Jesus is, of course, more than a great prophet. Elijah and Elisha both prayed earnestly for the dead boys and even laid themselves upon their bodies, but Jesus did not need to pray or go through any rituals. He simply commanded the young man back to life, thus exhibiting that He stands alone as the divine Son of God.

With shrieks of grief turned to shouts of joy, the funeral crowd became a festal crowd. The former pallbearers hoisted the miracle boy high on the former bier and fell into line behind Jesus in His victory parade. Both crowds were one now, and as the joyous procession with its single float proceeded back through Nain's gate, what exuberance must have filled the city. Jesus Christ had indeed turned their "mourning into dancing" (Psalm 30:11 NRSV).

People published this miracle widely. The news spread throughout Judea and to the surrounding country. John the Baptist, languishing in prison, heard the story. Needing his faith strengthened during this difficult time, he sent two of his disciples to Jesus with a question: "Are you the one who was to come, or should we expect someone else?" (Luke 7:19). Jesus said to them, "Go back and report to John what you have seen and heard: The blind receive sight, the lame walk, those who have leprosy are cured, the deaf hear, *the dead are raised,* and the good news is preached to the poor" (Luke 7:22, emphasis added). This report undoubtedly gave John hope and confidence as he faced his own early death.

The Spirit of the Sovereign LORD is on me, because the LORD has anointed me to preach good news to the poor. He has sent me to bind up the brokenhearted . . . to comfort all who mourn, and provide for those who grieve in Zion—to bestow on them a crown of beauty instead of ashes, the oil of gladness instead of mourning, and a garment of praise instead of a spirit of despair.

ISAIAH 61:1-3

LESSONS FOR OUR OWN HEARTS

A few months ago I joined my close friends at the graveside service of their precious granddaughter who died suddenly of SIDS. The little white coffin was the tiniest I had ever seen. Only hours before her death, the proud parents had brought home darling photos of their little angel for family and friends to coo over. Who could not wonder, *Why, God?*

Jesus told His disciples, "In the world you have tribulation" (John 16:33 RSV). And it doesn't take a rocket scientist to see that His assessment is true. Even when life seems smooth and everything is going our way, we don't know what is coming down the pike. When we least expect it, life can throw us some terrible zinger that hits like a sledgehammer. Instantly our hearts careen from contentment mode to crisis mode, from comfort zone to distress zone, from happy-go-lucky to grief-stricken. Matthew Henry said, "Our mountain never stands so strong but it may be moved, and therefore, in this world we must always rejoice with trembling."

We can count on two things in this life: *Life is short*—"What is your life? You are a mist that appears for a little while and then vanishes" (James 4:14). *Death is certain*—"Just as man is destined to die once, and after that to face judgment" (Hebrews 9:27). Truly, none of us can be sure of our next moment of life on this planet.

Crowds of people witnessed an awesome miracle one day in the town of Nain, but eventually they all entered their grave, the widow's son included. In fact, everyone Jesus ever healed in the New Testament died! The funeral business never dried up then, and it has never dried up since. Unless Jesus Christ returns first, death is a debt we must all pay. With 2,300,000 people estimated to die in America alone this year, The National Funeral Directors Association boasts that demand is great for people to enter their profession. All over the planet more people are dying, and more people are grieving than ever—and Death, riding his pale horse, may have barely begun his lethal errand (Revelation 6:8).

But God's Son came into this world of woe to bring us hope. After He told His disciples that troubles were a part of life in this world, He said, "But be of good cheer, I have overcome the world" (John 16:33 RSV). Moved by the pathos of human experience, Christ constantly exhibited His Father's compassionate heart. In His ministry to the widow of Nain, we glimpse His contempt for and power over death. Not only did He ruin that funeral procession, but He broke up every funeral He encountered! He hates death and can hardly wait to see this last enemy destroyed (see 1 Corinthians 15:25-26).

We saw it illustrated in our church a few weeks ago. It was a Friday afternoon when Lonna Haslam (a single mom) got a devastating call. Her seventeen-year-old son Rich had been in the wrong place at the wrong time when someone squirted a substance into his mouth. Soon Rich started convulsing, stopped breathing, and went into a coma. He was rushed to a hospital where they put him on life support equipment. Not expecting him to live, doctors asked Lonna about donating Rich's organs. For the next day he had severe seizures every ten minutes, and the doctor said that if he ever came out of the coma, he would be severely brain damaged. Police treated it as a criminal case.

Meanwhile the church prayed fervently, and on Sunday morning we prayed for him in our morning services. As Lonna prayed at the hospital, she suddenly felt peace. Looking at the time, she knew our service was in progress and that we must be praying. That night Rich came out of the coma and pulled out his breathing tube. Lonna was told that recovery from a coma takes days and even weeks, but she saw hourly improvement. Thursday Rich came home, Friday he went to school, and Sunday—exactly one week after we had united in prayer—he testified of his miracle before our cheering congregation.

Christ went into the tomb Friday and returned alive Sunday, and so had Rich. He had been as good as dead, and Christ restored him, handing him back to his grieving single mother. As I watched Rich standing before our congregation, tears streamed down my face. I knew, indeed, that I serve a living Savior who still works miracles.

Yet we cannot always count on dramatic miracles. Sometimes the Lord does them, but often He does not. In fact, He delights in taking His people home to heaven: "Precious in the sight of the LORD is the death of his saints" (Psalm 116:15). His primary mission was never to extend our temporal life here but to secure for us the hope of eternal life with Him in heaven. Here on earth we die, our loved ones die, and rare is the report of a dead person returning to life. There in heaven we live joyfully forever. He wants us to be assured in our "blessed hope" (Titus 2:13).

> *But our citizenship is in heaven. And we eagerly await a Savior from there, the Lord Jesus Christ, who, by the power that enables him to bring everything under his control, will transform our lowly bodies so that they will be like his glorious body.*
>
> PHILIPPIANS 3:20-21

Meanwhile the realities of this life can leave believers—just like everyone else—with grieving hearts. The pain can be especially severe for ones who, unlike the widow of Nain, have had to bury a child. What can compare with a mother's unfailing love—its tender compassion, selfless devotion, undying patience? Hers is a love that "bears all things, believes all things, hopes all things, endures all things" (1 Corinthians 13:7 NRSV). What, then, can be more heart-wrenching than a mother grieving the loss of her beloved child? I thank the Lord that I have not had to deal with this grief. However, I have two dear friends who have.

Jean Bailes, a close friend for many years, lost her only son. She and her husband, Jerry ("Doc"), prayed earnestly for their son. But he died. Unwilling to accept their tragedy, they prayed in faith that he be raised from the dead and even had his shoes with them at the funeral in hopes that he might need to wear them home. But he did not need his shoes. God chose instead to take him home to heaven. "Lord," Jean sobbed, "where were You? Why didn't You answer my prayers? I wanted to see him whole, happy, and healthy." Instantly she heard God's still, small voice reply, "He is." She cried, "But, Lord, You don't understand—he was my *only* son!" She knew at once what she had said, that she had it wrong, that God understood fully what it was like to lose an only son.

Jean surrendered her grieving heart to the Lord, and He healed her. Today, many years later, she says that she can still feel the pain of that time but rejoices in the happy memories, too. She saw lives changed for good because of her son's death, and she and Jerry grew through it. She admits that they might have become prideful if God had answered their prayers in the way they wanted. She has this advice for people who are grieving: "We can't dwell on what might have been and the expectations we had. God still has us here for some purpose, and we need to get on with whatever it is and not become absorbed in our grief." Jean and Jerry became absorbed in serving the Lord. After Jerry retired from his medical practice, they served for a time as missionaries and still serve Jesus together in many dynamic ways.

Marie Dainow is another dear friend, our former church secretary. Clay and I were in our kitchen sitting at the table one day four years ago when the phone rang. My cheery "hello" was met with an unearthly shrill voice shrieking at me. My first thought was that it must be a crank call. But suddenly the truth became all too real. It was Marie. She was extremely distressed, and she was crying, "John drowned!"

As Clay and I rushed to her house in a panic, we could not believe it was real. Marie, like the widow of Nain, was a widow, and John was her only son. She was our closest friend, a dedicated Christian who served God with her whole heart. John had returned to the Lord a number of years earlier and loved the Lord with all his heart. He was a high school teacher and was about to go to seminary in preparation for ministry. Marie couldn't have been more pleased.

Only a month before, he had sent her a birthday card expressing his gratitude for her prayers and example and confirming his intention to serve Jesus for the rest of his life. *It can't be; it just can't be*, I thought. But it was true. Vacationing amid the towering peaks and tumbling falls of Yosemite, John tried to rescue his dog from a swift current and drowned.

John was popular with his high school students, and it seemed that at least a hundred of them attended and wept at the large funeral. Seeing the lives he had touched, plus receiving cards and expressions of solace, gave Marie strength and comfort. She surrendered her sorrowing heart to God, and He carried her through the grieving process into recovery.

Hungering for her roots and sensing God's leading, Marie moved back to her native land of Ireland. While she does not understand why the Lord allowed her son to die, she sees how God has used it. She says, "God has used my testimony to help others in some small way to cope with the trauma of grief here in Northern Ireland, a place that has known unbelievable trauma. The sectarian violence of the past thirty-two years has left families devastated as loved ones were gunned down or killed in bomb explosions. For the past year and a half I have been part of the Christian Renewal Centre, which has been committed to reconciliation and has opened its doors to many hurting and devastated people in this province."

Gladys Staines recently lost her beloved husband and two sons in a savage attack in India. A mob of Hindu extremists, hating the Christian missionaries, burned them to death in their car. Despite her overwhelming grief, however, Gladys refuses to become bitter. Courageously forgiving the murderers and committing herself to continue the work among India's lepers, her action in the wake of such hatred has reverberated throughout the nation of over a billion people. The police commissioner said, "She is a remarkable one—a great Christian." A Hindu swami said she "has reached a spiritual height." Says Gladys, "That is the Christianity we are asked to practice; we have to work and show that Jesus is worth dying for."

She also says that she can now relate with women who have lost loved ones in plane crashes, road accidents, or caste-related violence. She has a thirteen-year-old daughter who also stunned the nation on numerous television interviews by saying, "God thought it worthy to take my father home."*(Source: www.newsroom.org. Used by permission.)*

Can you see how these grieving hearts let their trials make them better persons rather than bitter persons? Their victory came, not by denying their grief, but by surrendering it to the Lord and turning outward in service to others. Some with grieving hearts, however, stay angry and become bitter. Unable to understand why God failed to restore their loved one, their heart protests, *How dare You, God; it's not fair!"*

I certainly have no easy answers. But we need to have a higher regard for God, a deeper sense of His character—His holiness, righteousness, integrity—and a deeper sense of our finiteness. We see in a mirror dimly; we know in part (1 Corinthians 13:12), and finite flesh can never comprehend the ways of our infinite God. Just because we cannot understand Him does not hand us a reason to charge Him with injustice and cruelty. We simply do not have the resources for putting God on trial. Even confused and grieving Job, after having lost ten children in one day, had to confess, "Far be it from God to do evil, from the Almighty to do wrong. It is unthinkable that God would do wrong, that the Almighty would pervert justice" (Job 34:10, 12).

Here is what we know for certain about God: He is not negligent, unkind, or unloving; that being unjust in any way would be impossible for Him; that His ways are higher than our own; that He does not violate a person's free will; that the destructive influence of sin pervades our world; that, despite it all, God works everything for ultimate good in the lives of His people (Romans 8:28). He is the all-powerful and sovereign Lord of all.

While grief is not sin, and we need to allow ourselves both time and grace as we work through our grief, we also should watch our heart toward God. The devil works subtly in the lives of Christians. One of his favorite devices is to sow doubt. When we are grieving, he can incite us to ask, "If God is a God of love, why did He allow this?" We need to trust that the one who made us, the one who holds the whole universe together by His word, is a loving Father and a compassionate Savior who ultimately weaves all things for good. He never singles out and punishes His children by afflicting them with grief.

Perhaps you think that no one else in the world understands your grieving heart. God does. He has been there. The Stoics who viewed God as unfeeling and indifferent were completely wrong. As He watched His beloved Son die a torturous death—perfect innocence, purity, and love incarnate—what grief must have flooded His father-heart. Jesus Himself was "a man of sorrows, and acquainted with grief" (Isaiah 53:3 KJV). Look at Him stirred to the depths of His soul, so sympathetic, so tender, toward the grieving little woman of Nain. What an eloquent testimony that God cares!

This same quality of tender compassion drove Christ to lay His life down for our redemption. Let this encourage your heart, dry your eyes, and inspire you with eternal hope. Acknowledge His sovereignty, and, rather than getting angry and offended, let Him comfort you. See the raising of the widow's son as a dress rehearsal for what will soon come. Jesus, the Lord of life and death, could alone wipe away this mother's tears, and He will soon wipe away every tear from the eyes of those who trust Him.

When we offer our broken and grieving hearts to Him, His Spirit moves to give us some tender mercy, some sweet revelation of His love to comfort and encourage us. One Christmas Marie walked into church to the joyful strains of, "Angels We Have Heard on High." As she joined the joyous refrain—"Glo-o-o-ria"—her own heart got transported to heavenly realms where she knew she was joining the heavenly choirs, including her son John, in praising God for His Son's birth. She said, "I left church full of peace and with a deeper awareness that in God's eternal timeline death is indeed a very temporary separation. I can look forward to that great reunion some day soon when there will be no more tears or sorrow."

Yes, and heaven's choirs keep singing. If only we can grasp it! Jesus Christ did. He was acquainted with grief and knew He would die on the cross, but He had joy in His heart (Luke 10:21). Knowing the larger picture, the greater plan, the broader purpose, He saw the truth—that His grief and pain would ultimately resolve all the world's grief and pain and that His sacrifice would swallow our present agony in eternal ecstasy.

We think we see reality, but it is so small. In fact, it is not reality at all; it is "virtual" reality. The Bible constantly tries to implant within us true reality, the heavenly perspective. God wants us to listen as He tries to tell us, "You are stuck in your little present when I've got a glorious future for you. I promise that this will be over soon, that your pain will not last, and that you will love the future I have planned for you more than you can imagine. Catch a glimpse of reality!"

My friend Ellen Appleby caught hold of it. She was young but had many physical problems and suffered much under surgeons' scalpels. Yet her face radiated with a knowledge of the reality that I could not yet grasp. For to her, to live was Christ and to die was gain (Philippians 1:21). Her husband, Chuck, was not a believer, and more than anything, Ellen wanted to see him come to Christ. She slipped into a coma, and Chuck came to church and gave his heart to Christ. Clay and I visited her in the ICU and told her the good news. In her comatose state, we did not see the slightest response until a tear formed in her eye and dripped down her cheek. From then on she improved, and soon we had our dear friend back.

Chuck and Ellen became a wonderful blessing to our church together. But one day she went into the hospital again with heart trouble. She told me, "I'm going to die soon." In total denial, I shrugged it off. I couldn't believe her words. *I'll just have to pray more for Ellen,* I thought. Just as I had prayed, she came home.

But late one night we got a call from Chuck. It was Ellen. We rushed to their home in time to see the paramedics wheeling her out. Ellen's extended battle with ill health had ended. But she had not lost; she had won! She had shined Christ's light while imprisoned in a body riddled with handicaps, and she was ready to be with Jesus. I had selfishly wanted to keep her here, but she had shed her crippled earthly tent to soar unrestrained in heaven's heights.

Tonight I took a break from writing and went to a dinner in honor of a dear friend who had died recently. Ida Crotty had become like family to Clay and me, the grandma I had never known. She was eighty-six years young and had enriched our lives in many dimensions. We enjoyed going to her home on a day off, playing Scrabble and eating goodies. We educated her in spiritual things, and she educated us in the arts, science, and history. Truly, she was one of the most stimulating people we had ever known. After she suffered a massive stroke, we visited her often. I prayed and even fasted that God would restore her. I wanted her back for just a few more years. God took her home, though, and Clay and I still grieve our loss.

While Christians suffer grief, for us death—even death of our dearest—is not what it is to those in the world. We know there is eternal life and light behind the veil. Having defeated death, our risen Savior boldly proclaims, "I am the resurrection and the life. Those who believe in me, even though they die, will live" (John 11:25 NRSV). Christians do not really die; they shed their earthly tents, but the real persons go to another sphere, a wondrous place beyond human comprehension. Death is a mere comma, not a period in our lives. It gets us to our heavenly coronation to receive our crown; it ushers us to the ultimate family reunion where we will celebrate together forever. "One hour of eternity, one moment with the Lord, will make us utterly forget a lifetime of desolations" (Horatius Bonar).

When Jesus told the widow, "Don't cry," in essence He was saying, "Don't cry for a dead son, for I will make him a living one!" He says that to all of us who have loved ones who have fallen asleep in Jesus. Therefore, we should not sorrow as if we have no hope: "But we do not want you to be uninformed, brothers and sisters, about those who have died, so that you may not grieve as others do who have no hope" (1 Thessalonians 4:13 NRSV). The same divine and almighty Lord who miraculously raised the widow's son will one day awaken not just one but all of the dead. He will restore all who have fallen asleep in Him to the loved ones who mourned their loss.

Will you in faith surrender your grieving heart to the Lord? Will you offer Him your grief, loneliness, and loss? Will you let Him take your feelings of regret and guilt and failure? Will you turn over to Him your anger, your doubt, and rebellion? Will you praise Him in faith, trusting that the resurrection will come after this dying? Will you let His Spirit refresh your soul as you await the glorious day? If you let Him, He will touch and heal your heart, and you will know the peace that passes understanding and the hope of full surrender. He will turn your "mourning into dancing" (Psalm 30:11 NRSV).

My friend Marie wrote these two poems following her son John's death:

Grief

All hopes now dashed—a son is gone.
O God, it was too soon to die.
I sit and weep, empty in despair.
This wrenching pain, so difficult to bear.

He had such hopes, his world to touch.
Would he make a difference?
He wanted to—so much
Concerned for those in a dying world.

A heart touched by God, a life full of hope,
He shared God's plan with all who'd hear.
His great passion—to live for Jesus more,
To make an impact, try each open door.

Why, Lord, was this plan cut short?
So many questions try this broken heart.
Where can I go, Lord; is there a greater plan?
Heal my pain; I need your strong right arm.

Hope

The Source of Hope, He is not gone.
My beloved child, you are not alone.
I've felt your pain, each bruise I've borne.
Listen, while I sing My song.

A song of hope for you to hear:
Take courage, daughter, have no fear.
Take rest in Father's arms and know
My love secure; I'll never let you go.

See, the sun is shining through—
The warmth of My peace to comfort you,
The gentle wind, My Spirit's dew,
Healing for your wounded heart anew.

He will wipe every tear from their eyes. There will be no more death or
mourning or crying or pain, for the old order of things has passed away.

REVELATION 21:4

Heart Check

1. Are you suffering from a grieving heart?

2. Can you see ways in which God has tried to comfort you with His reality?

3. How has the story of the widow of Nain encouraged your heart?

4. In what ways can you more fully surrender your grief to the Lord?

5. Compose a prayer to God in response to this chapter's lessons.

Addendum to This Chapter

Often God makes me live the lessons I write about, even as I write them. When I began working on this last chapter, I felt nervous, knowing that I had never experienced grief to any real depth and didn't want to either. Upon concluding the chapter, I nearly drew a breath of relief that God had gotten me through it without incident.

Two nights after sending the manuscript in, however, I was jolted by my brother-in-law's call from southern California. "Your mom is in the hospital," he said. "We don't know what happened, but your dad called 9-1-1, and the ambulance came and got her." I immediately called the hospital and was told by the doctor that she had likely suffered a stroke. Clay and I were able to get on a flight early the next morning, but as it turned out, hers was a massive stroke that had completely destroyed her brain stem.

As I stood at her bedside stroking her hair, squeezing her hand, kissing her cheek, crying and praying over her, I kept begging and pleading with the Lord to bring back my beloved Mama. I wanted to tell her how much I loved her, how much I needed her, how much I appreciated her. This could happen to others but not to *my* mother, not to *me*. I kept expressing my displeasure to the Lord: "I hate this, Lord."

The rest of the family had been there most of the night before and had already accepted the inevitability of the situation. The doctor gave her zero chance of recovery. With her brain unable to even signal her lungs to breathe, the only thing that kept her alive was a breathing machine. But I wanted to keep on fighting in prayer, hoping against hope for a miracle. I was the last to yield to God's will.

As my mom lay there unconscious, her earthly tent shutting down, we had a sense that she was no longer there, that her spirit had already gone home to be with Jesus, that the pain and suffering of her life were behind her. But this didn't make it any easier. In fact, I felt no joy or relief. I only felt loss, regret, and a hundred different "if onlys." I hadn't seen my mom for six months and had planned to fly down for a visit a week or two before. Trying to complete this book though, I had dragged my feet and postponed my visit. If only . . . if only . . . if only. *Why, Lord, did You let me make this mistake? Why didn't I get down here? Why didn't You let her wait for me? Why, Lord?*

I had recently grieved the loss of my dear friend Ida—but not like this. Ida's death had been expected. She was quite elderly, and after her stroke she had lived an unhappy existence for fifteen months on a feeding tube, unable to swallow, speak, or think straight. It hurt when she died, but I was prepared to accept her release. But *this*—this was different. This was my one and only mother, the one who had conceived me, anticipated my birth, nursed me, cradled me; the one who had been my longest-standing friend in life.

The Lord has been comforting me and giving me strength. He has not yet answered my questions, however. Instead, I have had to ask myself some hard questions. Will I, like those sisters in Christ I told you about, let my grief make me a better person, not a bitter person? Will I answer positively to the challenging questions I posed at the end of the last chapter? I am working on it.

Whoever you are, dear sister with a grieving heart, please know that I am suffering with you. As we work through our process of recovery, surrendering our broken hearts into our God's loving hands, we will heal together. He is faithful!

God has definitely used this experience in my life to deepen my understanding and empathy for those who are grieving. I appreciate all the more His sustaining grace. We don't always understand our Father's timing and His higher purposes, but in His amazing sovereignty He weaves events together to coincide with His eternal scheme. Listen to the "The Divine Weaver" (author unknown):

My life is but a weaving
Between my Lord and me;
I cannot choose the colors
He works on steadily.

Often He weaves in sorrow
And I, in foolish pride,
Forget that He sees the upper,
And I the underside.

Not till the loom is silent
And the shuttles cease to fly,
Shall God unroll the canvas
And explain the reason why.

The dark threads are as needful
In the Weaver's skillful hand,
As the threads of gold and silver
In the pattern He has planned.

Appendix A:
Prayer of Full Surrender

We do not naturally like the word *surrender*. It evokes images of white flags, defeat, and captivity. Surrendering to Christ, however, means the exact opposite. It means liberation! Ours is a surrender to love, not to bondage. Christ sets us free from our enslavement to the worldly powers of sin and death.

If you have never let the saving grace of Jesus Christ liberate you, or if you are suffering some pain and loss that has made you withdraw from God, I urge you to open your heart to Him now. He loves you and cares about your pain. He may not give you all the answers, but as you trust Him, He will impress you with truth, perspective, comfort, peace, hope, and strength. Surrender your heart to Him in faith. Here is a prayer you can pray aloud:

> Lord Jesus, I see how my sins have separated me from Your love. Thank You for dying on the cross to pay the penalty for my sins. I have shut You out of my life, but now I humbly open my heart's door to You. Please come in by Your grace and take the throne of my life. Please forgive my sins, wash me clean, and carry my burdens. I surrender to Your will; I surrender to Your love. Make me a new person with a new perspective. Help me to live my life in a way that pleases You. I place my hope in You and trust You to work good through my suffering. Thank You for the difference You are making in my life. Amen.

If you have prayed this prayer either as a first-time decision or as a rededication of your life to Christ, congratulations! If you have not done so already, it is most important for you to find a good church to help strengthen and support you in your Christian life. A good church is one that honors God's Word and acts as a loving family. God does not intend for any of His children to suffer alone but to work together for mutual encouragement.

Dear sister in Christ, whatever we go through, we have hope that is "an anchor for the soul, firm and secure" (Hebrews 6:19). One day soon this pain-wracked world will pass away, and we will be transported to Christ's eternal kingdom where He will wipe away every tear from our eyes forever. Meanwhile we can look confidently to His presence and power to heal us, sustain us, and even give us wonderful victories in His Name. He is faithful. Praise the Lord!

Now may I pray for you?

> Father, I pray for my sister. I know You have healing for her heart. As she reads the pages of this book, let her become convinced, too. Show her what she needs to release to You, and enable her to surrender everything in her life—past, present, future—into Your loving hands. As she gives You the cares of her heart, empty her completely of her own solutions, striving, and self-effort. Fill her instead with the pure oil of Your Spirit, and let it flow to her deepest being—encouraging her, infusing her heart with hope, faith, and freedom. Thank You for doing a beautiful work in my sister. Help her to trust Your work and to rest in Your love, knowing You are restoring her. Let her see You working not only in her life but in the lives of those around her. Thank You, Jesus! Amen.

Appendix B: Additional Selected Scriptures

For no matter how many promises God has made, they are "Yes" in Christ . . . (2 Corinthians 1:20).

For Desperate Hearts (Hagar)

2 Sam. 22:7, 17-18; Ps. 18:1-19; 23:1-6; 34:6-7, 15-20; 55:22; 56:13; 118:5; 121; 138:7; 139:1-10; Prov. 18:10; Isa. 41:9-10, 17-20; Jonah 2:2-7; Matt. 7:7-11; 10:28-31; 12:20-21; Luke 12:22-31; John 14:27; Eph. 6:10-18; Heb. 13:5-6

For Harassed Hearts (Hannah)

Ps. 25:1-3; 27:1-3; 31:14-20; 55:16-18; 56:1-4; 60:11-12; 71:12-16; 108:12-13; 118:6-9; 120:1-21; Isa. 41:11-16; Matt. 5:11-12; Mark 13:9; Luke 6:22-23; 12:11-12, 51-53; John 15:18-22; Rom. 8:31; 1 Peter 3:9-17; 4:12-16; Col. 3:15; 1 Thes. 3:2-4; 2 Thes. 1:4-6; 1 John 3:13; 5:4, 19-20; Rev. 3:8-11

For Disappointed Hearts (Elizabeth)

Ps. 57:2; 62:1-2; 92:12-15; 103:5; 138:8; 145:18-21; Prov. 3:5-6; 11:23; Isa. 26:3-4; 54:1-8; Luke 6:20-21; 14:33; Eph. 1:6; 3:7-8; Phil. 4:6-7, 11-13, 19; 2 Thes. 1:11; Heb. 6:15; 11:11-12; 12:1-3, 7-12; James 1:2-4, 12

For Devastated Hearts (Naomi)

Ps. 27:13-14; 71:20-21; 102:17-20; 113:7-9; 119:49-50, 92-93; Isa. 30:18-21; 42:3; 43:1-3; 49:13-21; Lam. 3:18-26; Joel 2:25-27; Zech. 118:9-12; Luke 18:1-8; Rom. 8:28, 35-39; 2 Cor. 1:8-10; Phil. 1:6; James 5:10-11; Rev. 2:10-11

For Languishing Hearts
(Woman with the Issue of Blood)

Ps. 20:1-5; 37:3-6; 40:1-3; 119:49-50, 92-93; Isa. 40:11, 27-31; 46:4; 64:4; Matt. 8:17; 11:28-30; 20:29-34; Mark 10:46-52; Luke 11:5-13; Rom. 5:3-5; 8:18-26; Eph. 1:17-23; 2 Tim. 4:6-8; Heb. 10:32-37

For Crisis-stricken Hearts
(Widow of Zarephath)

Ps. 31:21-24; 33:18-20; 37:16-26; 46:1-3; 56:3-4, 10-11; 57:1, 23; 91:1-16; 94:17; 103:13; 121; Prov. 10:24-5; 30:5; Isa. 33:6; 51:6-8; Jer. 17:7-8; Nahum 1:7; Hab. 3:17-19; Mal. 3:17-18; Matt. 6:25-34; Mark 12:43-44; 2 Cor. 4:7-11; 1 Thes. 1:6-7; Heb. 3:7-14; James 5:13-18; 1 Peter 5:10-11

For Lovelorn Hearts (Leah)

Exo. 15:13; Deut. 3:12; 1 Kings 8:23; 1 Chron. 16:34; Ps. 6:4; 13:5; 17:8; 27:10; 36:5, 7; 57:10; 59:16-17; 63:3-5; 66:20; 86:13, 15; 94:18-19; 103:11; 147:11; Isa. 54:10; 62:3-5, 11-12; Zeph. 3:16-17; Deut. 7:9; John 16:27; 17:23; Eph. 1:3-5; 2:4-9; 3:16-19; Tit. 3:4-6; 1 John 4:10, 19; Rev. 3:9

For Exploited Hearts (Bathsheba)

Ps. 9:9; 10:1-18; 12:5; 14:6-7; 35:10; 37:8-15; 57:3-7; 119:45; 124:6-8; 146:5-10; Prov. 23:10-11; Isa. 33:22; 35:3-4; 41:11-13; 43:18-19; 51:12-14; 55:12-13; 61:1; Jer. 30:17-20; 31:16-17; Ezek. 34:20-28; Zech. 4:6; 9:15; Mal. 4:2-3; Luke 4:18; 2 Cor. 3:17; Gal. 2:4; 5:11; James 2:5-6

For Guilt-laden Hearts
(Woman Caught in Adultery)

Ps. 32:1-5; 34:22; 51:17; 103:8-12; 109:30-31; 145:8-9; Isa. 1:18; 44:21-22; 50:7-9; 54:17; John 3:16-18; Rom. 3:21-25; 5:1-2, 6-10, 17; 6:23; 8:1-3, 15-17, 33-34; 10:9-11; Eph. 2:4-9; 3:12; Col. 1:21-23; 1 Thes. 5:9-10, 23-24; Heb. 4:14-16; 8:12; 9:14-15, 27; 10:19-23; 1 John 5:11-13

For Grieving Hearts (Widow of Nain)

Ps. 10:14; 31:9, 14; 73:21-26; 103:13-18; 116:15; Eccles. 12:7; Isa. 25:8; 26:19; 57:1-2; Hosea 13:14; Matt. 17:22-23; 25:34; John 5:24-29; 6:44; 10:28-29; 11:25-26; 14:1-3, 19; 16:6-7, 20-22; Acts 7:59; 1 Cor. 1:9; 15:13-26, 42-44, 50-55; 2 Cor. 4:16-18; 5:1-8; Phil. 1:20-23; 3:20—4:1; 1 Thes. 4:13-18; 2 Tim. 1:10; Titus 3:4-7; Heb. 2:9, 14-15; 9:27-28; 1 Peter 1:6-7; Rev. 19:6-9

Gratitude for Deliverance

Exo. 15:1-3; 2 Sam. 22:1-21; Ps. 28:6-8; 30:1-3; 31:7-8; 34:1-6; 54:6-7; 56:12-13; 66:8-20; 95:1-7; 96:1-3; 98:1-3; 103:1-5; 107; 116:1-14; 118:13-21; Isa. 12:1-6; 25:9; 38:16-17; 2 Cor. 1:3-5